FUNCTIONS IN MIND

Functions in Mind

A Theory of Intentional Content

CAROLYN PRICE

CLARENDON PRESS · OXFORD
2001

OXFORD
UNIVERSITY PRESS

Great Clarendon Street, Oxford OX2 6DP

Oxford University Press is a department of the University of Oxford.
It furthers the University's objective of excellence in research, scholarship,
and education by publishing worldwide in

Oxford New York

Athens Auckland Bangkok Bogotá Buenos Aires
Cape Town Chennai Dar es Salaam Delhi Florence Hong Kong Istanbul
Karachi Kolkata Kuala Lumpur Madrid Melbourne Mexico City Mumbai
Nairobi Paris São Paulo Shanghai Singapore Taipei Tokyo Toronto Warsaw

with associated companies in Berlin Ibadan

Oxford is a registered trade mark of Oxford University Press
in the UK and in certain other countries

Published in the United States
by Oxford University Press Inc., New York

© Carolyn Price 2001

The moral rights of the author have been asserted
Database right Oxford University Press (maker)

First published 2001

British Library Cataloguing in Publication Data
Data available
Library of Congress Cataloguing-in-Publication Data
Price, Carolyn.
Functions in mind: a theory of intentional content / Carolyn Price.
p. cm.
Includes bibliographical references.
1. Intentionality (Philosophy) I. Title.
B105.I56 P75 2001   128–dc21   2001016402
ISBN 0–19–924200–3

1 3 5 7 9 10 8 6 4 2

Typeset by J&L Composition Ltd, Filey, North Yorkshire
Printed in Great Britain
on acid-free paper by
Biddles Ltd, Guildford & King's Lynn

PREFACE

This book had its very first origins in a meeting with David Charles, who was then supervising me for the Philosophy of Mind Paper, which I took as part of the B.Phil. course at Oxford. He asked me how intentional explanations explain behaviour. My answer, I suppose, was sufficiently teleological for him to recommend that I read Ruth Millikan's book, *Language, Thought and Other Biological Categories*, then a relatively recent publication. I was hooked both on the question that he had asked me, and on the prospect of developing a teleological theory of content that would answer it. In this book, I attempt to provide such an answer.

To my regret, this is not an easy book. It will appeal primarily to professional philosophers and cognitive scientists and to graduate students working in the philosophy of mind. I have included running summaries as I go along, in order to highlight the main points of the argument. And I have added an appendix that is intended to help the reader navigate through some of the complexities of Chapters 4 and 5.

The bulk of the work for this book was completed while I was a Tutorial Fellow at St Hugh's College, Oxford. I am very grateful to the college for providing me with such an educative and friendly atmosphere in which to work; and for the two terms of sabbatical leave that helped me to make progress at crucial points. The final polishing has been done while I have held a Lectureship in Philosophy at the Open University. I would like to thank my colleagues there for their understanding in providing me with the space to finish the book.

There are numerous individuals to whom I owe thanks for comments and support. David Charles, Tim Williamson, Adrian Cussins, Quassim Cassam, and Michael Woods were all involved in supervising the theses that provided the foundations for the book. Since starting work on the book proper, I have had valuable comments from many people, including Katherine Brading, Martin Davies, James Kinch, Rowland Stout, Ralph Walker, Andrew Woodfield, and three anonymous readers for Oxford University Press. There are three individuals that I would like to single out for special thanks: John Campbell, who did the bulk of the work in supervising my D.Phil. thesis, and whose trenchant criticism saved me from many errors and imprecisions that would have caused trouble later on; Ruth Millikan, whose generous encouragement has fortified me over the years; and Adrian Moore, my ever-supportive colleague at St Hugh's, who not only found time to comment on an entire draft, but could be relied upon to provide advice, encouragement, or solace whenever required. I would also like to thank Penny Brading for her kind assistance in preparing the manuscript for submission. Finally, I would like to thank Peter Momtchiloff, Charlotte Jenkins, and Hilary Walford for invaluable advice and for their hard work in getting the book to press.

C.P.

Oxford
August 2000

ACKNOWLEDGEMENTS

Some of the material in this book is foreshadowed in published papers of mine. I am grateful to Blackwell Publishers Ltd for permission to reuse material from my article 'Functional Explanations and Natural Norms', which appeared in *Ratio*, 8 (1995), 143–60; and from my article 'Determinate Functions', which appeared in *Noûs*, 32 (1998), 54–75. I am grateful to Kluwer Academic Publishers for permission to use material from my article 'Function, Perception and Normal Causal Chains', which appeared in *Philosophical Studies*, 89 (1998), 30–51. And I would like to thank Taylor & Francis Ltd, PO Box 25, Abingdon, Oxfordshire, OX14 3UE (website address: http://www.tandf.co.uk/journals) for permission to reuse material from my paper 'General-Purpose Content', which was published in *International Studies for the Philosophy of Science*, 14 (2000), 123–33.

CONTENTS

INTRODUCTION

Nature and Function

1. Why teleology?

The aim of this book is to offer a theory of intentional content; in other words, to give an account of what we mean when we say that a person is musing *about* something, or that she has a yen *for* something, or that she is supposing *that* such-and-such is the case.[1] When we say that someone is thinking that something is so, we seem to be asserting that there is some kind of relation—a relation of representation—between her thought and certain items and properties in her environment. We might wonder what the nature of this relation might be. This is a pressing question, because appeals to intentional content appear to play a crucial role in explaining people's behaviour. Unless we know what kind of phenomenon intentionality is, we cannot know how these explanations are supposed to work; or for that matter, whether they work at all.

The argument of this book begins from the following assumption: intentionality is a *natural* phenomenon. What I take this to entail is that thoughts, wants, and so on are physical occurrences; and that explanations that appeal to intentional phenomena are, at least in some sense, causal explanations. These claims are hardly uncontroversial; yet I do not intend to argue for them in this book. Although it is possible to offer some broad considerations in favour of naturalism, it is not clear to me that considerations of this kind are likely to appeal to anyone but the previously converted. Instead, my aim in this book is to lay the foundations for a naturalistic account of intentionality that is both plausible and coherent. To show that a naturalistic theory of intentionality succeeds, at least in its own terms, is perhaps the most convincing defence the naturalist can provide.

I take it that naturalism is a view that is friendly to the mind, because it takes claims about intentional phenomena to say something substantial—and falsifiable—about the way the world is; and because it takes such claims to have important explanatory work to do. Hence naturalism is opposed

---

[1] I say more about what constitutes an intentional phenomenon in Chapter 4.

both to views that regard intentional phenomena as useful fictions, and to epiphenomenalism, which treats them as real but powerless by-products of neural activity. But friendliness of this kind may also have its costs: if claims about intentional phenomena are falsifiable, they may, in fact, be falsified. Indeed, eliminativists suggest that we already have good reason to suppose that claims about intentional phenomena are never true.[2]

There are two different kinds of consideration that can be advanced in support of eliminativism. On the one hand, an eliminativist might accept that statements that ascribe thoughts and wants to people are perfectly coherent, but contend that there is evidence (for example, scientific evidence) that such statements are always false. Alternatively, the eliminativist might appeal to a priori considerations: she might argue, for example, that the idea that human behaviour is sometimes explained by intentional phenomena is inherently confused.[3] It was a worry of this kind that first set me off on my search for a theory of intentional content.

The worry might be summed up as follows. If we are to defend a naturalistic view of intentionality, we need to characterize intentional explanations as causal explanations of some kind. And yet intentional explanations have properties that appear to differentiate them from standard forms of causal explanation. First and foremost, intentional explanations have a normative ring. We say that William invaded England *because* he wanted to become king. But we also say that he invaded *in order to* become king. An explanation of this kind, arguably, does not work by presenting William's action as an instance of some causal law or regularity. Rather, it seeks to make sense of William's action as rational in the light of his aims and his beliefs.[4] Making sense of an action in this way is an essentially normative procedure. If we are to accommodate the normativity of intentional explanations without abandoning naturalism, we must find a way of reconciling the claim that intentional explanations are normative with the claim that they are causal explanations of some kind.

It is this aim that has directed me towards a teleological theory of intentional content. A teleological theory is one that attempts to account for the intentional properties of our mental states by appealing to the fact that these states, or the mechanisms that produce them, are biological items that have functions. I am using the word 'function' here just as I am using it when I say that the function of a spider's web is to snare prey or that a function of the liver is to store vitamin A. Statements of this kind should interest anyone who is puzzled by intentional explanations because, as I explain in Chapter 1, they appear to exhibit the same combination of normativity and explanatory

---

[2] See especially Stich (1983) and Churchland (1984, 1992).

[3] On the face of it, this is an argument for epiphenomenalism, rather than eliminativism. But it can be used to support eliminativism if we add the assumption that intentional phenomena, if they exist at all, are sometimes capable of explaining human behaviour. This is a claim that a naturalist is likely to accept.

[4] See Davidson (1963).

force. If we can provide an account of function statements that explains how they are both normative and (causally) explanatory, and if we can characterize intentionality as a functional phenomenon, then we will have found a way to naturalize intentional explanations without denying their normativity.

2. Teleological Accounts

The idea that we could give a teleological theory of intentional content is hardly a new one. Ruth Millikan developed a teleological theory in her book *Language, Thought and Other Biological Categories* (1984).[5] Other writers, including David Papineau (1987), Fred Dretske (1988), and Karen Neander (1995), have developed their own teleological approaches.

Millikan's original statement of the theory began with an analysis of what we mean when we say that a biological device has a certain function. She argued that the functions of biological devices are grounded in their evolutionary history. The content of an intentional device would depend on the function of the mechanism that produced it. The function of an intentional mechanism is to guide the workings of some further mechanism—for example, an executive mechanism in control of the organism's behaviour—in such a way as to ensure that the operation of this second mechanism coincides with the occurrence of some favourable condition in the environment. To give a now familiar example: the function of the frog's fly-detecting mechanism is to ensure that the frog's fly snaps occur when a fly is in range. And so the content of the devices that it produces concerns the presence of a fly within range of the frog's snaps. This account of content is a strongly externalist account: the content of the device is determined entirely by the causal relations that it is supposed to bear to the organism's behaviour, and by the causal relations that the organism's behaviour is supposed to bear to the environment.

Other proponents of the teleological approach have shown how the theory might be developed in ways that differ from the account presented by Millikan. One important controversy concerns the connection between intentionality and information. Millikan gives no special role to the idea that intentional devices are supposed to carry information about the environment.[6] Instead, she treats intentional devices as somehow picturing the

---

[5] A rather different approach, but one that also ties intentional content to function, has been suggested by Robert Cummins (1983). Cummins's approach differs substantially from Millikan's in that his account of functions is profoundly non-naturalistic.

[6] Millikan's views on this issue have recently been changing. See Millikan (2000: app. B, 217–37).

states of affairs that they represent. In contrast, Dretske has attempted to combine a teleological theory of content with the idea that intentional devices carry information about the environment.

A second dispute concerns the nature of the content a teleologist will assign to intentional devices. Millikan, as we have seen, ties the content of intentional devices very closely to their role in ensuring the success of the organism's behaviour. Neander, on the other hand, has developed a teleological account that ties the content of intentional devices to what the system is actually able to discriminate. According to Neander, the frog's visual system detects, not flies, but small, dark, moving things, because the frog is not able to distinguish between flies and other moving objects that are small and dark.

It should be clear to anyone who reads this book how much it owes to earlier proponents of the theory, and especially to Millikan. Indeed, I have used her account as a reference point throughout the book, and my account overlaps with hers in important ways. But my version of events either differs from or supplements Millikan's in some significant ways. I have taken very seriously Millikan's stricture (1991: 163) that a teleological theory of content needs to be underpinned by a well-developed and plausible account of biological functions. The account of functions that I develop is rather different from Millikan's, and leads me to reach some conclusions that diverge from hers in important ways, particularly with respect to the capacities exercised by the simplest intentional systems. Moreover, where I do agree with Millikan, it is often for reasons of my own. For example, my account of functions supports a view of content that is much closer to Millikan's than to Neander's; but this is for reasons that are peculiar to my account.

Secondly, like Dretske, I am attracted to the idea that intentionality is essentially grounded in information: the notion of an informational relation plays a central role in my account of how to attribute content to intentional states. In contrast, I find no role for the idea that intentional devices picture the state of affairs that they represent.

Finally, there is room for disagreement over the nature of specific intentional capacities. One type of intentional capacity that I will examine in this book is the capacity to represent particular items, such as physical objects and places. The account that I introduce draws on the approach developed by Peter Strawson (1959). Strawson's approach centres on the idea that a subject who is able to represent particular objects or places must be able to keep track of them through changes in spatio-temporal position. On this view, the content of an intentional state will depend not only on its relation to the external environment, but also on the way it is used in processes of inference inside the system.[7] As a result, my account is a little less robustly externalist than Millikan's.

---

[7] However, as should become clear in Chapter 10, the way in which inferential role features in my account is quite different from the way in which it features in 'inferential-role' theories of content.

Whatever the distinctive features of my account, it is confronted by many of the objections raised against teleological theories in recent years. There are three objections that I regard as particularly important.

(1) Dretske (1986) and Fodor (1990) object that we cannot say, determinately, what the function of a biological item is. Hence someone who attempts to give an account of intentional content that centres on the notion of a biological function will be unable to ascribe determinate content to intentional states.

(2) Christopher Peacocke (1992) argues that the teleologist is committed to the view that we are unable to think about items that we cannot, in principle, make use of. Hence, the teleologist is unable to allow that we are able to represent the world in a fully objective way: that is, as fully independent of us.

(3) Kim Sterelny (1990: 123–34), Radu Bogdan (1994: 181), and John Campbell (1994: 212) have all suggested that the teleological theory is unable to account for our capacity to think and reason in a way that is not directed to the satisfaction of our biological needs.

Each of these objections can be related to a single charge: the teleologist is quite mistaken to suppose that we can use the notion of biological utility to account for truth. If a teleological theory is to succeed, all these objections will need to be answered.

3. The Structure of the Book

The book is divided into three parts. In Part I, I attempt to develop a theory of biological functions. The theory is there in order to ground the account of content that follows, and we will find ourselves referring back to it throughout the book. Nevertheless, the question of what we are doing when we attempt to explain the presence of a biological system or bodily organ with reference to its function seems to me to be a fascinating issue in its own right. I spend some time on the claim that it is possible to ascribe determinate functions to biological items. This argument will enable me to find an answer to Dretske's and Fodor's determinacy objection. But it is worth pointing out that the debate about the determinacy of functions has repercussions for anyone who supposes that the notion of a function plays an important role in biology.

In Parts II and III, I attempt to develop an account of how we ascribe content to intentional systems. In Part II, I will be concerned with comparatively primitive intentional systems. In Part III, I turn my attention to more sophisticated intentional systems, whose owners might be characterized as having beliefs and desires. I will refer to these more sophisticated systems as *doxastic systems*. To make this distinction, I will exploit the idea that simple systems are *special-purpose systems*: that is, there is some specifiable set of biological needs or interests that they function to promote. Doxastic systems, on the other hand, are *general-purpose systems*: a doxastic system may assist its possessor to satisfy any interest that she may happen to possess, including interests that conflict with her biological needs. I will give a fuller account of this distinction in Chapter 9.[8]

Special-purpose systems will include simple signalling systems, such as the frog's fly-detecting mechanism, and systems to which we can ascribe more demanding capacities, such as the ability to represent goals, the ability to engage in learning, and the capacity to represent particular items. It is in the second part of the book that I will present the major part of my response to the determinacy objection: I will argue that even the simplest intentional devices may be ascribed determinate content. However, I will argue that these devices are not marked by the kind of objectivity with which Peacocke is concerned.

Again, this part of the book might be viewed as nothing more than a preparation for what follows, a chance to introduce the mechanics that will be needed to account for the more sophisticated forms of representation that we will encounter in Part III. But I believe that the discussion in this part of the book is important in its own right, too. If we can understand how intentional phenomena can appear at this level, where the workings of intentional systems may be relatively well understood, then we will have taken an important step towards demystifying the claim that intentionality is a feature of the natural world.

In Part III, I attempt to do three things. First of all, I try to make clear what doxastic systems are *like*: I attempt to give a specific meaning to the claim that doxastic systems are general-purpose systems, and I investigate the special capabilities, such as curiosity and theory-building, that such systems may be thought to have. Secondly, I outline a teleological account of doxastic content, drawing heavily on the suggestions made in Part II. At this point, I will confront Sterelny's claim that the teleological theory is unable to account for the capacity to think in ways unconnected to our biological needs. Finally, in Chapter 11, I discuss the determinacy and objectivity objections for the last time. I consider, and reject, the suggestion that the move from special-purpose to general-purpose representation introduces some indeterminacy of content; and I argue that at least some general-purpose systems are capable of representing items that are, in principle, useless to the subject.

---

[8] This idea has its origin in a suggestion of Millikan's (1986: 72). But it is also the idea that generates Sterelny's objection.

PART I

A Theory of Functions

1

Explanation and Normativity

1. Introduction

The teleological theory of content begins from the premiss that the content of an intentional device is determined by its function, or by the function of the mechanism that produced it. So, the first task that the teleologist must carry out is to explain what it means to say that an item has a certain function.

This is not an insignificant undertaking: many different theories of functions have been proposed in recent years, based on quite different assumptions about the nature and status of functional properties. But it is also a task that is of great importance to the teleologist. This is because the theory of functions that she adopts at the start will play a major role in moulding the theory of content that she goes on to develop. If she were to choose a theory of functions that treats function statements as essentially subjective—a matter of how we interpret the world—she will be committed to a theory of content that treats intentionality in the same way. A teleological theory of this kind will be of no use to someone who hopes to give a naturalistic account of intentionality. On the other hand, if our theory of functions tells us that functions are objective, natural phenomena, then a teleological theory of content will allow us to treat intentionality in the same way.[1]

The first three chapters of this book are dedicated to the task of providing a theory of functions. In this chapter, I will set out the difficulties that a successful account will need to overcome, and I will investigate two theories that currently dominate the literature: the dispositional theory and the aetiological theory. I will argue that neither theory is successful in its basic form.

Consider the theories of content proposed by Robert Cummins (1983) and Ruth Millikan (1984). Both theories centre on the idea that the content of an intentional state has to do with its function. But Cummins regards function ascription as interpretative and indeterminate, while Millikan takes functions to be natural, determinate features of biological systems.

In the next chapter, I will argue in favour of a modified version of the aetiological theory. In Chapter 3, I will continue to develop this theory, setting out a detailed account of how we ascribe functions to biological items. It is necessary to do this, I will argue, if we are to show that the functions of biological items are determinate. The claim that biological functions are determinate will be crucial in defending the teleological theory against the accusation that the teleologist is unable to ascribe determinate content to intentional devices.

2. Functions and Function Statements

2.1. The Nature of my Account

The theory of functions that I shall develop over the next three chapters is intended to be viewed as an account of the 'common-sense' notion of a function—the notion that is in play when we engage in everyday talk about biological items. As such, my account is meant to answer to common-sense intuitions about what we would say about the function of a biological item in a range of situations. In this respect, my approach differs from that of Millikan (1989*a*), who takes herself to be offering a theoretical definition of a function, and from that of Neander (1991*b*), who sets out to present an analysis of the concept of a function possessed by modern scientific biologists.

In the Introduction, I explained that my original motivation for exploring the teleological theory of content was a desire to investigate the nature of common-sense intentional explanations of human behaviour. Now, it would be perfectly possible to develop a theoretical notion of intentional content—one that might replace our everyday notion. And again, it might be argued that psychologists employ a technical notion of content that makes sense only within a certain psychological theory. However, I take it that the notion of content to which our common-sense intentional explanations appeal must itself be a common-sense notion. Moreover, it is natural to suppose that a teleological account of the common-sense conception of content should begin from a common-sense notion of function.

Nevertheless, my account should not be viewed as a 'pure' conceptual analysis, reflecting all the vagaries in our everyday talk about functions. Instead, what I would like to do is to give an account of what I take to be the basic concept underlying our everyday talk. It is this basic notion that we employ when we classify biological devices in terms of their functions, or attempt to explain their presence in functional terms. In these contexts, I believe, we do have quite sharp intuitions about what constitutes the function of a device. It is these intuitions that my account is intended to explain.

2.2. Function Statements

I will begin by trying to get clear about the problems that an account of functions needs to solve. I will start by considering the ways in which we use the notion of a function to describe and to explain certain types of situation.

Function statements come in a variety of forms, reflecting the different roles they play. Consider the following examples:

(1) The function of a rain butt is to collect rainwater from the gutter.

(2) The rain butt is there in order to collect rainwater from the gutter.

(3) The rain butt is made of waterproof material so that it will not leak.

(4) The rain butt is supposed to collect rainwater from the gutter.

The first of these sentences tells us what *kind* of thing a rain butt is by invoking its function. Artefacts are commonly classified, at least in part, according to their function. Biological items, too, often seem to be classified partly by their function.[2] Hearts, flippers, courting displays, and birds' nests are all examples of biological items that are categorized, in part, by their functional properties. Crests, feathers, and screeches, on the other hand, are classified by their physical structure or appearance, rather than the functions that they play.[3]

It would be inappropriate to conclude from this that the *meaning* or *intension* of the term 'heart' is a specification of the heart's function. We take the ancient Greek word 'καρδια' to have the same meaning as the English word 'heart', even though (some of) the ancient Greeks ascribed a rather different set of functions to the heart. Rather we can treat terms that refer to functional kinds in a way analogous to the way in which Putnam (1975) treats terms that refer to chemical kinds, such as 'gold' or 'water'. For Putnam, to be a sample of water is to share the same chemical structure—*whatever that may be*—as the substance that is found in the oceans and rivers on our planet. Similarly, we might suggest, to be a heart is, in part, to be a biological item having the same function—*whatever that may be*—as the mechanism that thuds away inside my chest.[4]

---

[2] I say 'at least in part' because it is not obvious to me that function is the only feature relevant to the classification of biological items: it may be that the way in which biological items normally perform their functions is also relevant. For example, it might be important that hearts are pumps.

[3] Amundson and Lauder (1993) suggest that there is a preponderance of biological kinds characterized by anatomical structure, rather than function. However, they accept that a number of important biological kinds are characterized by function. They go on to suggest that a scientific biologist might do without functional kinds; but this prescriptive claim goes beyond my concerns in this book. See also Griffiths (1996) for a defence of functional classification in biology.   [4] See also Saul Kripke (1972).

The second and third sentences offer a pair of functional explanations. We can appeal to the function of an artefact to explain why it is present, and why it has certain features. We also employ the notion of a function when we are trying to make sense of natural phenomena. In particular, we appeal to the functions of biological items to explain why they are present and why they possess certain properties.

The fourth sentence emphasizes another important feature of function statements. Function statements are normative: a function statement states what an item is supposed to do. The normativity of function statements seems to stem from two different contrasts. First of all, a function statement states what an item is supposed to do, as opposed to what it actually does. The rain butt is supposed to hold the rainwater inside, but it may leak. The optic lens is supposed to focus incoming light to provide a clear image, but that is not what my optic lenses actually do. Secondly, a function statement states what an item is supposed to do, as opposed to what it does fortuitously or by accident. The old bath tub we threw out last year collects rain; that is something (useful) that it does, but it is not what it is supposed to do. It is fortunate for me that my nose supports my glasses, but that is not one of its biological functions. An item that is performing its function contrasts, first, with a defective device and, secondly, with an item that benefits its owner in an eccentric way.

Notice that at this point I am committing myself only to the claim that function *statements* have a normative character. I have not made the stronger claim that functional properties are grounded in objective functional norms. Similarly, we might distinguish between the modest claim that moral statements have a normative ring and the rather more controversial claim that there are objective moral values. Of course, one possible explanation for the fact that function statements have a normative ring is that they invoke objective functional norms. We will consider a view of this kind later in this chapter. But there are other possible explanations, as we shall see.[5]

Normativity is a feature not only of sentences such as (4) above, but also of functional explanations such as (2) and (3). In developing this point, I will draw on a very helpful discussion by Philip Pettit (1986).

It seems to be generally agreed that causal explanations, at least in the standard cases, are what Pettit (1986: 25) terms *regularizing explanations*. In other words, they explain a sequence of events by showing it to be an instance of some causal law, or of some broader regularity underpinned by causal laws. Not all explanations are regularizing explanations: as we shall see later on, not all causal explanations are regularizing explanations; and it is possible that some explanations are not causal explanations.

---

[5] When I present my positive account of function statements in Chapter 2, I will not attempt to explain the normativity of function statements by appealing to objective functional norms.

Functional explanations are not regularizing explanations: functional properties do not feature in causal laws or regularities. I cannot infer from the fact that an item has a certain function that it will tend to perform that function: the device may be defective, or the environment in which it operates may not cooperate. For example, I cannot infer from the fact that my heart is supposed to move my blood that it will move my blood: it might be stopped by a faulty valve, or by an assassin's bullet. Nor is there a law-like connection between the possession of a certain function by items of a certain kind and the presence of such an item within a particular system. This is because there may be many ways to plug a particular gap within a system. For example, if my red corpuscles could move themselves—if they could swim like sperm, say—I might not need a heart. So it is impossible to predict that I will have a heart from the fact that my corpuscles need to move.

If functional explanations are not regularizing explanations, how do they explain? Pettit (1986: 38–42) distinguishes a second class of explanation that he terms *normalizing explanations*. According to Pettit, normalizing explanations do not seek to exhibit an event or a situation as an instance of some causal law or regularity. Rather, they set out to present it as part of a process that tends towards a particular outcome or goal. As Pettit points out, functional explanations appear to be normalizing explanations: to say that I have a heart in order to move my blood is to explain this situation by presenting it as tending to promote a certain outcome.

There is clearly much more to be said about the nature and force of normalizing explanations. At this point, it is far from clear what it means to say that a particular event or situation 'tends towards' a particular outcome; or how this fact could help to explain the occurrence of the event. It is hard to resist the assumption that the normativity of function statements and the normalizing nature of functional explanations are intimately connected. If this is the case, then the answers to these questions will depend on our account of the normative character of function statements.

2.3. Why are Function Statements Puzzling?

Why should there be any disagreement about the nature of functions? The existence of disagreement suggests that there must be something *puzzling* about the notion of a function. The puzzle arises from just those features that make function statements so interesting to the teleologist—their normativity and their explanatory force.

Neither of these features is puzzling taken on its own. It is when we put them together that the difficulty arises. The explanatory force of function statements suggests that they are concerned with objective, causally operative properties of the world. Normative features, on the face of it, do not look like objective, causally operative properties. Moreover, the fact that we can appeal to an item's function to explain why it is there right now might be taken to suggest that functions have to do with what has happened in the past: the explanatory force of function statements suggests a 'backward-looking' view of functions. The normative character of function statements, on the other hand, appears to encourage the opposite expectation. Function statements seem to be concerned with what the item is required to do now or in the future: normativity suggests a 'forward-looking' view of functions.

The puzzle is amplified by the fact that functional explanations are themselves normalizing explanations. This shows that the normativity and the explanatory force of function statements cannot be pulled apart. Indeed, as I explained in the Introduction, it is this feature of functional explanations that makes a teleological theory of intentional content seem so promising, for intentional explanations also appear to be normalizing explanations. If we can understand this feature of functional explanations, we may be closer to understanding how intentional explanations work.

In the case of artefacts, such as the rain butt, it is easy to see how we might resolve the puzzle. When we ascribe functions to artefacts, we seem to be relying on an implicit appeal to human wants and intentions.[6] Artefacts have functions because they are designed and manufactured with the intention that they should be used in a certain way, or perhaps just because they are used in that way. The notions of design and use seem to presuppose conscious human agency.

An appeal to human wants and intentions can help us to bridge the gap between the explanatory force of function statements and their normativity.[7] One suggestion might be that functions are normative because, when an agent makes something with the intention that it should perform a certain task, she makes it *in the expectation* that it should do so. But her creation may fail to live up to her expectations: it may leak, or tip over, or prove unsatisfactory in some other way; and, if it should do so, it can be classed as a failure, relative to the agent's expectations. Again, there may be other items in the vicinity that are capable of performing that particular task, but are not expected to do so by some agent. Moreover, it is these very same expectations that explain why the item is present: it is because the agent expected it to behave in a certain way that she made it or put it where it is.[8]

---

[6] 'Seem' is important: as Christopher Boorse (1976: 73) points out, the components of many artefacts may never have been consciously designed, but may nevertheless have functions. He gives the example of the use of yeast in brewing.

[7] My account of this issue owes much to a discussion by Karen Neander (1991*a*: 455–8).

[8] A solution of this kind would, of course, be deeply disappointing to the teleologist. If functions depend on intentional phenomena, we cannot account for intentional phenomena by appealing to functions.

But, if the only way in which we can solve the puzzle is by appealing to the purposes and expectations of some agent, then we will be forced to give up talking about biological functions. Biological items were not produced with the intention that they should operate in a certain way; nor do their owners consciously use them. If functions presuppose agency, then the idea that biological items have functions will turn out to be a mistake, left over from an earlier biology that assumed that organisms are artefacts, produced by a divine Creator. We would have to draw the conclusion that, unless the natural world has a Creator, there are no natural functions.

I think that this worry is a pressing one, but we need not begin by assuming that it is insoluble. To solve it, we need to find some more general account of the normative force of function statements that underpins our ascription of functions both to items that have been consciously designed or used, and to items that have not. This need not imply that we must treat statements that attribute functions to artefacts and statements that attribute functions to natural items as straightforwardly univocal. But we do need to find some single principle that will make it intelligible how both kinds of statement can be both normative and explanatory. Unless we can find a single principle that underlies both kinds of statement, we will be open to the objection that it is only artefacts that have genuine functional properties, and that biological items have functions only in a metaphorical sense.

2.4. Functions and Function Statements: Summary

In this first part of the book, my aim is to provide an account of our common-sense notion of a function. I have started by outlining the features of functions and function statements that such an account needs to accommodate. First, artefacts and biological items are often categorized, in part, by their function. Secondly, function statements have explanatory force: we appeal to the function of a device to explain its presence. Thirdly, function statements have a normative character. The normative character of function statements seems to rest on two contrasts: the contrast between a functioning device and a defective device; and the contrast between a functioning device and an eccentric device. Finally, functional explanations are themselves normalizing explanations. It is the combination of normativity and explanatory force that makes function statements so puzzling. In the case of an artefact, we might dispel the puzzle by appealing to the purposes and expectations of the designer. But, if the natural world has no designer, we cannot use this strategy to generate an account of biological functions.

3. The Basic Dispositional Theory

3.1. Function, Service, and Value

For the rest of this chapter, I will concentrate primarily on biological functions. My strategy will be to formulate basic versions of two opposing theories of biological functions: a dispositional account and an aetiological account. My discussion will owe a great deal to suggestions made by earlier writers, but I will try to develop each analysis in a way that abstracts away from the details of specific accounts.[9] In this way I hope to get clear about the intuitions that underlie each account, as well as its strengths and its weaknesses.

I will argue that neither the basic dispositional theory nor the basic aetiological theory succeeds in accounting for the peculiar features of function statements. Neither account is able to give a satisfying account of functional explanations as normalizing explanations. I believe that, once we can see why each of these accounts fails, we will be in a better position to construct a more successful analysis.

A dispositional theory of functions is made up of two key elements: the first is the idea that the functioning device *serves* some other entity by producing some outcome; and the second is the idea that the outcome produced by the functioning device has some *value*. I will discuss these two ideas in turn.

Peter Achinstein (1977) distinguishes between three different kinds of function: a *design function* is what something has been designed or created to do; a *use function* is what it is used to do; and a *service function* is what it happens to do, where its doing so confers a benefit on someone or somebody. As we saw in the last section, it does not seem possible to apply the notions of design and use to biological items, if we accept modern evolutionary theory.

Dispositional theories solve this problem by identifying biological functions with something akin to Achinstein's service functions. The idea will be that the function of a biological item is something that it does or is disposed to do, where its doing so benefits the organism or species by contributing to some biological end.

There is a great deal of room for disagreement about what might constitute a biological end. There are (at least) three proposals that have received wide attention among proponents of this kind of theory:

---

[9] I have drawn particularly heavily on the following discussions: for the dispositional theory, Woodfield (1976), Prior (1985), Bigelow and Pargetter (1987), and Bedau (1992a); for the aetiological theory, Wright (1976), Millikan (1984, 1989a), and Neander (1991b).

(1) a goal of the organism;

(2) some state or activity of the organism or species—such as survival or reproduction—that is, objectively, a biological end;

(3) some state or activity of the organism or species that we, as interested observers or investigators of biological entities, regard as a biological end.

Goal-centred theories face a number of serious objections. The main difficulty is that it is not clear whether it makes sense to attribute goals to plants and to simple animals. Certainly these organisms do not have goals in the sense of explicitly represented purposes; and other criteria of goal-directedness that have been offered have tended to attribute goals to systems that clearly do not have functions. To give an example, one proposal is that the behaviour of a system will count as directed towards a goal if its behaviour exhibits a certain amount of plasticity with respect to that goal. An objector will reply that a rock rolling down a hill exhibits a fair degree of plasticity with respect to the goal of reaching the bottom.[10] I believe that the problems for goal-centred theories are overwhelming, and I shall not give them any further consideration here.

This leaves (2) and (3). A proponent of (2) will claim that there are some ends, such as survival and reproduction, that can be regarded as distinctively biological ends, and that have this status independently of human interests and values. A proponent of (3), on the other hand, will insist that survival and reproduction will count as biological ends only because we view them in that light. Had human psychology been different, we might have regarded large size, or an attractive appearance, as biological ends.

On the face of it, (3) seems the more cautious position. A proponent of (2) needs to justify the claim that survival and reproduction are objective biological ends. One thought might be that survival and reproduction have this status because that is what the majority of organisms do. The obvious objection here is that most, if not all, organisms suffer pain and die, but that does not seem to be a good reason to suppose that pain and death are objective biological ends. A better solution might be to point to the definition of biology as the study of life, and then to claim that survival and reproduction are definitive of life: on this view, the claim that survival and reproduction are biological ends will be true by definition.

Both these versions of the dispositional theory begin from the idea that biological devices have functions in so far as they serve the organism or species by helping to produce some biological end. But this, by itself, will not account

[10] The best-known example of a goal-centred theory is proposed by Ernest Nagel (1977). I have taken the example of the rolling stone from Graham MacDonald (1992: 78). For further criticisms of the goal-centred theory, see also Bedau (1992*b*).

for the normativity of function statements. The dispositional theorist also needs to appeal to the idea that biological ends have some value.

To see this, compare a biological system with a thermal system. It could be argued that, just as survival and reproduction are biological ends, thermal equilibrium is a thermodynamical end: thermal equilibrium is the end to which all thermal systems, *as* thermal systems, tend. But, if thermal equilibrium is an end, it does not seem to be the right sort of end to give rise to functions. It does not seem very natural, for example, to say that an ice cube has the thermodynamical function to melt in a warm room—that ice cubes are *supposed* to melt

It should be fairly obvious what has gone wrong here: thermal equilibrium is not the kind of end that it is appropriate to characterize in normative terms. It is an end in the sense that it is an outcome to which thermal systems tend, but it is not an end in the sense that it has some value. If this diagnosis is correct, it suggests that the dispositional theorist cannot account for the normativity of function statements by appealing to the notion of service alone: she must also appeal to the idea that biological ends have value.

A proponent of (2) will be committed to the view that survival and reproduction have objective value for biological organisms. On this view the normative force of function statements will be explained by the fact there are objective functional norms, generated by states of affairs that have objective biological value. The proponent of (3), on the other hand, will regard functional norms as subjective, because she regards biological value as subjective. On this view, the value of survival and reproduction as biological ends will rest on our own attitudes or concerns. I take it that both these views are quite coherent, and I will take them both into account in what follows.

In the light of what has been said so far, we can formulate a dispositional analysis of function statements as follows. Where d is an item, and F is an activity, d has (or is appropriately viewed as having) the function to do F if and only if d belongs to a type of item, D,[11] such that:

D.1 (Some) items belonging to D do F.

D.2 By doing F, items belonging to D contribute to some state or activity of the organism or species to which they belong that has (or is viewed as having) intrinsic biological value.

3.2. *Types of Item*

A notable feature of this analysis is that it includes a reference to the *type* of item to which d belongs. This is because the dispositional theorist needs to

---

[11] I will explain why we need to refer to the type of device to which d belongs in the next section.

allow for the possibility that a device might be so defective that it never actually performs its function. Given that this is a possibility, she cannot insist that all items that function to do F are actually capable of doing F. The obvious solution is to accept that we do not ascribe functions to individual items, but to types of item. In this way the dispositional theorist can ascribe functions to defective devices by appealing to the functions performed by items of the same type. On this view, assigning a function to an individual item will be a two-step process: we will begin by grouping it with other items of the same type, and then ascribe a function to it on the basis of the function(s) performed by items of that type.

We need, therefore, to consider what would be the most appropriate way to group biological items into types before ascribing functions to them. The most obvious basis for this initial grouping would be physical similarity. It is not obvious, however, that we could be guaranteed to find a purely physical criterion that would be generous enough to include malformed devices, but strict enough to exclude all other items that we would intuitively wish to exclude. For example, it is not clear that we could find a physical criterion that would distinguish between, for example, a pulmonary artery and a (perhaps malformed) pulmonary vein, or between a hair and a (perhaps malformed) whisker.

An alternative approach focuses on the causal origin of the item. We can develop this idea by borrowing from Millikan (1984: 23–5) the idea of a *reproductively established family*.[12] A set of items will belong to the same family if they share similar physical characteristics, and if they do so because they are all descendants of a common ancestor and have all been produced in more or less the same way. A family will be a first-order family if each member is directly produced by another member of the family. A family will be a higher-order family if each member of the family is produced by a member of the same lower-order family.

Genes are members of a first-order family: each strand of DNA is produced by another strand of DNA by a process that ensures that the new strand is physically similar to the original strand. Biological organs are members of higher-order families. Each pulmonary vein, whether healthy or defective, has been produced in (more or less) the same way by genetic mechanisms that belong to the same first-order family.[13] Pulmonary veins and pulmonary arteries will belong to different higher-order families because that have been produced by genetic mechanisms belonging to

---

[12] This idea is borrowed from an aetiological theory of functions; but there is no reason why the dispositional theorist should not make use of it.

[13] The phrase 'more or less' is important. We need to leave enough latitude to allow for malformed veins. On the other hand, where things have gone very wrong, we might not wish to classify the results as an organ of any kind. There is room for vagueness here (Millikan 1984: 25).

different first-order families.[14] It would be possible for a dispositional theorist to stipulate that biological items will be items of the same type if they belong to the same higher-order family.

A question for the dispositional theorist is whether we should identify families of biological items with biological kinds. If we did so, we would have reversed the dependence of function and type that I have been assuming until now. In other words, we would have abandoned the view that biological items are classified in accordance with their function, and replaced it with the view that they are ascribed functions in accordance with their type. Such a reversal would have the consequence that two items that evolved independently, and so belong to different families, could not be said to belong to the same biological kind. But we can avoid this consequence by turning the dispositional theorist's two-step strategy into a three-step one: first group items together into families (for example, fruit bats' wings); then ascribe biological functions to them on the basis of what members of the family usefully do (provide lift for flight); and then appeal to their biological function to classify them as members of some biological kind (wings).

In the next two sections I will present two objections to the dispositional theory. The first objection is that the dispositional theorist cannot give a satisfactory account of eccentric items. The second is that the dispositional theorist is unable to offer a satisfactory account of functional explanations as normalizing explanations. I will argue that both these objections succeed and that the success of these objections undermines the claim that the normativity of function statements rests on the value, or the perceived value, of certain states of affairs.

3.3. Eccentric Benefits: A Problem for the Basic Dispositional Theory

As we have seen, the dispositional theory attempts to account for the normativity of function statements by appeal to the value, or perceived value, of the outcome that the functioning device is supposed to produce. It is because that outcome is valuable that the item is supposed to produce it.

The first objection that I would like to consider is that the dispositional theory fails to allow for the possibility that an item might produce some valuable outcome in an eccentric way—that is, without having the function to do so.

---

[14] I am assuming that veins and arteries are produced by distinct genetic mechanisms. An alternative possibility is that veins and arteries are produced by the same genetic mechanisms operating in different biochemical environments. If this were the case, veins and arteries would still belong to different types, on the suggested criterion, because they would have been produced in (more or less) different ways. If so, there could be circumstances in which it would be indeterminate whether a certain piece of tissue was a malformed artery or a malformed vein.

This is an important objection, because, as we saw earlier, the contrast between a functional and an eccentric item is essential to the normativity of function statements.

Suppose that an organism has a malformed eye that does not respond to light, but happens to resemble a warning mark carried by poisonous relatives of the organism. And suppose that, as a result of this resemblance, predators avoid the organism, so that it is able to survive and reproduce. According to the dispositional account as formulated above, this organ must be ascribed the biological function of a warning mark, rather than an eye; and so, presumably, must be classified accordingly. And yet this does not seem to be the natural way to describe this case: it seems natural to say that this organ is helping to secure a biological end, but that it is not doing so in the way that it is supposed to. Not every contribution to a biologically valuable outcome constitutes a biological function.

The problem will be aggravated further by the reference to types of item in the dispositional analysis. The dispositional theorist seems to be forced to claim not only that the malformed eye has the function to act as a warning mark, but also that the eyes belonging to other members of the same species are malfunctioning because they fail to scare off predators. It looks as if any contribution, no matter how eccentric, by a family member will count as a biological function of all the members of that family.

The most natural way for the dispositional theorist to exclude such cases is to appeal to their atypicality. The claim will now be that the biological function of a particular item will be whatever members of the same family typically do that contributes to some biological end. In other words, we should modify D.1 to:

D.1* Items belonging to D typically do G.

On this modified view, the normativity of function statements will rest, not only on the notion of biological value, but also on the idea that some activities are typically or standardly performed by items of a certain type.

Unfortunately, it is not at all obvious how this notion of typicality is to be understood. The problem is to find a formulation that will allow for two important facts: the first is that some biological devices have functions that they perform only very rarely; the second is that some biological devices have multiple functions.

One way to interpret D.1* is to understand it as insisting that most members of D do F. On this interpretation, the account will exclude devices that perform their functions only very rarely, such as sperm or ova. An alternative would be to interpret D.1* as claiming that members of D do F more frequently than anything else that they do that is of biological value. But this excludes devices, such as the liver, that have multiple functions, some of which they perform more frequently than others.

I am not at all certain whether it is possible to find an interpretation of D.1* that does not give rise to problems of this kind. If no such interpretation can be found, the dispositional theorist's attempt to account for the normativity of function statements by appealing to biological value will have failed.

3.4. Normalizing Explanations: The Basic Dispositional Theory

In this section, I will add fuel to the fire by arguing that the dispositional theory is unable to explain how functional explanations can be normalizing explanations. As we shall see, it is possible for a dispositional theorist to treat functional explanations either as non-causal or as causal explanations. I will argue that neither view is entirely satisfactory: the first because it fails to show that functional explanations are normalizing *explanations*, the second because it fails to show that they are *normalizing* explanations.

I will begin with the dispositional theorist who claims that functional explanations are non-causal explanations. The idea will be that we can make sense of the presence of an item by showing that it contributed to the satisfaction of some biological end. This would be a kind of 'normalization after the fact'. This kind of explanation takes the occurrence of the item as given, and then seeks to make it intelligible by showing that it promotes the accomplishment of some biological end. Such an explanation does not tell us anything about the origin of the item. It simply invites us to see how it was beneficial.

How might a 'normalization after the fact' explain the fact that an item is present? Perhaps the idea will be that we can see why its presence is appropriate, given that its being there usually helps to promote some valuable end. In other words, we will be able to make sense of its occurrence, not as an isolated incident, but as an instance of a more general pattern that consistently benefits the organism in a particular way.

We might concede that the dispositional theory is able to provide a coherent characterization of functional explanations along these lines. Moreover, it is an account that succeeds in explaining how such explanations might be normalizing explanations. Nevertheless, we might be left feeling that this account is not very convincing. The reason is, I think, that a functional explanation, so characterized, is not much of an *explanation* at all: it is really just a redescription of the event.[15]

To explain the occurrence of some event or state of affairs is to fit it into the pattern of our expectations about the world—to show, in some way, that we

---

[15] It might be suggested that all explanations are causal explanations. I am not sure that I would wish to make such an extreme claim: for example, I would not wish to deny that there are mathematical explanations. But it does seem to me to be plausible to suppose that any explanation of why some spatio-temporal entity—such as an object or an event—exists or occurs will be a causal explanation.

should not be surprised by it. According to the dispositional theory, to give a functional explanation of some biological device is to show that it belongs to a type of item whose occurrence usually benefits the organism. But why should knowing this lead us to be any less surprised that the item is present? Perhaps the idea is that we operate with a basic expectation that biological items usually benefit their possessors. But such an assumption would seem to be somewhat optimistic.

This suggests that the dispositional theorist should treat functional explanations as causal explanations. At first sight, however, it might look as if the dispositional theorist will be precluded from making such a move. According to the dispositional theory, the ascription of a function to an item does not imply anything about its causal history. Hence there will be no guarantee that there will be any causal connection between the presence of an item and the functional properties of items of that type.

In fact, there are two different ways in which it is possible to reconcile a dispositional theory of functions with a causal account of functional explanations. The first is to restrict the notion of a biological end to that of reproductive fitness, thereby ensuring that, whatever the function of an item may be, it will be one that helps to ensure the persistence of that type of device. The second is to reject the claim that function statements are intrinsically explanatory—the ascription of a function to an item will only sometimes provide an explanation of its presence.

It is possible, then, for a dispositional theorist to offer an account of functional explanations that does take such explanations to be concerned with the causal origins of the device. What we now need to consider is what kind of causal explanation the dispositional theorist will take functional explanations to be.

Earlier, I mentioned the possibility that there might be causal explanations that are not regularizing explanations. David Lewis (1986: 219–20) suggests that we should characterize a causal explanation as one that offers some information about the causal history of a certain event. But a causal explanation need not provide information about the causal laws or regularities that governed the production of a particular event. The explanation may simply cite one or more of the events that were the causes of the event; or it may indicate that the causal history of the event included a pattern of events of a certain kind; or it may give negative information—information about what the causal history does not include. All these explanations are causal, in that they provide information about the causal history of an event. Hence they all imply the existence of some regularizing explanation for the event's occurrence. Indeed, they may give some indication as to what that explanation might be. But they are not themselves regularizing explanations.

The suggestion is, then, that a causal explanation is one that gives some information about the causal origin of something. This includes statements that serve merely to identify some event or process as a cause, without indicating the explanatorily relevant features of that event. On this second version of the dispositional theory, functional explanations will be causal explanations of this kind: a functional explanation will serve to identify the cause of the presence of the item. To say that an item is present in order to do F is to say that it is there because other items of the same type have done F and their doing so did some good.[16]

On this view, the normative, functional features of the item are adding nothing to the force of the explanation. The force of the explanation would be unchanged if we simply said that the item is there because other items of that type did F and their doing F helped the organism to survive or reproduce. The point of using a normative function statement is to add the implication that a full explanation will refer to the fact that this is an outcome that is to be valued. Similarly, someone might attempt to explain a military victory by saying that it was due to the courageous behaviour of a particular group of soldiers. This explanation identifies the cause of the victory as the soldiers' fearless behaviour; and it makes the additional point that the soldiers' fearlessness is to be admired.

On this account, it seems to be a moot point whether functional explanations should be categorized as normalizing explanations. A functional explanation is a normalizing explanation in a weak sense, in that it appeals to normative features of an item in order to explain its presence. But it is not a normalizing explanation in the stronger sense that the distinctive force of the explanation has to do with the normative quality of those features. What is distinctive about a functional explanation is that it indicates the occurrence of a distinctive kind of causal process. But we could have done that just as well by saying that the item is there because items of that kind help the organism to reproduce by doing F. Similarly, we could have explained the victory by saying that it happened because the soldiers behaved in a fearless way. The point of using a normative function statement is to make an additional, non-explanatory point.

On this second view, then, the dispositional theorist has succeeded in showing how there can be functional explanations that are genuinely explanatory, but in a way that deprives them of a distinctively normalizing character. This is because, on this account, there is no connection between the normativity of function statements and their explanatory power. These two puzzling features of function statements are allowed to cohabit, but they lead independent lives. The explanatory force of function statements derives from the fact that the behaviour of certain items helps to promote some state of affairs—the element of service; but their normative character derives from the value of

---

[16] This account is taken from Andrew Woodfield (1976: 139). Mark Bedau (1992*a*) offers a rather similar account; he also discusses the worry that I raise here, but concludes instead that there are no 'full-blooded' teleological (i.e. normative) explanations in biology.

that state of affairs. There is nothing incoherent or impossible about this solution. But it does seem very unsatisfactory—unsatisfactory enough, I think, to cast doubt on the claim that, on this view, functional explanations really are normalizing explanations.

3.5. *The Basic Dispositional Account: Summary*

The basic dispositional account centres on the notions of service and value. According to the dispositional theory, an item d can be ascribed the function to do F if and only if items of the same type typically do F, thereby contributing to some outcome that has (or is viewed as having) intrinsic biological value. I have suggested that there are two difficulties facing the basic dispositional account. First, it is not clear that it is possible to find a satisfactory interpretation of the requirement that devices belonging to D should typically do F. Secondly, the theory fails to provide an attractive account of functional explanations: the view that functional explanations are non-causal 'normalizations after the fact' preserves the normativity of function statements at the expense of their explanatory force, while the view that functional explanations are causal explanations leaves a gap between the explanatory and normative features of function statements. All these difficulties appear to arise from the dispositional theorist's reliance on the notion of biological value to account for the normativity of function statements.

4. The Basic Aetiological Theory

4.1. *Function and Causal History*

The dispositional theorist began from the premiss that we cannot identify biological functions with design functions or use functions because biological items are not subject to conscious design or use. The aetiological theory aims to circumvent this obstacle by finding a way of characterizing design and use functions that avoids any explicit reference to conscious agency. Like the dispositional account, the aetiological theory begins with the claim that the biological function of an item is something that it does. It distinguishes the function(s) of an item from its other capacities by adding the idea that a function of an item is something it does that explains why it is present, or why it occurs.

The aetiological theory has traditionally been associated with the analysis of function statements offered by Larry Wright (1976). Wright suggests that a statement ascribing a function F to an item d should be analysed as making two claims:

W.1 d does F.

W.2 d is present because d does F.

Wright's analysis is deliberately vague, because he wishes it to cover a range of different cases. In what follows, I will focus on a modified version of Wright's formulation, one that makes a clear distinction between tokens and types, and is more precise with respect to tense. In fact, we can offer two versions of this modified formulation, one that applies to design functions and one that applies to use functions.

Where d is a particular item, and F is an activity, d has the design function to do F if and only if d belongs to some type of item D, such that:

AD.1 Items belonging to D have done F in the past.

AD.2 The fact that items belonging to D have done F causally explains the fact that d occurs.

Where d is a particular item, and F is an activity, d has the use function to do F if and only if:

AU.1 d has done F in the past.

AU.2 The fact that d has done F causally explains the fact that d continues to be present or to occur.[17]

Biological functions are design functions, not use functions. There are two reasons for insisting on this. The first is that there are some biological items, specifically those whose functions concern reproduction rather than survival, that do not have use functions: the fact that an ovary stores eggs, for example, does not explain the fact that it continues to exist. The second is that biological items may acquire eccentric use functions during the organism's lifetime. For example, an individual animal might have an unusual limping gait that confuses predators; and this might help to explain the survival of the organism and its gait. But we would not consider confusing predators to be a biological function of the organism's gait. For current purposes, then, we will be concerned exclusively with design functions: AD.1 and AD.2 can be regarded as constituting a basic aetiological analysis of biological functions.

This basic aetiological analysis avoids all mention of biological value, whether subjective or objective. It appeals only to the causal history of the

---

[17] There is a disparity between the proposed analysis of design function statements and the proposed analysis of use function statements. To assign a design function to an item is to imply something about the explanation for its existence. To assign a use function to an item is *either* to imply something about the explanation for its existence *or*, merely, to imply something about why it continues to be present—for example, why it remains as part of a larger system, or why it is kept as part of someone's toolkit, or simply why it is left where it is.

item in question. I take it that the aetiologist will regard it as a virtue of her account that she is able to avoid treating functions as subjective, without being committed to the claim that there is such a thing as objective biological value. In what follows, I will treat it as a constraint on the success of the aetiological account that it should remain free of these commitments. But it would be possible for an aetiologist to reject this constraint.

Notice that the basic aetiological account, as I have formulated it here, makes no reference to the process of natural selection. In this respect, it contrasts with many of the aetiological accounts to be found in the recent literature.[18] However, the basic account that I have presented here includes only those elements that are essential to an aetiological account; and I take it that a reference to natural selection is not essential to such an account. I will return to the role of natural selection in the next chapter.

Like the dispositional analysis, the aetiological analysis of design function statements needs to include a reference to the type of item to which d belongs, though for a different reason. Suppose that, in our analysis, we had relied simply on the claim that the presence of d could be explained by the fact that causal ancestors of d had done F in the past. If so, we would have been confronted by the following problem: the causal ancestors of a particular item will include not only earlier items of a similar kind, but *all* the organs, systems, and behaviours possessed by the organism's ancestors. The causal ancestors of my heart will include not only my ancestors' hearts, but also their livers, kidneys, bones, nervous systems, and so on: if any of these items had failed, my heart might not have existed. By including a reference to types in the aetiological analysis, we can rule out the claim that my heart has the function not only to move my blood, but to remove toxins from it as well. The aetiological theorist might try to group biological items into types by physical similarity. But a much more natural solution would be to type them by family, in the sense suggested earlier. On this view, causal origin, biological kind, and biological function will come in a single package.

In the next two sections I will consider two objections that might be brought against the basic aetiological theory. The first of these is the worry that the aetiologist will not be able to allow for the possibility that families of biological items might lose or change their functions over time. The second is the objection that the basic aetiological account will not be able to offer a satisfactory account of functional explanations as normalizing explanations. I will reject the first of these objections, but I will endorse the second.

---

[18] Buller (1998) distinguishes between strong aetiological accounts—those that include a reference to natural selection—and weak aetiological accounts—those that do not.

4.2. Changing   Functions: Problems   for   the   Basic   Aetiological
   Theory

Unlike the dispositional account, the aetiological account can easily allow for
the possibility of eccentric items. On this account, the malformed eye will not
have the function to act as a warning mark, because its presence cannot be
explained by the fact that earlier members of the same family acted as warning marks. Nevertheless, there is a cluster of objections that seek to undermine
the claim that the aetiologist will be able to draw a clear distinction between
functioning, malfunctioning, and eccentric items.

It has often been objected that the aetiologist is not able to allow that a type
of device has changed its function over the years or has lost a function that it
previously had. Unless the aetiologist can allow for change or loss of function,
she will be unable to make a distinction between devices whose functions have
altered or become redundant and devices that are malfunctioning: every
human being will have a defective appendix. The aetiologist also needs to
explain what it is for an item to gain a new function. In particular, she will not
want to be forced to claim that an item might have the function to do F simply because one of its ancestors happened to do F on a single occasion, and
thereby helped the organism to reproduce. This is the aetiological equivalent
of the problem of the eccentric item.

I think that the problem about change of function often arises as a result of
a confusion of types and tokens, fostered by the ambiguities in Wright's original formulation. Consider a situation in which a type of device gains a new
function (F_N) in addition to its original one (F_O). It may well be true that, if
we want to understand why that type of item is present in that type of organism, we need only consider the original function of the device: it was because
items of that type did F_O that it became prevalent in the population. But, if we
consider a particular example of that type of item belonging to a particular
organism, then we need to consider both the original and the novel functions
of the item. The fact that this particular item is present will be explained by
the fact that the parents and grandparents of the organism possessed an item
that did *both* F_O and F_N. So the fact that earlier items of the same kind did F_N
will help to explain the presence of items of that kind.

But this does not explain how a device could lose a function. After all, even
in the case of a type of item that has long since ceased to do F_O, the presence
of a particular item of that type will be explained by the fact that its distant
ancestors did F_O. It is not clear that we can give a very precise account of the
circumstances under which a family of items loses a function, but I think it is
clear where we should be looking. As generations of family members unable
to do F_O go by, the fact that earlier family members once did F_O will become
less and less significant in the explanation for the presence of their descendants, while other phenomena, such as genetic inertia or the fact that family

members now do F_N, will become more and more significant. Godfrey-Smith (1994) has suggested that we should adopt a 'modern-history' theory of functions, which takes the function of a type of item to be determined by its recent past. Such an account will exploit some notion of explanatory weight, which is lost as other, more recent phenomena join the causal chain. In other words, we need to modify AD.1 to:

AD.1* Items belonging to D have done F in the recent past.

There is clearly room for vagueness here, to match the vagueness in our intuitions about when a device loses its function. [19]

Some notion of explanatory weight is also needed to deal with the case of the eccentric item. The aetiologist ought to insist that functions take time and repetition to establish. Only then will the fact that earlier items of that kind did F_N carry weight in the explanation for the presence of this item in comparison with other factors such as genetic inertia, or the fact that earlier devices did F_O. Of course, this will leave the aetiologist in trouble with another group of objectors who worry that this kind of account denies functions to first generation items. On this view, the aetiological theory will deny functions to second, third, and even fourth generation items too. But I think that this is a point on which intuitions simply diverge.

Clearly, this notion of explanatory weight will require further development, preferably within a wider theory of causal explanation. But I take it that it is sufficiently clear for our present purposes. If so, the basic aetiological account has passed its first test—that of explaining how items may change, lose, or gain a function. However, I will argue in the next section that there is another objection that the aetiological account fails to answer.

4.3. Normalizing Explanations: The Basic Aetiological Account

In contrast with the dispositional theory, the basic aetiological theory begins with the notion of a functional explanation. For the aetiological theory, it seems, it will be the normativity of function statements that requires special treatment. As we have seen, the aetiologist tries to do without the idea that there are objective functional norms, while at the same time avoiding the claim that the normativity of function statements is purely

---

[19] It might be objected that I am being too kind to the aetiologist here. Why should the aetiologist be allowed a rather vague notion of explanatory weight, when the dispositional theorist was criticized for relying on an unexplained notion of frequency? But note that the problem for the dispositional theorist was not that the relevant notion of frequency might be rather vague. The problem was that it is impossible to find an interpretation of the frequency requirement that yields plausible results, no matter how vaguely it is applied. There is nothing wrong with a certain amount of vagueness in our account of functions, provided we are clear about what is going on.

subjective. To do this, she needs to explain what it is about the objective, non-normative features of such items that explains why it is appropriate to characterize them in normative terms. And this, on the face of it, is no easy task.

Nevertheless, it might be argued that the need to account for this feature of function statements poses little difficulty for the aetiological account. After all, the basic aetiological theory offers a perfectly clear criterion for distinguishing functioning devices from malfunctioning and eccentric items: a device will malfunction if it fails to do what its ancestors did; it will operate eccentrically if what it does is not what its ancestors did. A device is supposed to do what its ancestors did.

However, this is not by itself a very satisfying solution to the problem. A simple stipulation that malfunctioning is a matter of failing to live up to one's causal history will not help us to understand how the causal history of an item could make it appropriate to describe it in normative terms in the first place. In order to get any further with this problem, we need to understand what the aetiologist will say about the normalizing force of functional explanations.

The most natural approach for the aetiologist to take is to begin in the same way as the second dispositional theorist described above; that is, to treat functional explanations as causal explanations, in Lewis's broader sense. Once again, the point of a functional explanation will be to provide a very specific kind of information about the causal history of the device—namely, that it involved a certain kind of causal process. What is distinctive about this causal process is that there is a causal connection between the fact that an organism possesses a certain device and the fact that devices of that kind are able to produce a certain kind of effect. We might label this kind of process a process of *self-preservation*, because it involves a type of item being able to ensure its own persistence.

But why should the aetiologist regard this kind of explanation as a *normalizing* explanation? A process of self-preservation is just like any other causal process—a course of events governed by causal laws. The challenge for the aetiologist is to answer this question without relying on the idea that some states of affairs are intrinsically valuable, or seen as valuable by us.

The claim that a device is supposed to behave in a certain way seems to involve two elements. First, we need to be able to make sense of the idea that there is some standard that the device might meet or fail to meet. Secondly, we need to explain why it is appropriate to apply that standard to the device. The aetiologist might start from the idea that the device is required to live up to the past behaviour of its ancestors. But it is much less obvious why the fact that an item is the product of a process of self-preservation should impose this kind of requirement upon it.

There is an alternative starting point for the aetiologist. As we have seen, the normativity of function statements implies two different kinds of contrast: a contrast between a functioning and a malfunctioning device; and a contrast between a functioning and an eccentric item. The aetiologist might start from the suggestion that the normalizing force of functional explanations derives directly from these two contrasts.[20]

Where the causal history of a particular item involves a process of self-preservation, there is a strong sense in which it is *no accident* that the organism possesses an item that is able to produce a certain kind of effect: the item is there just because earlier items of the same type behaved in that way. The aetiologist can argue that the normalizing force of a functional explanation derives, at least in part, from this contrast. When I offer a functional explanation for the presence of my heart, I offer a piece of information about its causal history, information that shows that it is no accident that I possess a mechanism that is able to move blood around my body. The contrast will be with other features of my heart, and with other mechanisms, whose presence is quite fortuitous.

When we offer a functional explanation for the presence of a defective device, the contrast will be with other features of the device and other traits that are equally unhelpful. Here, the expectation will be that the presence of such a useless device must be an accident, a product of causal processes that have nothing to do with the capacities of devices of that kind. The point of the explanation will be to show that the *presence* of a malfunctioning device is no accident. What is accidental is its failure to behave as its ancestors behaved. The idea is, then, that functional explanations are normalizing explanations because they draw attention to the fact that the occurrence of an item of a certain kind is no accident, even when it is failing to behave in the way in which it might reasonably be expected to do.

Unfortunately, the account presented in this section is open to a fatal objection. The objection is that it is possible to find cases where an item appears to be the result of a process of self-preservation, but where it seems very unnatural to describe it in normative, functional terms. I think that Mark Bedau (1991) has proposed the neatest example of this kind of objection. Bedau uses the example of clay crystals to show that the aetiological theory will ascribe functional properties to items that patently do not have them.[21]

Clay is made up of tiny crystals. Crystals are built up of layer upon layer of atoms, and each layer builds on the layer below. A crystal grows because free-floating atoms or ions tend to stick to its surface, forming a new layer that matches the layer below. Crystals can form spontaneously in a solution

---

[20] See Wright (1976: 82–1).
[21] Bedau takes his example from Richard Dawkins (1986: 150–6). I have also drawn on Dawkins's account. Christopher Boorse (1976: 75) presents some more everyday counter-examples of the same kind, but the examples he gives concern putative use functions, so they are not directly relevant here.

or they can be seeded by particles of dust or small crystals. When a crystal seed is dropped into a solution, it will produce a population of crystals with similar physical properties: flat crystals will produce flat crystals and chunky crystals will produce chunky crystals. Naturally occurring crystals, like those in clay, have flaws. Once a flaw has appeared it will tend to be copied in the layers that accumulate on top. So the fact that the topmost layer has certain features can be explained by the fact that earlier layers have those features.

It will follow from this that the fact that a particular layer of clay is present and has the properties that it has can be causally explained by the fact that earlier layers with similar properties were able to replicate themselves. Indeed, it is possible to imagine a situation in which clay crystals become involved in a process of natural selection. Suppose that a family of clay crystals possessed a trait—a certain shape, say—that made them more efficient replicators. For example, suppose that chunky crystals growing on the bed of a stream slow the flow of water, with the result that they replicate more easily than flat crystals growing in the same stream and so use up a larger share of the minerals needed to create new crystals. In this situation, there would be selection for chunkiness over flatness (Dawkins 1986: 154).

It seems that the aetiologist ought to conclude that clay crystals might have the function to replicate themselves, or even to slow the flow of water around them. And yet, as Bedau protests, it does not seem to be appropriate to describe the behaviour of clay crystals in functional terms. Asked why a particular clay crystal is present, we can reply that it is there because earlier clay crystals were capable of replicating, but not that it is there *in order to* replicate. There is no implicit contrast with other traits that the crystals possess whose presence is purely fortuitous. The implication is that the aetiologist is wrong to suppose that functional explanations are normalizing explanations simply because they indicate that an item is the result of a process of self-preservation.

I believe that Bedau's objection is a very strong one: strong enough to show that we have not yet found a theory of functions that is able to give an adequate account of the normativity of function statements.

4.4. The Basic Aetiological Account: Summary

The basic aetiological theory centres on the idea that a function arises where the history of a device includes a certain kind of causal process—a process of self-preservation. On this account a device d can be ascribed the function to do F if and only if other items of the same type have done F in the recent past, and the fact that they did so helps to explain the presence of d. According to the aetiologist, the point of a functional explanation is to make sense of the presence of a device as no accident, given its history. But, in the end, the basic aetiological account fails to account for the normative force of function statements. This is because there are items, such as clay crystals, that are produced by a process of <u>self-preservation</u>, which we would not naturally describe in normative, functional terms.

I began by suggesting that a theory of functions must succeed in reconciling the normativity of function statements with their explanatory force. It seems that neither the basic dispositional theory nor the basic aetiological theory is entirely successful in meeting this challenge. In the next chapter, I will continue my search for a successful theory of functions.

2

The Core Account

1. Introduction

In the previous chapter, I suggested that a theory of functions must be able to reconcile the normative character of function statements with their explanatory force. In this chapter, I will attempt to develop a theory of functions that meets this challenge. The account that I shall propose is essentially a version of the aetiological theory, but it borrows an important element from the dispositional account. I will argue that this modified account is able to accommodate both the explanatory force and the normative character of function statements.

2. The Elements of the Account

2.1. A History of Service

According to the basic aetiological theory, as we have seen, the normative force of function statements can be explained by the fact that some biological items are produced by a causal process of a certain kind—a process of self-preservation. As we have seen, the theory fails because it is possible to find an example—clay crystals—where an item is the product of the right kind of causal history, but where it seems very unnatural to describe it as having a function.

The dispositional theory, on the other hand, does not have difficulties with this case. The dispositional theorist can deny that clay crystals, in replicating, are contributing to some state of affairs that has (or is viewed as having) biological value. For example, the dispositional theorist might suggest that our reluctance to ascribe functions to clay crystals is explained by the fact that no value attaches to states of affairs involving natural but non-living things.

One thought might be that we could try to supplement the basic aetiological theory by borrowing from the dispositional account. As we saw in the previous chapter, the dispositional theory is made up of two basic ingredients: value and service. Can we solve the problem by incorporating one of these elements into an otherwise aetiological theory?

Bedau (1991) himself suggests that the clay crystal objection demonstrates that it is impossible to account for the normativity of biological function statements without appealing to some notion of biological value. It would certainly be possible to develop a theory of functions that combined an appeal to causal history with an appeal to biological value. The theory would centre on the claim that an item can be ascribed the function to do F if its presence can be explained by the fact that its ancestors did F, where their doing so has (or is regarded as having) some biological value. A theory of this kind would be able to sidestep the clay crystal objection. Moreover, because it retains an appeal to causal history, it will be able to distinguish functions from eccentric benefits.

Nevertheless, a theory of this kind will not offer a complete solution to the problem. An aetiological theory that incorporates a reference to value will be no more successful than the basic dispositional theory in accounting for the explanatory force of function statements. Once more, the problem will be that the theory will make no connection between the normativity of function statements and their explanatory force. Indeed, any account that attempts to explain the normativity of function statements as arising either from objective biological value or from human wants and expectations will face a problem of this kind.[1]

I would like to develop an alternative approach. I would like to suggest that the most promising resource possessed by the dispositional account is not the notion of value, but the notion of service. According to the dispositional theory, items do not have functions on their own account. Rather, for an item to have a function is for it to be supposed to contribute to the workings of some second item. On this view, a function statement implies the existence of a means–end relationship between two items. I agree with the dispositional theorist that this means–end relationship is essential to our notion of a function.

If this is right, it suggests an alternative diagnosis of the failure of the basic aetiological theory. According to this alternative diagnosis, the difficulties encountered by the theory arise, not because of its exclusive reliance on causal history, but because it misidentifies the kind of causal process involved. The causal process to which the basic theory appeals—the process of self preservation—is too simple to play this role, because it fails to take account of the means–end relationship on which the existence of a function depends.

I believe that a version of the aetiological theory that incorporates a notion of service will be able to account for the normativity of function statements without having to appeal to the notion of biological value. Moreover, I hope to show that a theory of this kind will be able to offer a satisfying account of

[1] Bedau (1991) is aware of this point.

the normative character of functional explanations. I will refer to this modified aetiological theory as the *core account*, because it embodies the nucleus of the theory of functions that I would like to defend.

At the heart of the core account is the following claim: a device will have the function to behave in a certain way, if its presence can be explained by the fact that its ancestors, by behaving in that way, contributed to the workings of some second mechanism, which in turned helped to produce the device. On this view, a device will have a function when it is a product, not of a process of self-preservation, but of a process that we might label a process of *preservation through service*.

This suggests the following analysis of natural design functions. Where d is an item and F is an activity, d has the function to do F if and only if there is some family of items G; there is some family of items D, to which d belongs, and which consists of items produced by a member of G in some manner M;[2] there is some item g which belongs to G and which produced d by M; and there is some activity E, such that:

CD.1 Members of D have done F in the recent past.

CD.2 The fact that g produced d by M is explained partly by the fact that the doing of F by members of D in the recent past assisted g, or other members of G that are ancestors of g, to do some further thing E.

To give an example: my heart has the function to move the blood because, first, the hearts possessed by my recent ancestors moved the blood; and, secondly, by doing so, they assisted the genetic material inside my ancestors' germline cells to replicate, thereby setting in train a sequence of events that ended with the production of my heart.[3]

Since I will draw on the notion of a natural use function in a later chapter, I will include an analysis of natural use functions here. Natural use functions can be analysed as follows: where d is an item and F is an activity, d has the use function to do F if there is some second item g which maintains d and some activity E such that:

CU.1 d has recently done F.

CU.2 The fact that g maintains d is explained partly by the fact that d's recently doing F has assisted g to do some further thing E.

There are two features of these analyses that require explanation. The first is that it is important to bear in mind that, whenever I use words such as

---

[2] It is always necessary to understand the phrase 'produced in manner M' as including the proviso 'more or less'.

[3] In fact, in this case, almost any of the organs inside my ancestor's bodies could have played the role of the second mechanism in this analysis: in almost all cases, their activities feature on the causal chain that leads from the operation of my ancestors' hearts to the production of my heart. I make this clearer in my discussion of 'governors' in the next section.

'produce', 'assist', or 'contribute to' in this context, they are to be understood in rather a stark sense. One item will count as producing another if it contributes some event to the causal chain that eventuates in the occurrence of the second. In this sense of the word, a particular rain shower will be produced not only by a cloud, but also by the ocean, the sun, and earlier showers. An item will count as assisting or contributing to the operation of some other item if something that the first item does is a cause—perhaps a rather distant one—of something that the second item does. Similarly, if I describe one item as benefiting from the operation of another, or as needing another item to behave in a certain way, I am to be understood as claiming that the latter, by behaving in that way, would help the former to do some further thing.[4]

Secondly, the analysis does not require that the behaviour of earlier members of D affected g itself, but only that it should have affected g or ancestors of g. This is to allow us, for example, to ascribe a function to the eyes of children born to blind parents. In this case, the eyes of the child's parents did not enable them to see; but what is important is that the eyes of the child's earlier ancestors did enable them to see. In this case, then, it is the ancestors of g, rather than g itself, to which earlier members of D made their contribution.

In Chapter 3, I will introduce some further modifications to this account. But the analysis given here encapsulates the essential spirit of the account of functions that I would like to defend. The core account incorporates both the backward-looking intuition that a function arises when the presence of a device can be explained by something that it or its ancestors did, and the forward-looking intuition that a function involves a means–end relationship between two devices. The additional modifications that I shall introduce will answer to these two basic intuitions.

2.2. Introducing Governors

By performing its function, d is supposed once again to assist some further item to do E. I will refer to an item that a particular device is supposed to assist as its *governor*. The notion of a governor is central to the theory of functions that I will develop in this and the next chapter, so I would like to say something about it here. But I will give a more detailed account of what constitutes a governor in the next chapter.

[4] It is important not to interpret the claim that members of G need members of D to do F if they are to do E as implying that members of G will *only* be able to do E if some member of D does F. There may be some other way of enabling members of G to do E. Rather, the performance of F by some member of D is, as Mackie would put it, 'necessary in the circumstances'. See Mackie (1974: 38).

Which items will count as the governors of a functioning device? We can begin by insisting that a governor of d must be a member of some family that plays the role of G in the analysis above. For example, my liver belongs to the same family as my ancestors' livers. Moreover, my ancestors' livers helped to produce my heart. But, clearly, this is not strong enough: for my brother's liver will also belong to this family, and we would not want to say that my heart is supposed to help deliver oxygen to my brother's liver. We must also insist that the governors of a device d will be items that are *equivalent* to those members of G that helped to produce d. An item will be equivalent to one of these earlier items if it is causally related to d in much the same way as those earlier items were related to earlier members of D that assisted them to do E.[5] My liver, unlike my brother's, is causally related to my heart in much the same way as my ancestors' livers were related to their hearts. Given that my ancestors' livers helped to produce my heart, and given that my liver is equivalent to my ancestors' livers, we can say that my liver is a governor of my heart—it is an item to which my heart is supposed to contribute.

In a complex system, such as an organism, there may be a long string of governors to which the device is supposed to contribute, either on its own or in concert with other mechanisms. The governors of the heart will include those organs that, like the liver, benefit directly from the operation of the circulatory system. But they will also include the governors of those organs, and the governors of those governors, all of which benefit from the operation of the heart, until we come to the genetic material inside the germline cells of the organism.

2.3. Clay Crystals and the Core Account

Once we have replaced the basic aetiological theory with the core account, we can rule out the suggestion that clay crystals function to replicate themselves, and we can explain why this suggestion seems so counter-intuitive. It seems counter-intuitive because, although the persistence of clay crystals can be explained by the fact that they replicate themselves, this explanation does not go via the workings of any second mechanism. The tendency of clay crystals to replicate themselves does not serve any end beyond itself.

Nevertheless, there are two objections that could be made to this proposed solution to the problem posed by the clay crystals. First of all, it might be argued that, in replicating, a layer of crystals does contribute to the workings

---

[5] 'Causally related' here means 'related with respect to causal origin'. The processes that produced my heart and my liver were related to each other in more or less the same way as the processes that produced my ancestor's heart and her liver. This relationship does not hold between the processes that produced my heart and my brother's liver.

of some second item—namely, the new layer of crystals that results. If this second layer in turn produces a third layer of crystals, it might be thought that this third layer could be ascribed the function of replicating. This would be the case if we gave the third layer the role of d in our analysis, while the second layer took on the role of g. In this case, we could say that the presence of d (the third layer) can be explained by the fact that it was brought into being by g (the second layer), as a result of the fact that an ancestor of d (the original layer) was able to replicate, so affecting g.

However, there is a simple solution to this problem: we can insist that affecting the producer g should not include bringing it into being. This prohibition reflects the fact that the relationship between D and G is asymmetrical: members of G have a certain causal priority over members of D.[6]

The second objection is prompted by the possibility that the clay crystals might possess features that enable them to facilitate replication by altering their environment. At the end of the last chapter, I described a situation in which chunky crystals are able to slow the flow of water in the stream, thereby increasing the availability of the minerals that they need to replicate. It might be objected that, in this case, the crystals ought to be ascribed the function of slowing the stream, according to the core account: the fact that this layer of crystals is present can be explained by the fact that earlier crystals slowed the stream, thereby causing the stream to deposit more of the minerals required for replication.

I think that this is a good objection, and one that cannot be answered by the core account as it stands. However, I believe that it can be answered by a fully developed version of the account that I shall set out in Chapter 3. For this reason, I will defer my response to this objection until Chapter 3.

2.4. *Two Rival Aetiological Strategies*

A number of writers have suggested modified versions of the basic aetiological account. In this section I would like to consider two other versions of the aetiological account that have been suggested by other writers. These are accounts that focus on the process of natural selection and accounts that centre on the idea that functioning devices are supposed to be part of a larger system. I would like to distinguish the core account from these alternative accounts and to explain why I prefer the core account.

According to the core account, we can say that a bat's wings have the function to enable the bat to fly, and we can do so in virtue of certain facts about

---

[6] Note that an effect of including this provision is to rule out ascribing to genes and to organisms the function of producing each other. We can still describe organisms as having the function to provide materials and energy to enable genes to replicate, but it does not seem obvious that genes will have any functions in relation to organisms.

the bat's history. The first fact is that the bat possesses wings partly because it possesses a genetic structure that specifies wings. The second fact is that the presence of an organism that possesses a genetic structure of that kind can be explained in part by the fact that the wings possessed by the bat's ancestors enabled them to fly.

On this account, a type of trait may develop a biological function provided that it is able to contribute to the organism's capacity to survive and to reproduce, and provided that it is heritable. Hence, this account is consistent with a story in which evolution occurs through natural selection. But it is also consistent with a story in which the species have always been as they are now, or have changed very slowly as a result of genetic drift, provided that their continuing existence can nevertheless be explained by the operation of their organs and other traits. Someone who believes that the species are eternal and changeless does not have to deny that if bats' wings stopped flapping there would soon be no bats.

In contrast, many recent proponents of the aetiological theory have proposed accounts that centre on the idea that the function of a biological device is what it has been naturally selected for.[7] Natural selection can occur only where traits vary within a population: where there is variability within a population, individuals will possess different traits that *compete* against each other. But the notion of competition is not central to the core account. According to the core account, all that is important is that a trait is present because of what it has done in the past: it does not need to have competed against rival traits.[8]

Of course, many items that are the products of natural selection will also be the products of a process of preservation through service. But this need not always be the case. In particular, we have already seen that clay crystals may possess traits that are selected for, without these traits possessing functions. If my diagnosis of this problem is correct, this is because a process of natural selection will not necessarily involve a means–end relationship of the kind that generates functions.

The second strategy that I would like to consider is similar to the core account, in that it does make use of the idea that a function involves a means–end relationship between two items (Griffiths 1993: 410–11; Godfrey-Smith 1994: 347–50). But it differs from the core account in that it centres on the claim that a device will have a function only if it contributes to the workings of some larger system of which it is a part. It is important to distinguish this claim from the one that I am proposing here. The heart belongs to a larger

---

[7] Millikan (1989*a*), Neander (1991*b*), and Godfrey-Smith (1994) amongst others. In general, these theorists are not attempting to give an account of the common-sense notion of a function.

[8] Buller (1998) labels aetiological accounts that do not rely on the process of natural selection 'weak aetiological accounts'. The core account is a weak aetiological account.

system in the body, the circulatory system. But the circulatory system will not count as a governor of the heart. The governors of the heart will be those organs and structures to which the heart is supposed to contribute, whether directly or indirectly: the kidneys, brain, liver, and so on, which are supplied with oxygen and nutrients as a result of the heart's operation, and other items to which those organs go on to contribute.

I believe that this is a better way of incorporating the notion of service into our account, because the notion of a larger system, if interpreted strictly, is not applicable in all cases and, if interpreted leniently, might seem to let in too much. For example, it is not obvious in what sense a simple tool, such as a tin opener, can be said to belong to a larger system. It might be replied that we can take the human agent and the tin opener together as constituting a system, but this would seem to be a rather gerrymandered solution. Moreover, if we can take a cook with a tin opener to be a system, there seems to be no reason why we should not take a stream clogged with clay to be a system, and describe clay crystals as contributing to this larger system of stream and clay.

If we make this move, we will be unable to answer Bedau's worry in the way in which I have suggested. The fact that the clay crystals replicate will ensure that the stream stays clogged with clay. Moreover, the presence of clay in the stream will help to facilitate the production of new clay crystals. The source of the problem is easy to identify. If we insist that a functional device must contribute to some larger system of which it is a part, rather than to some separate governor, there will be no guarantee that the part of the system that is responsible for replicating the device is not identical with the device itself. This is what is happening in the clay crystal story: the same items are both filling the stream with clay and, as a result, producing new clay crystals.

2.5. The Elements of the Account: Summary

The account that I have proposed is a version of the aetiological account that incorporates the notion of service introduced by the dispositional account. According to the core account, an item can be ascribed the function to do F if its presence can be explained, in part, by the fact that earlier items of the same type did F and by doing so assisted a second item to do some further thing. A device that has the function to do F is supposed to contribute to the workings of its governor(s) by doing so.

This account will be able to resolve Bedau's clay crystal objection, because the clay crystals replicate themselves, and so do not rely on some second item to produce them. However, there are situations in which clay crystals are able to affect some other entity in a way that helps them to replicate. I have yet to explain why this does not imply that, in this situation, clay crystals would have the function to behave in that way.

Finally, the core account must be distinguished from two other modified versions of the aetiological account: the core account makes no reference to natural selection, nor does it rely on the idea that a functioning device is supposed to contribute to a wider system of which it is a part.

3. The Normative Character of Function Statements

3.1. *Normalizing Explanations: The Core Account*

Like the basic aetiological theory, the core account will characterize teleological explanations as a kind of *causal* explanation. The point of a functional explanation will be to indicate that the history of a device includes a causal process of a certain kind—a process of preservation through service. But we have yet to explain why the occurrence of a process of this kind should make it appropriate to characterize the operation of biological devices in normative terms.

The problems that face the core account at this point are exactly the same as those encountered by the basic aetiological account. A process of preservation through service may have a more complex structure than a process of self-preservation, but, nonetheless, it is still just a sequence of events, governed by natural laws. Why should a natural process of this kind be characterized in normative terms?

It is possible to divide this question into two parts. First, we can ask why items that are products of *this* kind of causal process should be characterized in normative terms. We want to say that fur is supposed to insulate and hearts are supposed to move the blood, but not that the sun is supposed to shine, or that clay crystals are supposed to replicate. But what is the difference between these cases? Secondly, we need to consider why the fact that an item was produced by a particular kind of natural process should ever make it appropriate to describe that item in normative terms.

In this section, I will give some attention to both these questions. I will argue that the difference between a process of preservation through service and a process of self-preservation has to do with the relation between the functioning device and the mechanism that produced it. And I will attempt to forestall the objection that this is just another way of importing human values into the situation by anthropomorphizing the producing mechanism. In answer to the second question I will appeal to Wright's idea (1976: 106) that the normativity of function statements arises from a *dead metaphor*, and I will try to throw some light on the nature of this metaphor.[9]

I will begin with the first question. As we saw in the previous chapter, the claim that a device is supposed to behave in a certain way seems to involve two elements: the idea that there is some standard that a device might meet or fail to meet; and a rationale for applying that standard to the device. The suggestion will be that it is the special, causal relationship between the functioning device (d) and the mechanism that produced it (g) that both sets the standard and imposes it on d.

There are two sides to the relationship between d and g. First, if d were to do F, this would assist some member of G to do some further thing, E. In other words, members of G have a need that would be satisfied by the presence of an item that does F.[10] It is the existence of this need that makes doing F into a standard other devices might meet or fail to meet. Secondly, g produced d; moreover, g produced d partly *because* members of D are capable of assisting members of G to do E by doing F. It is the fact that d is causally dependent on g that imposes doing F as a standard upon d. Note that all that is important here is the causal relationship between g and d: members of G are assisted to do E by the fact that members of D do F, regardless of whether we regard doing F as a good thing; and g produced d because members of D have done F, regardless of whether we expect or want d to do F.

There is an obvious parallel with artificial functions that makes it tempting to lapse into anthropomorphic language at this point. We are tempted to say that d is supposed to do F because g produced d *in the expectation* that d would do F. This is a dangerous temptation because it suggests the following picture. We began by assigning functions to artefacts. Artefacts are supposed to behave in a certain way because they are produced by human designers in the expectation that they will do so. We then applied the notion of a function to natural devices in the mistaken belief that they were artefacts. Now that we understand that organs are produced by genes, and not by God, we ought to accept that it is inappropriate to characterize biological devices in normative terms. To suppose otherwise is to think of genes as little agents with their own purposes and expectations.

However, I believe that this objection rests on a mistaken view of the normative force of artificial function statements. We do not need to suppose that a designer confers a function on an artefact by somehow imposing or projecting her expectations onto the device. Rather, we can hold that what makes

---

[9] Wright suggested that the metaphor in question involves comparing natural functions to artificial functions. I will make a rather different suggestion, one that will apply to natural and artificial functions in just the same way.

[10] Recall that the claim that g needs d to do F if g is to do E implies only that d's doing F is necessary in the circumstances for g's doing E.

it appropriate to describe an artefact in normative terms is the causal relationship between the device and its designer, the (objective) fact that the
designer produced the device because she intended that it should be used in a
certain way.[11] On this view, we can allow that the normative character both of
statements that ascribe functions to biological devices and of artificial function statements derives from a perfectly objective state of affairs.

The answer to the first question, then, is that the normativity of function
statements has to do with the structure of the causal relationship between the
device and the mechanism that produced it. But I have yet to consider the second question: why should the existence of this causal relationship make it
appropriate to describe the device in normative terms? Why should we talk of
'standards' or 'requirements' here at all? I think that the most natural explanation is that the normative force of function statements derives from a dead
metaphor.

In this case, the metaphor derives from a moral or social relationship: it is
a metaphor of *obligation*.[12] The idea will be that a device 'owes' it to the mechanism that produced it to perform its function. A defective device will count
as defective because it is failing to meet its 'obligation' to its 'maker'. In contrast, behaviour that the device produces quite fortuitously will be behaviour
that is not 'owed' to any other mechanism. It is the notion of service that
makes this metaphor pertinent. As the story of the clay crystals demonstrates,
we do not represent the relationship between an item and its ancestors in the
same way. An item that is the product of a process of self-preservation is not
thereby 'obliged' to meet the standard set by its ancestors. This suggests that it
is the device's dependence on the mechanism that produced it that the
metaphor is designed to spotlight.

If this is correct, normativity is a feature, not of biological items themselves,
but of statements that we use to ascribe functions to them. Such statements
are normative because they trade on this analogy with obligation.

---

[11] A full account of artificial functions would have to be much more sophisticated than
this in order to deal with a number of complications. In particular, the account would have
to allow for the possibility that artefacts may have functions that are novel or unique. We
cannot appeal to the behaviour of earlier devices of the same kind in order to determine
the functions of these devices. For this reason, the core account cannot be applied directly
to artefacts. Nevertheless, I do think that it is possible to give a closely analogous account
of artificial functions. I do not have space to develop it properly here, but it turns on the
idea that an artificial device has the function to perform a certain task if it has been produced by some second mechanism because a similar device would have the capacity to perform that task.

[12] My line of thought here has been inspired in part by Andrew Woodfield's suggestion
that function statements should be analysed using a deontic operator: semantically, to say
that d has the function to do F is to say something like 'd has the duty to do F'. (Private
communication; see also Woodfield 1990: 204.) But I am not sure how far Woodfield
would go along with the suggestion made here.

3.2. Metaphorical Norms

The claim the normative character of function statements derives from a dead metaphor requires further investigation. I need to make clear what I take the implications of this claim to be.

It might seem that, by explaining the normativity of function statements in terms of a dead metaphor, I have failed to do what I set out to do at the beginning of this discussion—that is, to refute the suggestion that biological devices have functions only in a metaphorical sense. I have, of course, argued against the view that the sentence 'The heart is supposed to move the blood' should be viewed as treating the heart, metaphorically, as an artefact. But now it might seem that I am treating all function statements, whether they are concerned with natural devices or artefacts, as merely metaphorical.

It is important to clarify what my proposal is. The core account implies that to say that a device has a function is to say that it is the product of a process of preservation through service. It follows that, on this view, the sentence 'The heart has the function to move the blood' will be quite literally true. In this respect, my account differs from the one I described earlier, because, on that account, the heart cannot literally be said to have the function to move the blood: on that account, only devices that are expected to behave in a certain way by some agent can literally be ascribed a function.

On the other hand, I have suggested that the sentence 'The heart is supposed to move the blood' is metaphorical. In other words, although natural devices literally have functions, there literally are no functional norms in nature: normativity is a feature, not of biological devices, but of function statements.

Nevertheless, it might be thought that my account commits me to even more than this—that is, that it implies that function statements are not really normative at all. The answer to this depends on what we understand a dead metaphor to be. And this in turn will depend in part on what account we give of metaphorical discourse in general. The issues are both controversial and complex, and I cannot explore them properly here. Nevertheless it may be helpful for me to make it clear where I stand.

There are two opposing views of the status of metaphorical discourse to be found in the literature. What we might regard as the traditional view holds that metaphorical sentences, although they are usually literally false, may nonetheless be true. For example, the sentence 'United has a leaky defence' might be true, even if it is literally false. On this view, a sentence can be used to express different propositions depending on how it is interpreted. And so a sentence is true or false only relative to a particular interpretation. To be literally true is to be true under a particular kind of interpretation: to say that a sentence is literally true is to say that, if every phrase in the sentence were interpreted literally, it would express a proposition that is true. Hence, to say that a sentence is literally false is not incompatible with saying that it is true under some other, non-literal, interpretation.[13]

On this view, sentences that include dead metaphors may be treated in just the same way. Dead metaphors will be regarded as metaphors that are so embedded in our language that they have a well-established conventional meaning. When I describe someone as a warm person, I may literally be interpreted as saying that she has a high temperature. But if my sentence is interpreted in a conventional way—as speakers conventionally use it—its meaning is that she has a sympathetic and demonstrative personality. On this conventional, metaphorical interpretation the sentence may be perfectly true.

Davidson (1978) rejects the traditional view. He argues that there is no additional metaphorical meaning attaching to metaphorical sentences. Most metaphorical sentences are literally false, and there is no alternative sense in which they are true. When we endorse a metaphorical sentence, we endorse it as apt or powerful, not as true.

However, Davidson does not wish to give the same account of sentences that contain dead metaphors. If he were to do so, he would have to insist that a very large proportion of what we say in everyday conversation is straightforwardly false. Instead, Davidson argues that a dead metaphor is no longer a metaphor: when a metaphorical expression dies, it gains a new literal meaning. On this view, the sentence 'Alice is a very warm person' should be regarded as straightforwardly ambiguous. It may mean either 'Alice is a person with a high temperature' or 'Alice is a sympathetic, demonstrative person'. Taken in either sense, it may literally be true.

On the traditional view, then, a dead metaphor is a metaphor that has ossified; a sentence that contains a dead metaphor may be true, even if it is not literally true. In contrast, Davidson holds that, when a metaphor dies, it simply disappears; a sentence that contains a dead metaphor, if true, will be literally true.

We are now in a position to see why someone might suggest that, in claiming that the normative character of function statements derives from a dead metaphor, I have implied that function statements are not really normative at all. If we were to accept Davidson's account, it would be difficult to insist that a sentence such as 'The heart is supposed to move the blood' is really norma-

---

[13] I do not think that a proponent of the traditional view needs to be committed to the claim that we can always find a straightforward non-literal interpretation of a metaphorical sentence. In particular, the metaphors that we encounter in a literary context will not always yield a single proposition that can be assessed for truth or falsity. Nevertheless, the traditional theorist may point to the fact that the metaphors we encounter in everyday conversation usually express relatively simple ideas; in these cases, we can characterize metaphorical sentences as true, if literally false. For some recent statements of the traditional view, see Tirell (1991), and Scholz (1993). See also Black (1954) and Goodman (1968).

tive in character. This is because, on Davidson's view, the metaphor that is supposed to underpin the normative character of the sentence is no longer there. A supporter of Davidson's view might well suggest that, if I want to insist that a sentence such as 'The heart is supposed to move the blood' has a normative ring, then I should give up the view that its normative character depends on a dead metaphor.

However, I think that there are good reasons to reject Davidson's account of dead metaphors. As Reimer (1986) has argued, the metaphorical force of such expressions continues to play a crucial role in structuring the way we think about the states of affairs that they describe; moreover, the fact that this is so explains why they remain embedded in our language. It is true that the metaphorical status of such sentences is no longer *conspicuous* to the speakers who use them, but this is not to say that the metaphor has disappeared.[14]

For this reason, I would prefer to adopt some version of the traditional view. On this view, although the sentence 'The heart is supposed to move the blood' is not literally true, it is nevertheless true. It is true because there is a perfectly well-established, conventional way of interpreting the sentence on which it means that hearts were produced by some other mechanism because earlier hearts moved the blood. Nevertheless, the normative flavour of the sentence remains, because the metaphor remains.

3.3. The Normativity of Function Statements: Summary

The normative character of function statements serves to highlight a certain feature of the heart's causal history—the interdependent, yet asymmetrical relationship between earlier hearts and the mechanisms that produce them. When we characterize this relationship in normative terms, we are invoking a dead metaphor of social obligation. To say this is not to say that the claim that a device has a function is metaphorical. It is the claim that a device is supposed to perform its function that trades on a metaphor. We can combine this account of the normativity of function statements with the claim that function statements are genuinely normative only if we reject Davidson's claim that a dead metaphor is no longer a metaphor.

---

[14] I am not claiming that metaphors never disappear; I am only claiming that dead metaphors are not metaphors that have disappeared. See Bredin (1992) for a discussion of the degrees of ossification suffered by metaphorical expressions.

4. Two Important Notions

I will end this chapter by introducing two notions that are of central importance in what follows. In the next section, I will explain Millikan's notion of a
normal explanation. In the final section of this chapter, I will explain what I
mean when I say that an item is *minimally competent* to perform a certain task.

4.1. Normal Performance

In developing her teleological theory of intentional content, Millikan introduces a distinctively teleological notion of *normality* (Millikan 1984: 33–4). As
we shall see, this notion provides the teleologist with a very powerful and useful tool. So it is important to explain it with some care.

Associated with each function possessed by a device is a normal explanation
for the proper performance of that function: a normal explanation specifies
the way in which the ancestors of the device performed that function in the
past. For example, a normal explanation for the performance of the heart's
function will mention the fact that, in the past, hearts have moved the blood
by pumping it, and that they have pumped at a particular rate, depending on
the body's requirements. The function of a device is concerned with *what* a
device is supposed to do; a normal explanation is concerned with *how* that
function is performed. Note that this explanation might vary from species to
species: hearts of different species normally pump the blood at different
speeds.

An important point to bear in mind is that the notion of normality is an
explanatory, not a statistical notion. A normal explanation is concerned with
just those aspects of a device's performance that help to explain its success.
Hearts usually make a thumping noise when they pump. A particularly quiet
heart would be behaving unusually, but it would not be operating abnormally:
the noisiness of hearts has not, in the past, helped to explain their success. A
heart that pumped too slowly, on the other hand, would be operating abnormally. Because the notion of normality is an explanatory notion, it is also a
normative notion: a normal explanation tells us how the device *is supposed to*
perform its function.[15]

It is important that a normal explanation is pitched at the right level of generality. A normal explanation must be general enough to provide a *unified*
account of the way in which a device has contributed to its governors over many
generations. We would not say, for example, that a woman's heart normally

---

[15] In the next chapter, we will have to do some work to distinguish the function of a
device from the normal conditions of the performance of that function.

works in a different way from a man's heart because her heart normally pumps blood around a female body, whereas his heart normally pumps blood around a male body. This is because there is a way of characterizing how the heart works that treats these two cases as instances of a single phenomenon—that is, a heart pumping blood around a body (Millikan 1984: 33–34, 44; 1995: 287–8).

On the other hand, a normal explanation must be specific enough to avoid redundancy: we would not want to say that my heart will be behaving normally when it is pumping blood at an appropriate speed *and decibel level*. As we have seen, the amount of noise that the heart makes as it moves the blood is redundant in the explanation for its success in performing its function (Millikan 1990b: 336). A normal explanation, then, must be sufficiently general to provide the most unified possible account of the device's performance, yet specific enough to avoid any redundancy in the explanation for its success.

It is quite possible for a device to fulfil its function in an abnormal way. For example, a defective camouflage pattern might protect an organism from a predator, not by helping it to blend in with the background, but by leading the predator to confuse the organism with one of its own conspecifics. Conversely, a device may operate normally, at least in some respects, without fulfilling its function: a heart might be pumping but failing to move the blood around the organism's body because it is no longer connected to the aorta.

Whenever I use the words 'normal', 'normally', or 'normality' in what follows, I will always be referring to this explanatory, normative notion, and never to the merely statistical notion of what usually or typically happens.

4.2. Minimal Competence

A second notion that I would like to introduce at this point is the notion of minimal competence. The function of a device, as we have seen, is determined by what its ancestors did that ensured their survival, *via* the activity of their governors. It follows that, for a device to have the function to do F, it must be the case that some of its ancestors were able to do F. This is a very modest requirement: it need not have been the case that those ancestors were particularly good at doing F—they need not have done F particularly efficiently, or very reliably, or with *panache*. All that is required is that they were minimally competent to do F—that they were able sometimes, somehow, to get the job done. It is because they were at least minimally competent to do F that they can properly be described as surviving because they did F.

An item may be minimally competent to do F without having the function to do F. My heart is minimally competent to act as a paperweight, but that is not its function. Nevertheless, an item cannot be ascribed the function to do F unless some of its ancestors were minimally competent to do F. Moreover, it is this standard of minimal competence that a particular device has to meet if it is to count as performing its function.

It is important to emphasize the minimal nature of minimal competence. In particular, we will always need to bear in mind that an item may meet some set of minimal competence conditions, even though those conditions do not characterize the way in which it typically or generally operates. All that matters is that the item meets those conditions on occasion. A cat's pounce, perhaps, is not generally quick or precise enough to secure a meal. Nevertheless, it is at least minimally competent to do so.

The notions of normality and minimal competence will be of central importance when we turn to the task of developing a teleological theory of intentional content. Before that, however, we need to complete our theory of functions.

3

Determinate Functions

1. Introduction

The core account is intended to capture the central intuitions that lie behind our ascriptions of functions to biological devices. As such, it can be taken as providing necessary conditions that a device must satisfy if it is to have a function. But it is not by itself strong enough to underwrite the ascription of determinate functions to biological devices. In this chapter, I will attempt to solve this problem by proposing some additional constraints on function ascription.

I can explain the problem most effectively if I begin by making some assumptions about the functions of some familiar biological devices. I will continue to assume, as I have done so far, that the following are all plausible claims:

(1) The function of the heart is to move the blood around the body.

(2) The function of a wing is to provide lift in flying.

(3) The function of a nest is to shelter the organism, its young, or its eggs.

Moreover, I take it that hearts, wings, and nests are all items that are classified, in part, by their functions.

According to the core account, all the ascriptions of function listed above will be perfectly legitimate. However, there are many other ways in which we could specify the functions of hearts, wings, and nests, all of which are equally consistent with the account. We can divide these rival function ascriptions into four separate groups.

The first group includes ascriptions that concern things an item has to do before it can perform its function. Before it can move blood around the body, the heart has to grow to an appropriate size and it has to convert oxygen and nutrients to energy to enable it to work properly. Similarly, a wing may have to unfurl before it can assist the organism to fly; a nest may have to balance on a branch before it can shelter the organism's young. These events will feature on causal chains leading to the successful operation of the governors of these devices. For example, the fact that earlier hearts have grown will help to explain why this heart is present. According to the core account, then, growing will count as a function of the heart.

The second group consists of ascriptions that concern activities *by means of which* the device performs its function. The heart moves the blood around the body *by* making squeezing motions; the wing provides lift *by* flapping. The flapping of earlier wings contributed to the workings of their governors, because it is just by flapping that they provided lift for flight. So the fact that this particular pair of wings is present can certainly be explained by the fact that earlier wings flapped: according to the core account, it will be perfectly legitimate to say the function of wings is to flap.

The third group is concerned with consequences that a device *helps to bring about* by performing its function. By providing lift for flight, wings help the organism to feed and avoid predators. By moving the blood around the body, the heart helps to distribute oxygen and nutrients to other organs. By insulating the organism's eggs, the nest helps to produce healthy adult offspring. Moreover, all these devices help the organism to reproduce. Once again, all these activities will count as functions of the device, according to the core account: if the workings of earlier hearts, wings, and nests had not given rise to these further consequences, this particular heart, wing, or nest would not exist.

There is one final group of rival function ascriptions we need to consider. These are ascriptions that characterize the function of a device in a particularly *fine-grained* way. For example, it will be an important feature of the functioning of the human heart that the blood that it moves around the body is free of clots. If the blood moved by the heart contains a clot, a blood vessel may become blocked and the organism may die. So one possibility is that we should say that the function of the heart is not simply to move the blood, but to move blood that is free of clots. The core account fails to make it clear how precisely we should characterize the function of a biological device.

We can represent the causal structure of events with a diagram (Figure 1). The black arrows represent causal relations linking distinct events; the white arrows link different descriptions of a single activity, and represent the relation that we denote by the term 'thereby'. All the phrases in bold type represent possible functions of the heart according to the core account. Note that growing is a separate activity of the heart, whereas making squeezing motions, moving the blood, moving clot-free blood, and helping to circulate oxygen are all different ways of describing a single activity.[1]

---

[1] I am presupposing a view of event individuation on which events are treated as concrete particulars that may be described in a variety of ways. See Davidson (1969).

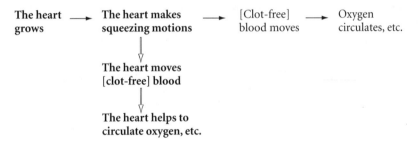

FIG. 1. *Possible Functions of the Heart*

The problem is, then, that the core account will not enable us to make any distinction between the function of a device and a normal precondition for the performance of its function. It will not distinguish between a device's function and the means by which it normally performs its function, or the consequences that it normally helps to bring about by performing its function. Nor will it help us decide how precisely we should specify the function of a device. The function of a device will include everything earlier devices have done or brought about that feature on the causal chain leading to the production of that device. In every case, we can say that, had those earlier devices not done those things—had the heart not grown, or not made squeezing motions, or not helped to circulate oxygen, or not moved clot-free blood—this device would not have been here now.

2. Lines of Response

We could respond to this situation in a number of different ways. First, we might reject the idea that there is some important distinction between the function of a device and the preconditions, means, or consequences of its performance, and conclude that the function of a device will be *indeterminate* between all these different possibilities. The suggestion will be that there is an unresolvable vagueness in our notion of a function that prevents us from saying with any precision what the function of a biological device is.[2] If we took

---

[2] Most of the debate on this issue has focused on the functions of intentional mechanisms, such as the frog's visual system, which I will not discuss until a later chapter. But many of the arguments and positions presented in this more specialized context will apply equally well to the issue of biological functions in general. Jerry Fodor (1990: 64–5) argues that biological functions are indeterminate. See also Dretske (1986), Hall (1990), and Sullivan (1993).

this route, we would not have to make any modifications to the core account, but could leave it as it stands.

A second response would be to claim that all biological devices have a *multitude* of different functions. The functions of the heart, for example, will include moving the blood, moving clot-free blood, making squeezing motions, helping to circulate oxygen and nutrients, and many others. Of course, the heart does not have multiple functions in the way that the liver does. It is rather that the heart has a large cluster of functions, all of which are intimately connected with its capacity to move the blood around the body.[3]

A slightly different version of this kind of solution is to say that biological devices have very *complex* functions.[4] Neander (1995: 114–19) points out that we can describe a biological device as contributing to a hierarchy of ends: the heart contributes to gene replication, *by* helping to circulate oxygen and nutrients, *by* moving the blood, *by* making squeezing motions. This could be taken to suggest that, in order to provide a complete specification of the function of the heart, we would need to mention the fact that it contributes to all these ends. On this version, the heart will have only one function: making squeezing motions, moving the blood, and helping to distribute oxygen and nutrients will all be different *aspects* of that function. Perhaps we might characterize these different aspects of a device's function as concerned with different *kinds* or *levels* of explanation for the presence of the device.[5] Once again, someone who responded to the problem in this way would not need to modify the core account.

The third response is to accept that these difficulties demonstrate that the core account by itself does not provide sufficient conditions for the ascription of biological functions. We still need to find some further conditions that will distinguish between the function of a device and these other activities, and so exclude these rival function ascriptions.

Our choice of response will have very important implications for how we proceed in future chapters. If we were to accept that biological functions are indeterminate or multiple or many-layered, then it would be natural to expect the contents we ascribe to intentional devices to be indeterminate or multiple or many-layered in the same way. At any rate, if we wished to avoid this conclusion, we would have to put in some work; and we might well need to import some non-teleological considerations to help us to extract simple, determinate content from vague or very complex functions. If, on the other

---

[3] Surprisingly, Millikan sometimes seems to take this view. See Millikan (1991: 161). But elsewhere she rejects it (Millikan 1993a: 101).

[4] For an example of this kind of response, see Agar (1993).

[5] See Griffiths and Goode (1995) for a suggestion of this kind. Neander's view is slightly more complicated, in that she takes certain levels of description to be privileged in talk of functions (Neander 1995: 118–20).

hand, we were able to show that it is possible to give an account of function ascription on which biological functions turn out to be determinate and relatively simple, then we would be in a rather better position to make the same claims about intentional content, without having to bring in additional, perhaps non-teleological, considerations at some later stage.

It should be clear by now that I would favour this third position. Nevertheless, this preference requires some justification: it is certainly not *obvious* that biological functions are determinate, or that biological devices do not have a whole host of interrelated functions. Nevertheless, it is possible to give some good reasons for rejecting the claim that these rival function ascriptions should be viewed as identifying genuine biological functions.

The first reason is simply that many of these alternative function ascriptions seem flatly counter-intuitive. We would not normally say that the function of the heart is to grow, or that the function of a wing is to unfurl. These are things that hearts or wings normally do, but to say that hearts or wings are present *in order to* do these things seems wrong. The same is true of the claim that the function of the heart is to make squeezing motions or the claim that the function of a wing is to flap. Of course, the fact that hearts have made squeezing motions helps to explain why we have hearts, but making squeezing motions is not what hearts are *for*. Again, the suggestion that the function of the human heart is to move blood that is free of clots does not seem very natural: when a clot lodges in a blood vessel this is not because *the heart* is malfunctioning.

Nevertheless, it is not so obvious that the same level of implausibility attaches to the third group of candidate function ascriptions. The claim that we have hearts to help circulate oxygen and nutrients, or that organisms build nests to help produce healthy offspring does not seem particularly unnatural. Even the claim that any biological device is there in order to help the organism to reproduce seems to make some sense. Nevertheless, I do think that there is a good reason for denying that we should treat these claims as describing the functions of these devices, except in a very loose sense.

At the beginning of Chapter 1, I began my discussion of functions with the idea that we sometimes appeal to functional properties to help us to categorize items into biological kinds. If the notion of a function is to provide a basis for classifying devices into kinds, then clearly it must be a notion that will *differentiate* between different biological devices. A notion of a function that will allow us to say that the function of any biological device is to help the organism to reproduce will not do this job. For this reason, I would like to suggest that the claim that we have hearts in order to help circulate oxygen and nutrients or in order to help us to reproduce is best taken as a claim about the unified functional structure of the human organism, rather than a claim about the function of the heart.

As we shall see, it is not only this third group of rival function ascriptions that gives rise to this kind of problem. In fact, if we were to accept any of the alternative ascriptions that I have described, we would run into serious difficulties in attempting to categorize biological items in accordance with their functions. I will highlight these difficulties as I go along.

3. The Proposed Solution

3.1. *Additional Constraints*

In what follows, I will attempt to formulate some additional constraints on function ascription that will enable us to distinguish between the function of a device and the preconditions, means, and consequences of the performance of that function. I will propose three additional constraints governing the ascription of functions, together with one additional constraint that will apply only to devices that have what I will call 'relational functions'.

I take it that these additional constraints have some intuitive force, and I will try to indicate what I take that force to be. They are not intended to be merely stipulative. Nevertheless, I can imagine someone protesting that my discussion splits hairs to an unnatural degree. I would not wish to imply that polite usage is as precise as my argument suggests. But I do think that, when we are focusing on the question 'What is the function of this device?' for the purposes of explanation or classification—in other words, when the question is important—there is available a precise answer that is both intuitive and capable of principled explanation.

As I promised in the previous chapter, these additional constraints are intended to answer to the two basic intuitions underlying the core account: the backward-looking intuition that a function arises when a family of devices does something to ensure its own survival; and the forward-looking intuition that in performing a function a device does something that contributes to the workings of some other mechanism. To determine the function of a device we need to determine what it is that *that* type of device does that contributes to the workings of its governors.

As well as trying to explain how each of my constraints is motivated by these considerations, I will also try to support each one in two other ways: first by illustrating each constraint with actual examples, showing how it excludes what I take to be implausible function ascriptions in everyday cases; and, secondly, by attempting to demonstrate how a failure to include each of these constraints in a complete theory of function ascription would undermine any attempt to categorize biological items in accordance with their function.

3.2. *Subcomponents, Fellow Components, and Governors*

The organs, behaviours, and subsystems possessed by an individual organism are related to each other in a variety of ways. In what follows, I will rely on some distinctions between the different ways in which devices may be related to each other, as governor, subcomponent, or fellow component. In this section, I will attempt to make these distinctions clear, and I will illustrate them using the example of the circulatory system.

I take it that the relationship between a device or system and its subcomponents is relatively clear. A device (d) will count as a subcomponent of a larger device or system (d*) if d is a part of d* and if d's performing its function is partly constitutive of d*'s performing its function. For example, the left atrium is a part of the heart; and, when the left atrium pushes blood into the left ventricle, this activity partly constitutes the heart's activity in moving the blood. So the left atrium is a subcomponent of the heart.

As we saw in the previous chapter, the governors of a device will be those items to which that device is supposed to contribute by performing its function. For example, when the heart moves the blood, this is supposed to contribute to the workings of other organs, such as the liver, that receive oxygen and nutrients via the circulatory system.

A group of fellow components will be a group of devices that work together to make a joint contribution to a single, shared set of governors. Together, they can be described as forming a system, such as the circulatory system or a sensorimotor system. The relation between fellow components is a reciprocal one: the components are dependent on each other. This relation of mutual dependence is quite unlike the essentially asymmetrical, means–end relationship between the device and its governors. The components of a system have functions only because together they produce some output that is used by some item outside and separate from the system. Each component makes a different contribution that helps to ensure that the contributions made by the others are helpful to the governors that they share. For example, the fact that the blood vessels channel the blood around the body helps to ensure that the heart's activity in moving the blood has the effect of distributing nutrients and oxygen around the body.[6]

In this case, the contribution made by the blood vessels is essential to ensure that the activity of the heart is able to produce some useful result. But in other cases fellow components may work to ensure only that the activity of the device is more effective than it would have been. For example, the digestion of

---

[6] Note that one device may be related to another both as fellow component and as governor: the blood vessels are not only fellow components of the heart, but also governors, because they receive oxygen and nutrients as a result of the activity of the heart.

food by the stomach is facilitated but not dependent on the production of saliva by the salivary glands.[7]

In most cases, fellow components will operate concurrently to produce a certain effect. For example, the heart, the blood vessels, and the blood operate concurrently to ensure that oxygen is carried around the body. But, in some cases, components belonging to a single system operate successively, one device helping to control the operation of another. For example, the heart is dependent on the sinoatrial node—our natural pacemaker—to control the contraction of the heart muscles, thereby enabling the heart to move the blood in the right way.

This possibility threatens to blur the distinction between a fellow component and a governor. We need to make clear why the heart counts as a fellow component, not as a governor, of the sinoatrial node. The reason is that the heart is directly dependent on the node to ensure that, in performing its function, it is helping to produce some useful outcome—the circulation of nutrients and oxygen. Hence, it makes sense to regard these two devices as working together to produce this result. Contrast the relation between the heart and one of its governors, a leg muscle, say. In this case, what the heart immediately enables the muscle to do is to convert the oxygen and nutrients it receives into energy: this is not a function of the muscle. As a result, there is no single outcome that is produced as a *direct* result of their performing their functions. In this sense, the activity of the heart does not mesh with the activity of the muscle in the intimate way in which it meshes with the activities of other components of the circulatory system.[8]

With these distinctions in place, I am now in a position to introduce my four additional constraints.

3.3. The Immediacy Condition

The immediacy condition can be stated as follows: where a device d is present because earlier devices of the same type did F, d will have the function to do F only if there is nothing else that those earlier devices did that provides a more immediate explanation for the presence of d.[9]

---

[7] I owe both the point and the example to an anonymous reader for Oxford University Press.

[8] We can make this distinction more formal by saying that an item g* will count as a governor of d only if what d immediately enables g* to do is not an activity that constitutes a function of g*. Since this definition appeals to the notion of a function, we will have to be careful that any appeal to the distinction between governor and fellow component later on does not introduce a circularity into the account. I will return to this in n. 10.

[9] This condition has an analogue in Millikan's account of intentional content, where she requires that the state of affairs represented by an intentional state should be the one

The effect of this constraint is to exclude the first group of rival function ascriptions that I described: ascriptions that fail to distinguish between the function of a device and activities that are preconditions for the performance of its function. For example, the immediacy condition will rule out the claim that the function of my heart is to grow. Although it is true that the fact that my ancestors' hearts grew helps to explain the presence of my heart, this is only because growing enabled them to do something else—namely, move the blood. The fact that my ancestors' hearts moved the blood provides a more immediate explanation for the presence of my heart than the fact that they grew. The effect of the immediacy condition, then, is to eliminate contributions that occur too early on the causal chain to constitute the function of a device.

Note that the point of this condition is to help identify *which* event the device functions to contribute. It is not concerned with the way in which the device's contribution is described. Hence the immediacy condition will not rule out the claim that the function of the heart is to make squeezing motions, given that the heart's making squeezing motions is the same event as its moving the blood. As we have seen, this distinction is a distinction between not different events, but between different ways of characterizing a single event.

The rationale behind the immediacy condition has to do with the means–end character of a function. To know the function of a device, we need to know how it normally helps to promote the operation of its governors. A device will assist its governors *by* behaving in a certain way. What is important here is that the 'by' relation links different descriptions of a particular event. It does not link chains of events. Compare: I frightened the burglar by turning on the light, by flicking the switch, by moving my finger; but I did not frighten the burglar by entering the room, even though I needed to enter the room before I could turn on the light. In the same way, the heart needs to grow before it can help its governors; but this is not to say that it is *by growing* that it helps them. If we want to know how a device contributes to its governors, we need to focus only on behaviour that affects them directly; and we need to distinguish this from other things that the device needs to do before it can behave in this way.

Ignoring the immediacy condition would lead us to differentiate between devices to which we would not normally assign differing functions. For example, there are species of birds that build their nests on the ground. The nests built by these birds do not need to balance on branches. But it would seem strange to conclude that these nests lack a *function* possessed by other nests.

---

mentioned in 'the most proximate' normal explanation for the success of the behaviour it prompts (Millikan 1984: 100). Millikan's condition applies only to devices with relational functions, and it is not equivalent to the immediacy condition. Rather, it is equivalent to the extended immediacy condition, which I will introduce in Section 3.7.

The function of both kinds of nest, I take it, is to shelter the bird and its young. They differ only in the properties they need to have in order to perform that function.

It is the immediacy condition that will enable us to deal with the remaining difficulty raised by the clay crystals left over from the previous chapter. The problem was that the clay crystals might help to ensure their own survival by slowing the stream, thereby ensuring that the stream deposited more of the minerals the crystals need to replicate. If so, the core account on its own implies that the crystals have the function to slow the stream. Once we add the immediacy condition, however, we see that this no longer follows: for there is something else that the crystals do that provides a more immediate explanation for their survival—namely, to replicate. Although the clay crystals are dependent on the stream to help them to replicate, the nature of this dependence is not the same as the nature of the dependence between the heart and the mechanisms that produced it.

I believe that the core account, supplemented by the immediacy condition, will enable us to identify which of the activities performed by a device constitutes a function.[10] The remaining problems concern how those activities are described. In the next three sections, I will attempt to show that the activities of a device will count as functional only under a particular description, and that this description can be picked out in a principled way.

3.4. The Independence Condition

In the last section, I suggested that the heart could not be ascribed the function of growing because it was not *by* growing that it contributed to its governors. Nevertheless, as we have seen, there will be many things *by doing which* the heart assists its governors. As we saw earlier, we can describe the heart as contributing to a hierarchy of ends: the heart contributes to gene replication, *by* helping to circulate oxygen and nutrients, *by* moving the blood, *by* making squeezing motions.

Neander (1995: 118–20) suggests that, although all these descriptions could be taken to characterize functions of the heart, it is the lowest level of description that has priority. She points out that, as we move up to higher and higher levels of description, we are describing the activities of larger and larger systems: it is the circulatory system, not the heart alone, that circulates oxygen and nutrients. This suggests that, if we want to specify the function of the heart, we need to find an activity that involves the heart alone. She goes on to

---

[10] It is for this reason that the appeal to the distinction between governor and fellow component in Section 3.6 will not introduce a circularity: the account so far has not appealed to this distinction, and it gives us enough to determine whether what d immediately enables g* to do is a function of g*.

make the point that, the lower the level at which we characterize the function of a device, the more information we will have when we are told that it has malfunctioned. If we identify malfunctioning with failing to function at the lowest level of description, then, when we say that someone's heart is malfunctioning, we will know something very specific about what has gone wrong.

I would like to travel a little way with Neander on this point, although, as we shall see in the next section, not all the way. Where I agree with her is in the claim that, in characterizing the function of a device, we need to focus on something that the device is capable of producing on its own, without the cooperation of other devices.

The motivation for this condition, in my account, has to do with the thought that a function arises when the persistence of a certain type of device is explained by its own behaviour. On this view, the function of a type of device will be something peculiar to it, something that arises from its particular contribution to the workings of its governors, in contrast with the contributions made by other components of the same system. When we ask for the function of a device, we want to know what *it* does, what *it* contributes, not simply what it helps to contribute to.

I shall dub this second condition the independence condition. It can be formulated as follows: where a device d is present because earlier devices of the same type did F, d will have the function to do F only if F is something that members of D are capable of doing on their own, without the cooperation of fellow components or governors of the device.[11]

The independence condition will rule out the claim that the function of the heart is to distribute oxygen and nutrients and the claim that its function is to help the genes to replicate. The heart is capable of distributing oxygen and nutrients only in so far as it is assisted in doing so by the blood, which carries them, and by the veins and arteries, which channel the blood around the body. My genes are helped to replicate not by the operation of my heart alone but by the workings of a very large number of devices operating in concert. The independence condition leaves only the claim that the function of the heart is to move the blood and the claim that its function is to make squeezing motions. It is only these two ascriptions that characterize the activity of the heart in terms of something that it is capable of achieving on its own.[12]

---

[11] This leaves it open that the contribution of the device might be dependent on the activities of its subcomponents or of devices of which it is the governor.

[12] It might be objected that moving the blood is not something that the heart can do on its own: without the arteries and veins to channel the blood, it would not move in any direction, let alone the right one. All this shows is that we need to be more careful in specifying exactly what it is that the heart is supposed to do: what the heart does is to provide the motive force that gets the blood to move.

There are two ways of illustrating the importance of the independence condition for the classification of biological devices. The first is to point out that it is possible for two devices of the same type to belong to larger systems with quite different functions. For example, the heart of a lion helps it to catch antelopes; the heart of an antelope helps it to escape from lions. Without the independence condition, it would follow that, although the hearts of lions and the hearts of antelopes would both function to move blood around the organism's body, the hearts in these species would also have different functions: in one species, to help to provide the organism with food; and, in the other, to help it to avoid predators. But then we would not know that function would be relevant when it came to typing them. It would certainly seem unnatural to say that these are organs of different types. If we were able to focus on what the hearts are able to do on their own, on their particular contribution to the organism's survival, we would be able to focus on what they have in common: the capacity to move the blood.

Another danger of ignoring the independence condition is that, as we saw earlier, we might find ourselves classifying all biological devices as devices of the same type: hearts, wings, and birds' nests all contribute to their governors by helping the organism to reproduce. They make this contribution in conjunction with all the other organs, behaviours, and tools made by the organism. This could hardly be the notion of a function that underpins the classification of biological devices into distinct types.

3.5. *The Abstractness Condition, Clause One*

At this point, we have ruled out a number of rival function ascriptions. But we have yet to decide between the claim that the function of the heart is to move the blood, and the claim that its function is to make squeezing motions. Nor have we considered the claim that its function is to move blood that is free from clots. To resolve these issues we need to call on my third condition.

My third condition introduces the idea that when we ascribe functions to devices we do so at a certain level of *abstractness*. As we have seen, to specify the function of a device, we need to know what it contributed to its governors, given the contributions made by its fellow components. In other words, we need to know the function and design of the system as a whole. But we do not need to know *how* d's fellow components make their contributions—we do not need to know anything about their design. Nor do we need to know about the design of the device itself.

We could state this condition as follows: where the presence of a device d is explained by the fact that earlier devices did F, d will have the function to do F only if that explanation does not depend on specific features of the design of members of D, or of other devices that operated as fellow components on those occasions.

In this section I will discuss the requirement that, in ascribing a function to a device, we must abstract away from the design of the device itself. In order to make use of this requirement, we need to know how to distinguish between the design of a device and its function. The suggestion will be that, when we characterize the behaviour of a device in terms of its function, we will characterize it in terms of some *effect* that it produces. When we characterize its behaviour in terms of its design, this will not be the case. When we describe the heart as moving the blood, we characterize its operation in terms of some effect that it brings about; and so we describe it in functional terms. But when we describe the heart as making squeezing motions, we characterize it in terms of its design.

Why should we insist that the function of a device must be characterized in terms of some effect that it brings about? As with the immediacy condition, the rationale has to do with the means–end character of a function. As we have seen, for a device to have a function it must be the case that the survival of that type of device can be explained by the fact that it contributes to its governors in some way. So, to characterize the behaviour of a device as functional is to say what it was about the behaviour that is useful to its governors. The behaviour of a device will be useful to its governors only in virtue of producing a certain effect. It is the production of this effect that *constitutes* a device's contribution to its governors. So, to characterize the device in terms of the contribution that it makes to its governors is to characterize it in terms of some effect that it produces.

Compare: I frightened the burglar by turning on the light, by flicking the switch, by moving my finger. All these are descriptions of the action that immediately affected the burglar. But, if we want to know what was frightening about my action, I have to describe it in terms of some effect that it produced—the effect that frightened the burglar. In other words, I have to describe it as *my turning on the light*. Similarly, if we want to know what is functional about the activity of the heart, we have to describe it as *the heart's moving the blood*.

If we describe the heart as making squeezing motions, we are describing its behaviour in terms of its design, not in terms of its function. Of course, it is certainly true to say that the heart contributes to its governors *by* making squeezing motions. But this is not to say that the squeezing motions *constitute* its contribution. Its contribution must be something that those squeezing motions bring about, such as moving the blood.

In this way, we can rule out the claim that the function of the heart is to make squeezing motions; or that the function of a wing is to flap; or that the function of a nest is to be hollow and well lined. By applying this clause of the abstractness condition, we will be able to make a distinction between the function of a device and the way in which it normally performs its function.

It is at this point that my analysis diverges from Neander's account. This is not surprising, since Neander's theory of functions centres on the process of natural selection, not on the process of preservation through service. Hence, the claim that motivates the abstractness condition—the claim that the notion of a function is a means–end notion—does not feature in her account.

As we saw in the previous section, Neander's proposal is that, when we are describing the function of a device, the lowest level of description at which we can characterize its activity has a privileged role to play. It seems to follow from this claim that the most privileged characterization of the heart's function will treat the heart as having the function to make squeezing motions.[13] I have to say that I find this result counter-intuitive. But I also believe that it is based on an incorrect view of what a function statement tells us. Neander's reason for taking this line is, as we saw in the previous section, that, the lower the level of description, the more informative the claim that the device is failing to perform its function. But why should this be the only relevant consideration? After all, the lower the level of description, the less information we are given about what the device achieves when it succeeds in performing its function. If we take seriously the idea that a function statement tells us what a device is supposed to contribute to its governors, then it will be the second kind of information, rather than the first, that we will expect such a statement to provide.

For this reason, I believe, we need to distinguish between the claim *that* a device has failed to perform its function and an explanation that tells us *how* or *why* it has failed. To say that the heart is failing to make squeezing motions, or that it is leaking, or that it is no longer connected to the blood supply, is to tell us more than that it is failing to perform its function. It is to tell us the nature or cause of its failure. If so, we do not need to move to the very lowest level of description when we characterize the function of a device. The level must be low enough to meet the independence condition; but it must be high enough to tell us what effect the device produces by functioning as it should. This is because of the means–end nature of a function.

3.6. The Abstractness Condition, Clause Two

We must now consider the second clause of the abstractness condition, the requirement that an ascription of function to a device must abstract away from the design of its fellow components. To abstract away from the design of other components of the same system, we need to insist that the device's contribution is characterized in a certain way. It must be characterized in terms of

---

[13] It is far from clear to me that Neander would wish to endorse this claim. I am suggesting only that it appears to follow from her account as it stands.

features that help to explain the survival of the device, given the effects produced by the device's fellow components, but regardless of their physical composition or structure. It is this part of the abstractness condition that will enable us to deal with the suggestion that the function of the heart is to move clot-free blood. Clots are dangerous because of the design of the blood vessels. That design could be changed—by making them smoother or more elastic, or by incorporating some mechanism to break down or bypass blockages as soon as they occur—without altering the immediate contribution that the blood vessels make to their governors.[14]

Once again the motivation for this part of the abstractness condition has to do with the means–end character of functions. To see how the behaviour of a device is functional we need to focus on the way in which it answers the needs of its governors. The need to move clot-free blood is not in the first instance a need of the governors of the heart. It does not arise out of features of their design or their environment. Rather, it arises out of the design of the blood vessels, which are fellow components of the heart. To say that the function of the heart is to move clot-free blood is to focus on the requirements of its fellow components, rather than on the requirements of the governors that they share.

The relation of mutual dependence that holds between fellow components is not the right kind of relation to give rise to functions. The design of an efficient device will be well adapted to the design of its fellow components; but answering their needs is not what the device is there to do. In ascribing a function to a device we need to abstract away from features of its operation that are adaptations to its fellow components, in order to concentrate on the asymmetrical, means–end relation between the device and its governors.

It is important to be clear precisely what is ruled out by the second clause of the abstractness condition. As I have said, the effect of this clause is to rule out overspecific function ascriptions such as the claim that the function of the heart is to move clot-free blood. But now consider a device, such as the sinoatrial node, whose role is to control the behaviour of some other device. The function of the sinoatrial node is to stimulate the heart muscles to contract in such a way as to enable the heart to move the blood. Clearly, what constitutes the right sequence of contractions will depend on the design of the heart itself. So we cannot describe the function of the sinoatrial node without making some kind of reference to the heart's design.

But this case need not be viewed as a counter-example to the abstractness condition. What the abstractness condition will rule out is the claim that the

---

[14] It might be objected that the function of the heart does depend on the design of the blood, because, if the blood were not a liquid, incapable of moving itself, the heart would not need to move it. But, if oxygen and nutrients were normally carried around the body by a substance that was capable of moving itself, that substance would differ from blood, not only in design, but also in function.

function of the node is to ensure that the heart muscles contract in some specifiable way: first the atria, then the ventricles, and so on. To characterize the function of the node in this way would certainly involve a failure to abstract away from the specific details of the heart's design. But there is no reason why we should not say that the function of the sinoatrial node is to ensure that heart muscles contract in the right way, *whatever that may be*. We can make this claim without presupposing anything about the design of the heart, and hence without accepting that the function of the node might vary with the heart's design. I mention this point here because, as I will explain later, it has important implications concerning the content of intentional states.[15]

I have already rehearsed the difficulties that we would face if we tried to base an account of biological categories on the notion of a biological function without first eliminating the rival ascriptions of function discussed in this section and the previous one. The claim that the function of the heart is to make squeezing motions would force us to classify apparently disparate devices together; while the claim that its function is to move clot-free blood would compel us to distinguish between devices that we would naturally place in the same category. In order to avoid these difficulties, we need to take seriously the idea that the notion of a function is a means–end notion, and that ascriptions of biological function answer to the abstractness condition.

3.7. The Extended Immediacy Condition

The last condition that I shall introduce is a rather specialized one, as it is relevant only to devices that possess what Millikan terms relational functions. It is a very important condition for a proponent of the teleological theory, because the notion of a relational function is going to play a major role in our account of intentional content. So the first thing we need to do is make clear what Millikan means by a relational function.

According to Millikan (1984: 39–40), a device will have a relational function when its function is to produce some item or state of affairs that bears some relation to some other item or state of affairs. To borrow Millikan's own example, the pigment-arranging mechanisms in the skin of the chameleon have a relational function: they function to make the chameleon's skin bear the relation *same colour as* to the surface on which the chameleon is sitting. It is not difficult to see that relational functions are likely to give rise to difficulties in specifying the exact nature of the relation that the device is supposed to bring about.

Imagine that a species of chameleon-like creatures evolved in an environment where all surfaces are either green or red. And suppose that, in this

---

[15] These implications will be discussed in Chapters 5 and 11.

environment, all green surfaces are green because they contain chlorophyll and all red surfaces are red because they contain iron oxide. Should we say that the function of the chameleons' pigment-arranging mechanisms is to correlate skin colour with surface colour, or should we say that their function is to correlate skin colour with chemical composition?

Suppose that the explanation for the survival of this type of mechanism has to do with the chameleons' need to avoid predators that rely on vision to find their prey. If so, the fact that these mechanisms are able to match skin colour with chemical composition seems to be beside the point, a result of a correlation in the environment that has no relevance to the organism's needs. Nevertheless, it is still possible to insist that these mechanisms survived because they correlated skin colour with chemical composition. Given that the composition of a surface explains its colour, the fact that the mechanisms successfully matched skin colour with chemical composition explains the fact that they successfully matched skin colour with surface colour, and so explains why they survived.

Once again, we can see how failing to solve this problem will get us into difficulties in categorizing biological devices. Different populations of chameleons might live in environments where there might be all sorts of different correlations between the colours of objects and their surface colours. Perhaps in one rather drab environment, differences in the colour of objects are caused exclusively by how damp they are; in another, by the amount of sunlight to which they have been exposed; in another, by their temperature. In these environments, the chameleons' pigment-arranging mechanisms will effectively track these various conditions. But it seems clear that all these mechanisms have the same *function*, and that function has to do with the colours of things, not their chemical composition or their dampness or their temperature.

It is very tempting to make an appeal to the immediacy condition here. After all, the fact that the chameleons' pigment-arranging mechanisms are able to match skin colour with chemical composition helps to explain their survival only because chemical composition explains surface colour. Hence, there is only an indirect relationship between chemical composition and the presence of these mechanisms. But the immediacy condition proper will not help us here, because that condition is designed to distinguish only between different activities of a device: to solve the problem with the chameleons' pigment-arranging mechanisms, we need to find a way of distinguishing between different relational properties of a single activity.

To do this, we need to introduce a fourth condition, which I shall call the extended immediacy condition, because it is intended as a principled extension of the immediacy condition to cover relational functions.[16] It can be

---

[16] This condition is, I think, equivalent to the condition that Millikan (1984: 100) places on the content of intentional states.

expressed as follows: where a device d is present because earlier devices of the same type produced some relational state of affairs S, d will have the function to produce S only if there is no other relational condition produced by those earlier devices that features in a more immediate explanation for the presence of d.

Suppose that earlier pigment-arranging mechanisms correlated skin colour with chemical composition. And suppose that the occurrence of this correlation helps to explain the chameleons' survival only because it explains the occurrence of a further correlation between skin colour and surface colour. Then the fact that those earlier mechanisms correlated skin colour with chemical composition will fail to provide an immediate explanation for the presence of this pigment-arranging mechanism.

The rationale for the extended immediacy condition is just the same as for the earlier condition: the need to stress how the activity of a type of device helps to satisfy the requirements of its governors. To do this, we need to characterize the relation produced by the device in terms of events that provide the most immediate explanation for the governor's success. In this way, we will be abstracting away from contingencies in the environment that have no direct bearing on the needs of the governors of the device.

4. Summary

Putting the core account together with the additional conditions introduced in this chapter, we can construct the following theory of biological function ascription: where d is a device and F is an activity, d has the function to do F if and only if there is some family of items G; there is a second item g, which is a member of G and which produced d in manner M; there is some family of devices D, to which d belongs and which consists of devices produced by a member of G in manner M; and there is some activity E, such that:

CD.1   Members of D have done F in the recent past.

CD.2   The fact that g produced d by M is explained partly by the fact that the doing of F by members of D in the recent past assisted g or some other members of G that are g's ancestors to do some further thing F.

CD.3a There is nothing that members of D did in the recent past that would provide a more immediate explanation of g producing this d (the immediacy condition).

CD.3b Where the doing of F by members of D consisted in their bringing about some relational state of affairs, there is no relational state of

affairs that members of D recently brought about that would provide a more immediate explanation of g producing d (the extended
immediacy condition).

CD.4   F is characterized in terms of some effect that members of D were
able to bring about by themselves (the independence condition).

CD.5   The truth of the explanation referred to in CD.2 does not depend on
specific features of the design of members of D, or of any other
devices that worked in conjunction with members of D to bring it
about that g or g's ancestors did F (the abstractness condition).

I have tried to show that this account can be motivated in terms of two
essential features of function statements: the function of something has to do
with what *it* does; and the function of a device is what it contributes to its governors. I have also tried to show how the additional conditions that I have
added to the original core account are required to support functional categor-
izations of biological devices. And I have illustrated how these conditions will
enable us to lay claim to what I would take to be common-sense claims, such
as the claim that the function of the heart is to move blood around the body
or that the function of a nest is to shelter the organism, its eggs, or its young.
We might now feel inclined to conclude that it is possible to supply plausible and principled criteria for the ascription of functions that will underwrite
determinate function ascriptions. Nevertheless, I cannot claim to have established this conclusion, because I have not ruled out the existence of other rival
function ascriptions that could not be rejected by my account as it stands. It
may turn out that we will need to add new constraints, or amend the ones we
have. However, by setting out this account, I hope at least to have provided
support for the claim that biological devices have determinate functions, if
only by indicating the kinds of consideration that might be used to establish
this thesis.

Part II

Special-Purpose Systems

4

Minimal Intentionality

1. Introduction

A teleological theory of intentionality will begin from the following claim: a system will be able to represent or signal some state of affairs only if it possesses a certain kind of function.[1] Moreover, the content of the devices produced by that system—what it is that they represent or signal—will be determined in some way by the function of the systems that produce and use them.[2]

My task in the second part of this book is to investigate the workings of a range of simple intentional systems. My examples will include the frog's fly-detecting system, which helps the frog to direct snaps at flies; the bee dance mechanism, which guides bees to nectar; and the mechanisms that enable the rat to learn to avoid poisonous substances. All these systems are examples of what I shall refer to as *special-purpose systems*: that is, systems that function to control a particular kind of behaviour—behaviour directed towards the satisfaction of a specifiable need or set of needs.[3]

As we shall see, special-purpose intentional systems may be credited with a range of different intentional capacities. For example, some special-purpose systems operate by detecting the presence of a certain feature at some location, while others are capable of representing particular objects or places. Some systems are only able to register the occurrence of certain conditions, while others are also able to represent goals. Some systems, though not all, are able to learn or to engage in inference. According to the teleologist, these differences will derive from differences in the functional properties of these systems.

---

[1] Note that this is a necessary, not a sufficient condition: there may be more to intentionality than function. For example, a teleologist might suppose that an intentional system is one that normally carries out its function in a particular way.

[2] In what follows, I will refer to signals or representations as 'intentional devices' or, occasionally, 'states'; I will refer to the mechanisms that produce signals or representations as 'mechanisms' or 'systems', never as 'devices'.

[3] I shall offer a more precise account of the distinction between special-purpose and general-purpose intentional systems in Chapter 9.

A teleological account of these different intentional capacities will centre on the notion of minimal competence, which I introduced at the end of Chapter 2: to know what it is for an intentional system to possess a particular intentional capacity, we need to determine the minimal conditions a system must meet if it can be said to have survived by exercising that capacity. This feature of the teleological theory not only constrains the teleologist's account of particular intentional capacities, but also gives rise to some distinctive conclusions.

My task over the next few chapters will be to investigate what possession of these different intentional capacities requires. My strategy will be to consider each capacity in turn, treating more complex capacities as developments or modifications of more primitive abilities. By taking this step-by-step approach, I will be able to introduce the basic ingredients of my account one by one, helping to keep track of what is going on and ensuring that important distinctions are kept clear.[4]

In this chapter, I will be concerned with a fundamental question: what is it that distinguishes an intentional system from a non-intentional system? In order to answer this question, I will have to set out the minimal requirements that a system must meet if it is to count as an intentional system. To know what is distinctive about a system that meets these minimum conditions is to know what is distinctive of intentional systems in general.

The chapter falls into two halves. I will begin by discussing what the function of a minimally intentional system will be. I will argue for a very modest view, one that will allow us to count some very simple mechanisms as intentional systems. In the second half of the chapter, I will consider whether there are any constraints on the way in which an intentional system performs its function. I will argue that there is one such constraint: an intentional system must make use of information about how things are in the environment.

2. The Function of an Intentional System

2.1. 'Intentionality'

If we are to investigate what it is for a system to be an intentional system, we first need to know what is meant by 'intentionality'. The term 'intentionality' is, of course, a term of art, and one with too long a history to have an agreed use. Some philosophers are happy to ascribe intentional properties to very simple systems, including bacteria and thermostats. Others regard this as too liberal, and some would prefer to apply the term 'intentional' only to states

---

[4] For a fuller defence of this 'bottom-up' approach to intentionality, see Lloyd (1989: 8–9).

that could reasonably be described as beliefs, desires, or intentions. How far these are issues of substance is open to dispute. But, because this is such a contentious matter, I would like to say a little about how I am going to understand the term 'intentionality' in what follows. I am helped here by a very useful discussion of intentionality by Dretske (1995: 28–9).

Dretske identifies a number of features that characterize intentional devices. First, an intentional device can be described as being *about* or *directed onto* some feature or item. Secondly, an intentional device *presents* its object as being a certain way—as occurring, or as having some property, or as worth obtaining or doing. Thirdly, an intentional state can *mispresent* its object: an intentional state can present a feature as present when it is absent, or it can present an object as possessing some feature that it does not possess.

To count as an intentional device, an item has to fulfil all three of these requirements. It is for this reason that philosophers have often rejected the idea that moods, such as euphoria or depression, count as intentional phenomena: a feeling of euphoria might be characterized as presenting things in a certain way, and even, if it is inappropriate, as mispresenting them; but a feeling of euphoria is not *about* anything: it does not pick out any particular chunk of the world. Conversely, a spotlight or a pointer might be described as being directed onto some particular object; but a spotlight does not present its object in any particular way: it simply presents it. Hence, a spotlight is not an intentional phenomenon.

An account of intentionality also needs to accommodate the point that the intentional properties of an intentional device will feature in explanations of the behaviour to which it gives rise. At this point, I will leave it open exactly what the nature of these explanations might be. But I take it that any adequate account of intentionality must give some account of the intentional explanation of behaviour.

At this point, then, we can provide the following very general characterization of intentional devices. An intentional device is supposed to pick out some feature or object beyond itself, and to present it in a certain way. It can fail to do what it is supposed to do, and so it can mispresent its object. Where a device does have these properties, the fact that it does so has some explanatory force.

2.2. The Proposed Account

In this section, I will explain what I take the function of an intentional system to be. My account of this issue is heavily influenced by the account proposed by Millikan (1984). However, as will become clear in a later section, my account is rather weaker than hers.

On my proposed account, a mechanism will count as an intentional mechanism if its function is to control the operation of some second functioning mechanism in such a way as to ensure that the behaviour produced by that second mechanism coincides with a certain condition or set of conditions in the environment. Consider the frog's visual system. The system operates in such a way as to ensure that the frog responds to the presence of something small and dark by launching a snap. The visual system controls a second mechanism—the mechanism that controls snaps—and it does so by prompting this mechanism to produce a snap when there is something small and dark nearby.

The frog's visual system functions to coordinate a single behavioural response with a single condition in the environment. More complex intentional mechanisms will function to coordinate a *range* of behavioural responses with a *range* of conditions. An example is the bee dance mechanism, which functions to ensure that, when the bees fly to one of a range of locations around the hive, this coincides with the presence of nectar at that location.[5]

The notion of behaviour has a crucial role to play in this account, so I should explain how I am using this term. I will use the term 'behaviour' to refer to a physical response that has a function.[6] For example, the frog's snap is a complex physical response that has the function to ensure that the frog swallows a fly. In the case of the very simple intentional systems discussed in this chapter, the function of the responses that they control will be determined by the function of the executive mechanism that produces them: the frog's snaps have the function to capture flies because this is a function of the mechanism that produces them. Successful behaviour will be behaviour that succeeds in performing its function. When I describe a piece of behaviour as appropriate in the circumstances, I mean simply that it has taken place in circumstances that favour the success of behaviour of that kind.

There are two ideas that are central to the account that I have proposed. The first is that intentional mechanisms have relational functions. An intentional mechanism functions to produce a relation of coincidence between the response of the second mechanism and some condition or set of conditions in the environment (Millikan 1984: 97–100). The claim that intentional mechanisms have relational functions will have an important role to play in explaining the

---

[5] We need to add the proviso that it should not be the case that the behaviour prompted by the intentional mechanism normally coincides with some condition in the environment only because that behaviour causes that condition. This proviso is necessary in order to rule out cases of the following kind. The swallowing mechanism functions to introduce food into the oesophagus. Moreover, by doing this it prompts the oesophagus to produce the muscular contractions that move the food towards the stomach. It might be suggested that the swallowing mechanism functions to ensure that the oesophagus's contractions coincide with the presence of food. But the swallowing mechanism produces this coincidence only because it causes the contractions by moving the food into the oesophagus. In contrast, the frog's visual system does not prompt a snap by causing there to be a fly nearby. A device that causes the occurrence of a certain condition cannot also signal its occurrence.

[6] I shall not distinguish between behaviour that we tend to describe as produced by the whole organism—such as the frog's snap—and behaviour that is produced by a particular organ or system—such as the beating of the heart.

idea that intentional devices are directed onto some item or feature in the environment. On this view, we can begin our explanation of why a signal is *about* some feature by pointing to the fact that its function relates it to that feature. In at least a minimal sense, a signal picks out a specifiable chunk of the world; it is directed onto something.

The second element that is central to this account is the idea that intentional mechanisms are supposed to control the behaviour of some second mechanism (Millikan 1984: 96–8). I will borrow Millikan's terminology, and refer to this second mechanism as the *cooperating mechanism*. A cooperating mechanism might be a further intentional mechanism, or an executive mechanism in direct control of the organism's behaviour. As we have seen, in the case of the frog's visual system, the cooperating mechanism will be the executive mechanism that controls the production of fly snaps.

The claim that an intentional mechanism functions to control the behaviour of some further mechanism helps to account for the idea that an intentional device presents some item or feature in a particular way. The important point here is that the role of a signalling system is not simply to prompt a piece of behaviour at intervals, but to coordinate it with the presence or absence of some feature in the environment. The function of a signalling system can be viewed as a *communicative* one: not only is it itself sensitive to whether the relevant feature is present or absent; it is supposed to make its cooperating device sensitive to that fact. So, not only can it be described as focusing on that feature, as a spotlight might; it can also be characterized as conveying a message about it, as presenting it *as* present or absent; in other words, as making an assertion of some kind. And, of course, if this is conceded, there will be a clear sense in which a signalling signal can *mispresent* the environment: it may produce a signal under the wrong circumstances, triggering the cooperating device to produce behaviour that fails, or succeeds only in an abnormal way.

What kinds of system will have a function of this kind? It might be thought that the definition will include any system that can be described as reacting sensitively to its environment. But, in fact, there are some very simple systems that could be characterized in this way that the definition will exclude. For example, consider a small marine organism that does better if it stays in cooler water and that propels itself by vibrating cilia at one end of its body. The warmer the cilia become, the more rapidly they vibrate, so that when the organism is in a patch of warm water it tends to move out of it fairly quickly, and when it is in a cool area it tends to stay put. An organism of this kind can be said to react sensitively to the surrounding temperature, but it will not count as using intentional devices on this account. This is because, in this organism, the mechanisms that respond to environmental conditions and the mechanisms that control the organism's behaviour are the *same* set of mechanisms: there is no division of labour, and so no separate cooperating device. As a result, the organism cannot be described as possessing a mechanism that functions to register changes in temperature.

On the other hand, there are some very simple mechanisms that can be ascribed a function of this kind. I will refer to these mechanisms as *signalling systems*. Signalling systems are mechanisms that trigger stereotypical behavioural responses. They do not engage in even the simplest forms of inference; they do not represent goals; they may not even be capable of learning. An example of a signalling system is the sensory mechanism possessed by the arrow worm: this system helps the worm to move towards prey by detecting vibrations in the water. Other signallers use crude environmental cues to release pre-programmed patterns of behaviour. I have already mentioned the visual system of the frog. Another example is the visual system of the female stickleback, which, at a certain time of year, responds to the presence of something red by prompting the performance of a courtship dance.[7]

At this point, I cannot claim to have shown that these systems are intentional systems. All I have shown is that they share a function with intentional systems. Nevertheless, for simplicity's sake, I will assume that these systems are intentional systems in what follows. In fact, this assumption will have been vindicated by the end of the chapter.

2.3. Intentional Explanation

What view of intentional explanations is implied by this account of the function of intentional mechanisms? In this section, I would like to say a little about this issue. It is, of course, important to bear in mind that, at this point, we are dealing with very simple intentional systems. What I say here cannot be regarded as a comprehensive account of intentional explanation. In particular, it does not cover behaviour prompted by systems that are capable of representing goals.

How will an explanation that appeals to the intentional properties of a simple signal explain the response produced by its cooperating mechanism? One thought might be that the fact that a system actually succeeds in coordinating the response of its cooperating mechanism with conditions in the environment can at least help to explain the success of that response. But this does not seem to be the kind of explanation we are looking for. First of all, the fact that the system has this as its *function* will not be relevant to this explanation: it is what the system actually does, not what it is supposed to do, that will have explanatory significance.[8] Moreover, when we offer an intentional explanation

---

[7] In what follows I will maintain a terminological distinction between the term 'signal' and the term 'representation': I will reserve the term 'representation' for the devices produced by systems that are at least capable of engaging in some form of inference. There is nothing principled about this terminological divide; it is there primarily as a reminder of the unsophisticated nature of signalling systems.

[8] There is a similar problem with Dretske's attempt (1988: 79–80) to account for the explanatory significance of intentional properties by suggesting that intentional states are

of a creature's behaviour, we are usually interested in why that behaviour occurred, not why it was successful.

The teleologist will respond to this worry by pointing out that it rests on a false conception of the nature of intentional explanation. The problem arises from the assumption that, in explaining a piece of behaviour in intentional terms, we are offering a regularizing explanation of that behaviour. It is open to the teleologist, however, to insist that intentional explanations are normalizing explanations: the point of saying that the frog snapped because it detected a fly nearby is not to indicate the existence of some kind of regularity connecting events of these kinds. The point of the explanation is to make sense of the frog's behaviour as appropriate, given how it senses the world to be.

In Chapter 1, I tried to give some sense of how a proponent of an aetiological theory of functions would account for the force of functional explanations. I suggested that such explanations work by showing that it is no accident that an organism possesses an item that is able to produce a certain kind of effect. We can treat explanations that appeal to the content of a simple signal as following a similar pattern. When we say that the frog snapped because it saw a fly, the point of this explanation is to show that it is no accident that the frog snapped when it did. It is no accident, because the fact that the frog snapped at that time is explained by the fact that its snap was prompted by a certain type of visual signal; and the fact that this signal prompted the snap is explained by the fact that signals of that kind are capable of coordinating snaps with the presence of a fly. In the case of a snap that was prompted by an incorrect signal, the point of the explanation will be to show that it was no accident that the frog snapped in response to that signal; what was accidental was that it snapped when no fly was present. In this way, the explanation makes sense of the frog's behaviour as a normal response to the signal produced by its visual system, given that the function of its behaviour is to capture a fly.

2.4. *Minimal Content: A Preliminary Sketch*

In the remainder of this chapter, I will need to make some assumptions about the content of particular intentional devices that are under discussion. In this section, I will give a rough, preliminary sketch of the account of content that is naturally suggested by the account of the functions of intentional devices that I have offered. At this point, I will not attempt to defend this account—I will leave that task to the next chapter.

Where we are dealing with a very simple signalling mechanism—such as the frog's visual mechanism—we could present the account as follows. Where

---

structuring causes of behaviour. See also Millikan (1990c: 807–9). My account here is closer to that offered by McGinn (1989). See also Millikan (1986) and Sehon (1994).

I_C is a type of device produced by a signalling mechanism and C is a type of condition; I_C will signal the occurrence of C if and only if there is some relation R such that:

(S.1) In the past, instances of I_C sometimes bore R to instances of C.

(S.2) The fact that instances of I_C bore R to instances of C sometimes helped to explain the fact that the behaviour normally prompted by I_C coincided with an instance of C.

(S.3) On some of those occasions, the fact that that behaviour coincided with an instance of C helped to ensure its success.

In order to understand what constitutes successful behaviour by the cooperating mechanism, we first need to know the function of that mechanism. Consider the example of the visual mechanism that controls the frog's snaps. Very roughly, the function of this mechanism will be to ensure that the frog swallows flies. In order to identify the precise function of this mechanism, we need to consider which properties of flies help to explain the fact that the frog's snaps help it to survive. What makes flies relevant to frogs is their biochemical properties—the properties that make them nutritious to frogs. So the function of this mechanism is to ensure that the frog swallows items that have certain biochemical properties, those biochemical properties that make flies nutritious to frogs.[9]

In this and future chapters, I will talk a little more loosely than this. I will describe the frog as needing to catch flies, and I will describe other organisms as needing to capture prey or to avoid predators. This is necessary if I am to keep my sentences to a reasonable length. But all these terms need to be regarded as shorthand—shorthand for expressions that would pick out just those properties of the items in question that make them suitable to eat, or capable of killing, or whatever.

Now, consider the visual signals produced by the frog's visual system when there is something small and dark nearby. There is a set of conditions with which these signals have coincided in the past: the presence of a small, dark object in range of the frog's tongue; the presence of a fly in range of the frog's tongue; the sun shining as the signal is produced; and so on. There is a set of conditions that have helped to explain the success of the snaps prompted by those signals: the absence of a predator close to the frog; the presence of sticky fluid on the frog's tongue; the presence of a fly in range of the frog's tongue; and so on. Only one of these conditions—the presence of a fly in range of the frog's tongue—appears on both these lists.[10] Moreover, it is just because the

[9] See Sterelny (1990: 125–6) and Shapiro (1992) for alternative proposals.
[10] At this point it is far from clear why the absence of a predator or the presence of sticky slime on the frog's tongue are not conditions to which the frog's visual system normally bears some relation. This will become clear only by the end of this chapter, when I have said more about the nature of the relation that it is supposed to hold between a signal and the condition that it signals.

signals coincided with the presence of a fly within range that the frog's snaps occurred when a fly was present. So this is the condition that these visual devices will signal.

Note that, on this account, the content of the visual signal has a spatio-temporal aspect. The content of the signal concerns not simply the presence of a fly, but the presence of a fly within range of the frog's tongue at the time the frog snaps. This is because the normal explanation for the success of the frog's behaviour will include a reference, not only to the presence of the fly, but also to the time and location, relative to the frog, at which this condition occurred.

On this account, we can determine the content of the frog's visual signals by considering how devices of the same type were produced and used in the past. However, even in the case of relatively unsophisticated intentional systems, we will not always be able to appeal directly to the past history of the devices produced by the system. This is because some intentional systems possess relational functions; and mechanisms that possess relational functions have an important property: they can produce novel devices.

At first glance it might seem that the core account will preclude the possibility of novel devices having biological functions. This is because the function of a device will depend on its history, and therefore, we might assume, on what was done by earlier devices of the same type. But in the case of devices produced by a mechanism that has a relational function, this assumption will break down. It will break down because the workings of the mechanism will be characterized by a set of *rules* that determine how the devices produced by the mechanism are supposed to correlate with conditions in the environment; and these rules may be projected to cover new cases (Millikan 1984: 40–5).

We can make this clearer using the example of the bee dance mechanism. The operation of the bee dance mechanism is governed by a set of rules that relate specific features of the dance—the vigour, speed, and angle at which it is performed—to certain features of the nectar source that the bee has discovered—its quality, its distance from the hive, and the direction in which it lies. These rules capture the common factors operative on all the occasions in the past when bees have benefited from the operation of the bee dance mechanism. Hence, we can say that the rules *normally* govern the operation of this mechanism.

Now, suppose that the bee discovers a high-grade source of nectar exactly two miles north of the hive. The bee returns to the hive and dances a vigorous, moderately paced, vertical dance. It is possible that no bee has ever performed a dance with just that combination of features before. Hence we cannot assign a content to this dance by appealing to the way in which dances of the same type were produced and used in the past. Nevertheless, in producing this dance, the bee dance mechanism is operating in accordance with the rules that normally characterize its operation. Hence, as Millikan (1984: 41) points out, we can assign a content to this dance—its content will be derived from the function of the bee dance mechanism, *together with* the rules that normally govern its operation.

We can assign a function to the bee dance mechanism in just the same way as we assigned a function to the frog's visual system—by identifying the conditions with which the dances produced by the mechanism normally coincide, and the conditions that normally help to explain the success of the behaviour that the mechanism prompts. This will tell us that the function of the mechanism is to ensure that the bees' flights take them to locations where they will find sources of nectar. But it is the rules by which the mechanism normally works that determine which location is signalled by each type of dance.

This gives us the following, slightly more complex account to cover signalling mechanisms that can produce novel devices. Where S is a signalling mechanism, I_c is a type of device produced by S, and C is a type of condition, I_c will signal the occurrence of C if and only if there is some relation R; there is some rule or set of rules L; there is a range of types of devices *I* produced by S of which I_c is a member; and there is a range of types of condition *C* of which C is a member; such that:

(SS.1) In the past, instances of devices belonging to *I* sometimes bore R to instances of conditions belonging to *C* in accordance with a pattern characterized by L.

(SS.2) The fact some instance of a member of *I* bore R to some instance of a member of *C* sometimes helped to explain the fact that the behaviour prompted by that device coincided with that condition.

(SS.3) On some occasions, the fact that behaviour coincided with that condition helped to explain its success.

(SS.4) If S were operating in accordance with L, I_c would bear R to C.

This preliminary account of content is close to the account offered by Millikan (1984: 100). But it contrasts with accounts of content offered by other proponents of the teleological theory, such as Neander (1995). Neander argues for a more modest account of the content of simple intentional devices, one that takes more account of the organism's actual discriminatory capacities. The frog cannot discriminate flies from other small, dark objects. Hence, Neander suggests, we should treat it as signalling the presence of something small and dark nearby. Neander labels her account a 'Low Church' teleological theory, in opposition to Millikan's 'High Church' view.[11] In the next chapter, I will address issues about content in some detail. For the time being, it is enough to note that I will argue in defence of a High Church teleological theory—a slightly elaborated version of the account proposed here.

---

[11] This disagreement about content has its origins in the disagreement about functions that I discussed in Chapter 3. This will become clearer when I discuss these issues in more detail in the next chapter.

2.5. Intentionality and Articulate Structure

This account of the function of intentional mechanisms is a very modest one. In this section and the next, I will consider two possible amendments to the account. These amendments are interesting to me because they preserve the assumption that intentionality is a fairly modest achievement, though not quite as modest as I have suggested. In this section I will discuss Millikan's argument for the claim that intentional devices must have a certain structural complexity. In the next section I will investigate the idea, due to Fodor and Beckermann, that an intentional system must be capable of engaging in some form of inference. I will argue that neither of these amendments is needed.

As we have seen, Millikan argues that intentional devices will possess relational functions and will be used by some cooperating device. But she also adds a third criterion: intentional devices, she suggests, possess *articulate structure* (1984: 116–17; 1993*a*). She explains this idea as follows: every intentional device possesses an invariant aspect and one or more variant aspects. Transformations of the device with respect to one of its variant aspects will correspond to transformations of the state of affairs represented by the device. She illustrates her point using the example of the bee dance mechanism: although the dances produced by the mechanism share a basic structure, individual dances vary in certain ways. These variations correspond to variations in the state of affairs that the dance represents. For example, the speed and angle at which the dance is performed vary with the location of the nectar source. These correlations are captured by the rules that normally govern the workings of the mechanism. An intentional device, Millikan (1984: 116) suggests is "'articulate' in that it is 'articulated'; it divides into significant aspects, its significant variant or variants and its invariant aspect. Also it is 'articulate' in the sense that it "says" something: qua intentional icon it *contrasts* with other icons of the same family that are significant transforms of it." Millikan regards the possession of this kind of structure as an essential feature of intentional devices. She describes intentional devices as *mapping onto* the states of affairs that they represent or signal. In other words, she sees representation as a kind of picturing relation (1993*b*: 11).[12]

If we accept this view, it appears to follow that we ought to adopt a more conservative account of minimal intentionality than the one that I have proposed. On my proposed account, signals will count as intentional devices. But there is no requirement that signals possess articulate structure. For example,

---

[12] The idea that intentional states are, in some sense, pictures of what they represent is not, of course, original to Millikan. For some familiar examples, see Wittgenstein (1961), Sellars (1962), and Armstrong (1973). A distinction between variant and invariant aspects of a representation is made by Walton (1970: 337–42), though for a rather different purpose.

the signals produced by the arrow worm's sensory mechanism have no internal structure: the mechanism is able to register the occurrence of only a single type of condition in the environment—that is, the presence of prey ahead of the organism; and so the signals that it produces take exactly the same form each time they are produced. As a result, we might well expect Millikan to insist that we should not treat these signals as intentional phenomena.

Millikan, however, does not draw this conclusion. Instead, she suggests that we can regard unstructured signals as significant *parts* of intentional devices: the whole device, she suggests, is *the signal being produced at a certain place at a certain time*. This is because the signal produced by the arrow worm's sensory mechanism signals that there is prey ahead of the organism *here* and *now*—the spatio-temporal content of the signal is fixed (in part) by the time and place at which it is produced (Millikan 1984: 116–18). If we accept Millikan's account of unstructured signals, then we must accept that a bee dance, too, is only a part of an intentional device—for it will be true of the bee dance that its spatio-temporal content is determined in part by the time and the place at which it is performed.

An initially puzzling feature of this suggestion is that it is not clear that it will rule anything out. It might be thought that it will rule out the possibility that there could be an intentional device that an organism normally produces only once in its lifetime. For example, suppose that a species of amoeba possesses a mechanism that normally registers when conditions are right for the organism to divide. Each individual mechanism will normally operate only once in the amoeba's lifetime, so that it will not normally produce the same signal at different times or places. It might be suggested that this type of mechanism, at least, would be excluded by Millikan's criterion. But, of course, the signals produced by this type of mechanism do have one variable aspect: that is, the identity of the organism to which the mechanism belongs. We can treat these mechanisms as having the function to detect when conditions are right *for this organism* to divide, so that the identity of the organism helps to determine the content of the signals that they produce.

If this is correct, it seems that the only claim that will be excluded by Millikan's requirement will be the claim that there could be a type of intentional mechanism that operates only once in history. But of course, as far as biological devices are concerned, this claim is already excluded by the claim that intentionality is a matter of function: for, as we saw in Chapter 1, a function cannot be established without repetition.[13]

---

[13] The claim that functions require repetition applies only to biological devices. If we allow that artificial functions may also underpin intentionality, Millikan's criterion will exclude the claim that an artificial device designed to signal the imminent destruction of the world, say, will count as an intentional device. But I would regard this as a counter-intuitive consequence of her account.

It looks, then, as if this requirement would add very little to our account, at least in the sense that it does not rule out any cases that would be permitted by our initial account. We might wonder what the motivation for this requirement might be. It turns out that this condition is concerned, not with a worry about what constitutes an intentional system, but with a worry about the content of intentional devices.[14]

Earlier, I outlined a preliminary account of how content might be ascribed to the devices produced by signalling systems. According to this account, the content of a signal will concern some condition in the environment about which it normally carries information and which normally helps to explain the success of the behaviour which it prompts. The worry is that it might look as if this preliminary account is too weak: there are a number of conditions that meet these criteria that we would not wish to regard as represented by the device.[15] These will include certain conditions that are permanent features of the organism's environment.[16]

For example, the production of a bee dance will normally carry the information that acceleration due to gravity on the surface of the earth approximates 9.81 metres per second. Moreover, this fact about gravity will normally help to explain the success of the behaviour prompted by the dance—if the strength of the earth's gravitational pull were to change, it is unlikely that the bees' flights would succeed in taking them to sources of nectar. It seems, then, that we should take each bee dance to represent, among other things, the fact that acceleration due to gravity on the surface of the earth approximates 9.81 metres per second. Millikan seeks to solve this problem by appealing to the structural properties of the dance. The idea will be that there is no variable aspect of the bee dance that correlates with changes in the earth's gravitational pull. Hence, bee dances do not 'map onto' states of affairs involving gravity, and so they cannot be taken to represent such states of affairs.

However, there are problems with this solution. One worry is that mappings are all too easy to find. Even if a particular bee dance does not map onto the fact that acceleration due to gravity on the surface of the earth approximates 9.81 metres per second, we could still treat it as mapping onto the fact that acceleration due to gravity *in the area in which the nectar is located* approximates 9.81 metres per second. Moreover, the fact that this condition holds will help to explain the success of the behaviour prompted by the dance. Similarly, we could

[14] Millikan, private communication.
[15] There is a range of problems of this kind, a number of which will be discussed in Chapter 5.
[16] In one paper, Millikan (1995: 289) appeals to the relation of 'mapping onto' as a means of excluding rival content ascriptions concerning temporary states of affairs in the environment, such as the absence of a predator. But it is hard to see why bee dances could not be characterized as mapping onto such states of affairs: transformations of a particular bee dance will correspond to transformations in the location of the predator-free zone represented by the dance.

claim that the arrow worm's signals map onto the fact that acceleration due to gravity on the surface of the earth approximates 9.81 metres per second *at a particular time*—that is, the time at which they are produced. It is worth considering, therefore, whether there is any other way of dealing with the problem.

In fact, a closer investigation of the example reveals that the claim that the bee dance represents facts about gravity is not supported by the preliminary account that I set out earlier on. It is certainly true that the occurrence of a bee dance bears some relation to the fact that acceleration due to gravity on the surface of the earth approximates 9.81 metres per second—for example, there is a causal relation between these two conditions. It is also true that the fact that the bees' flights are adapted to the strength of the earth's gravitational pull helps to explain their success. However, there is no explanatory connection between these two facts. The fact that the bees' behaviour is suited to the earth's gravity is explained by the design of the bees' bodies—for example, the fact that the bees' wings are large enough to lift them from the ground. The fact that the bees' flights are triggered by bee dances has no part to play in this explanation.

I suggested earlier that the function of a signalling mechanism is to ensure that the organism's behaviour coincides with the occurrence of a certain condition in the environment. For a device to signal the occurrence of a certain condition, it is not enough that the behaviour that it prompts depends on the presence of that condition. It must also be the case that the fact that the organism's behaviour was suited to that condition is explained by the fact that it was triggered by that device. What is important here is not the internal structure of the device but its role in explaining the success of the behaviour that it prompts: the claim that bee dances signal facts about gravity violates clause (SS.2) of the account suggested above.[17]

I am certainly not attempting to deny that many intentional devices possess articulate structure. Nor do I wish to dispute the claim that this will be a functionally significant feature of some intentional devices, particularly those that are involved in processes of inference. The point I wish to make is simply that there is no pressing reason to insist that articulate structure is a *criterion* of intentionality.

2.6. Intentionality and Inference

The second proposal that I will consider has been suggested by a number of writers, including Fodor (1986) and Beckermann (1988).[18] They argue that a

---

[17] This is not intended to show that there could never be an intentional mechanism that functioned to detect some permanent state of affairs in the organism's environment. It is just that it is hard to imagine why any such mechanism would evolve. It seems far more likely that the organism's body would have adapted to that state of affairs.

[18] Fodor (1991: 257) has since modified his position and it is unclear whether he would still endorse this line of argument.

system will not count as an intentional system unless it is capable of engaging in at least a simple form of inference. By this I mean simply that the system must be capable of using devices that have a certain content in order to generate further devices that have a different content. I will argue that a proponent of a non-teleological theory of intentionality might have good reasons to accept this more conservative proposal, but that these reasons need not be shared by a teleologist.

The argument for this alternative proposal runs roughly as follows. We cannot ascribe intentional content to natural devices unless we can show that it is necessary to do so in order to explain the working of the system of which they are a part. But we need not explain the workings of a simple signalling system, such as the arrow worm's sensory system, in this way. Instead, we can offer a straightforward non-intentional explanation of the arrow worm's behaviour: we can say that the arrow worm heads towards prey because the small animals on which it feeds cause vibrations in the water, which cause the arrow worm's sensory device to send out a chemical impulse, which in turn causes the worm's fins to move in certain ways, with the result that it darts towards its prey. None of this makes any reference to intentional states.

On this view, it is only in the case of organisms that engage in processes of inference that we need to appeal to intentional states to explain behaviour. The idea, I think, is that, in the case of an organism that engages in inference, the explanation of its behaviour will refer to properties in the environment other than those that directly impinge upon it. The organism's behaviour need no longer be explained exclusively in terms of the push and pull of physical forces with which it is in direct contact. For example, imagine a more sophisticated cousin of the arrow worm, which is able to distinguish between different kinds of prey by combining information about the vibrations it senses with information about the visual appearance and scent of the source. A non-intentional explanation of the organism's response, an explanation that referred only to the vibrations, light waves, and chemical traces reaching the organism, and the various chemical impulses interacting inside it, would leave out something important. In the case of the imaginary arrow worm there is available an alternative kind of explanation for its behaviour, one that is somehow more illuminating than a non-intentional explanation.

Note that the argument, as I have set it out, does not trade on the idea that it would be impossible to give a non-intentional explanation of the behaviour of the more complex organism. This would clearly be an unwarranted claim. The idea is simply that, in the case of an organism that is capable of engaging in inference, a non-intentional explanation leaves something out, something that it would not leave out in the case of the simpler organism.

What the explanation would leave out, it seems to me, would be anything that made sense of the organism's behaviour as an appropriate response to conditions in the environment. If all we knew was that the behaviour was triggered by vibrations, light waves, and chemical traces, we would not be any the wiser about what made the creature's behaviour an appropriate response to those stimuli. What we need to add in is what those stimuli 'mean' to the organism. And now the idea will be that what those stimuli 'mean' to the organism is equivalent to how the organism *interprets* them. But the organism can only be described as interpreting the stimuli that reach it if it infers something from them. Mere vibrations do not mean anything to the real arrow worm because it does not interpret them. It simply reacts to them.

On this view, then, the difference between an explanation that makes sense of an organism's behaviour as an appropriate response to how things are and one that simply indicates how it arose has to do with the complexity of the causal process involved. In both cases, the organism's behaviour arises out of a certain kind of causal process. But only in the case of a system that is capable of inference does the process possess the right kind of complexity to justify describing it in intentional terms.

I think that this would be a powerful line of thought for a proponent of a non-teleological account of intentionality. But, as we have seen, the teleologist is able to offer a quite different account of what it means to make sense of an organism's behaviour in intentional terms. For the teleologist, the difference between these two kinds of explanation will be the difference between a teleological and a non-teleological explanation of the organism's behaviour. In the case of the arrow worm, for example, we can offer a non-teleological explanation of its behaviour by saying that it swam towards its prey because a sequence of chemical impulses caused its fins to work in a certain way. Or we can make sense of its behaviour in teleological terms by saying that it was produced in response to a device that signalled the presence of prey over there—in other words, that it was produced in the normal way by a device that has the function to ensure that it coincides with a condition (the presence of prey) that favours its success.

This teleological explanation does not simply characterize the organism's behaviour as a response to properties that directly impinge upon the organism. Rather, it presents the stimuli that reach the organism as having a certain significance for it. They have this significance, not because they are interpreted in a particular way, but because they are used to generate a device that functions to convey a certain message to the cooperating mechanism. The same point will apply both to systems that are capable of inference and to those that are not. In both cases we can make sense of the organism's behaviour as a response to stimuli that are normally used in a process that helps to ensure the success of its behaviour. If this is correct, the teleologist does not have to deny that the arrow worm is capable of signalling the presence of prey.

2.7. The Function of Intentional Mechanisms: Summary

I have suggested one condition that must be met by all intentional mechanisms: an intentional system must have the function to ensure that the
responses of some second, cooperating mechanism coincide with the occurrence of some condition or set of conditions in the environment. Simple signalling systems are the simplest mechanisms that have a function of this kind.
We can understand intentional explanations that appeal to the content of simple signals as showing that the fact that the organism produced a certain
response is no accident, given that it was prompted to do so by a signal that
functions to register the occurrence of some favourable condition.

This account of the function of intentional mechanisms can be used to generate a preliminary account of the content of simple signals. The notion of
content that emerges from this preliminary account is what Neander terms a
'High Church' notion of content. That is, it ties the content of a signal to the
explanation for the success of the organism's behaviour, rather than to the system's actual discriminatory capacities. I will defend this approach in the next
chapter.

The account that I have offered is modest in the extreme. I have considered
two possible amendments: the suggestion that intentional devices must
have articulate structure and the suggestion that they must be involved in
simple processes of inference. I have found no reason to accept either of these
amendments.

3. Intentionality and Information

3.1. The Intentional Relation

Up to this point, I have been concerned with the function of the minimally
intentional system. I would now like to turn my attention to a different issue.
I would like to investigate whether there are any constraints on the way in
which an intentional mechanism normally *carries out* its function. If there are,
then this creates the possibility that there are some kinds of mechanism that
fail to count as intentional mechanisms, not because they have the wrong
function, but because they perform their function in the wrong way. I would
like to argue that this is indeed the case.

As we have seen, the function of a minimally intentional mechanism is to
produce a certain relation—a relation of coincidence—between the response
of a cooperating device and some condition in the environment. It will follow
from this that there will also be some spatio-temporal relation that normally

holds between the devices produced by the mechanism and the condition that
they signal. One possible view is that this is the only relationship that is supposed to hold between a signal and the condition that it signals. But it might
be claimed that the signal will normally bear some *causal* or even *informational* relation to this condition. In this part of the chapter, I will argue in
favour of a version of this stronger view.

The idea that the teleologist should make use of a notion of information is
hardly a new one. The best-known attempt to combine teleology with information has been made by Dretske (1986, 1988).[19] However, as we shall see
later on, the notion of information that I shall exploit will be much weaker
than that proposed by Dretske.

I will begin by explaining why I believe that we need to include a reference
to information in our account of minimal intentionality. I will then consider
how best to characterize the notion of information that is required. In what
follows, I will continue to use the set of schematic letters introduced earlier,
namely:

S   the signalling mechanism;

I_C a type of intentional device produced by S;

C   the environmental condition that S is supposed to signal by producing
I_C;

R   the relation that is supposed to hold between I_C and C.

Our question is: is R an informational relation?

3.2. *Introducing Information*

In this section I will say something about what I take the nature of the informational relation to be. First of all, it is important to note that informational
relations hold between *types* of events: an individual event x will carry the
information that an event or condition of a certain type occurs or is about to
occur. Moreover, x will carry that information in virtue of being an event of a
certain type.

In general, information theorists are agreed that informational relations
consist in relations of *conditional probability* between types of event. In other
words, the occurrence of an event of a particular kind—an event of type X,

---

[19] For some other interesting suggestions, see Godfrey-Smith (1991), Bogdan (1994),
Ross and Zawidzki (1994), and Jacob (1997). Millikan's views on this issue are complex.
She appears to reject informational theories in Millikan (1989b: 286); but in a later paper,
she hints that her objection is primarily directed against accounts that centre on information in Dretske's sense (Millikan 1993a: 100 n.). In a very recent paper (Millikan 2000) she
expresses interest in the idea that intentional mechanisms will make use of information, in
some sense.

say—will carry the information that an event of type Y occurs if the occurrence of Y was more probable, given that an instance of X occurred. Nevertheless, there has been plenty of disagreement among philosophers about the strength of the conditional probabilities involved.[20] In this discussion, I would like to focus on two possibilities, a stronger and a weaker account.

On a strong account, information is to be identified with the relation that Dretske (1981: 115–16.) calls *indication*:

(I.1) Where X and Y are types of event and x is an instance of X: x indicates that an instance of Y occurs iff the probability of Y given X is 1.[21]

At first glance it looks as if, on this strong formulation, there will be no room for the information carried by an event to be misleading: if events of type X carry the information that an event of type Y occurs, then every instance of X will be accompanied by an event of type of Y. If so, this will give rise to a problem: it is hard to see how a theory of content based on such a strong formulation will allow for misrepresentation, because it will not be possible for an instance of X to occur that does not carry the information that a Y has occurred.[22]

However, as Pierre Jacob (1997: 52) points out, we do not need to read the formulation in this way: we can allow that x will indicate the occurrence of Y provided that the probability of Y, given an instance of X, is 1 *ceteris paribus*. Jacob does not set out in detail what kinds of condition he would class as *cetera* in this context, but his example suggests that these will include the kinds of condition that Dretske labels 'channel conditions' (Dretske 1981: 111–23; Jacob 1997: 54 n.). If this is right, then, on this view, a signal will indicate the occurrence of some condition in the environment if the occurrence of the signal is sufficient for the occurrence of that condition, provided that the signal has been produced in the normal way.[23] With this proviso in place, we can treat intentional devices as indicators while still leaving room for misrepresentation. Misrepresentation can occur where the intentional system malfunctions.

Dan Lloyd (1989: 64) has proposed a rather weaker account of the informational relation:

---

[20] This is a point I failed to recognize in Price (1998).

[21] In his formulation, Dretske relativizes the probability of Y given X to the subject's knowledge. For the sake of simplicity, I will ignore this feature of Dretske's account.

[22] Dretske's original solution to the difficulty turns on a distinction between the period during which the organism is learning to recognize some condition in the environment and the period during which it is making use of its recognitional capacity (Dretske 1981: 194–5).

[23] It is important that 'in the normal way' is not interpreted in a way that presupposes what information the signal normally carries. Otherwise, a teleological account that employs this notion of information will fall into a circularity.

(I.2) Where X and Y are types of event and x is an instance of X: x carries
       the information that an instance of Y occurs iff an instance of Y does
       occur and the probability of Y given X is greater than the probability
       of Y *tout court*.

In other words, an occurrence of an event of type X will carry the information
that an event of type Y occurs if an occurrence of an instance of Y is more
probable, given the occurrence of an instance of X. Given this weak definition
of information, there is plenty of scope for instances of X to occur that fail to
carry the information that an instance of Y has occurred. And so an account
of content that relies on this notion of information can easily leave room for
the idea that an intentional device might fail to carry the information that it
is supposed to carry, and so misrepresent how things are.

Later on in this chapter, we will need to adjudicate between these two
accounts of information. For the time being, however, I will simply assume
what is in common between the two accounts: informational relations rest on
relations of conditional probability between types of event.

I take it that the relations of conditional probability must be distinguished
from merely statistical correlations. The obvious way to do this is to insist that
these relations hold in virtue of the causal links between types of event. However, as Dretske (1988: 57) points out, there is a complication. In many cases
where there is some causal link between X and Y, the fact that the occurrence
of a Y is more probable, given the occurrence of an X, will not depend solely
on the existence of this causal link. It will also depend on how things happen
to be in the environment. For example, suppose that the presence of prey
ahead of the arrow worm is more probable, given the occurrence of a certain
kind of vibration in the water. Although there is a causal link between these
two conditions, it is not a matter of causal law that the presence of prey is
more probable, given the occurrence of a vibration. This is because the probability of prey, given a vibration, will also depend on certain contingent facts
about the environment, for example, the fact that similar vibrations are not
constantly being produced by geothermal activity on the ocean bed, or by the
engines of fishing boats on the surface.

Nevertheless, as Dretske goes on to point out, it does not follow that we cannot distinguish between this type of correlation and a merely accidental correlation. In this case, the existence of the correlation can be explained, at least
in part, by the causal link between vibrations and the movements of prey:
given how things are in the environment, it is not an accident that the correlation exists. We need, then, to distinguish between merely accidental correlations and correlations that exist, at least in part, as a result of a causal
connection between two types of event. It is only in the latter case that there
may be an informational relation between these two types of event. In this
sense, informational relations are grounded in causal relations.

It is important that we should not understand this claim in a way that would entail that events carry information only about their causal ancestors. It is certainly true that, where an event x carries the information that an event of type Y occurs, it will sometimes be the case that the occurrence of x is causally explained by the fact that an event of type Y has occurred. But this need not be the case: x may also carry information about its own causal descendants, and about its causal cousins—events with which it shares a common causal ancestor. In this way, we can allow that an event may carry information, not only about the past, but also about the present and the future (Goldman 1967; Dretske 1981: 38–9).[24]

At this point, then, we can identify the informational relation with some relation of conditional probability holding between types of event and explained, at least in part, by the causal links, direct or indirect, that help to generate that relation. My next task is to argue that the teleologist has good reason to accept that the relation that is supposed to hold between a signal and the condition that it signals is a relation of this kind.

3.3. Guessing Systems

The relation that we are looking for is R—the relation that *normally* holds between a simple intentional state and the condition that it represents or signals. In other words, the fact that this relation sometimes holds will help to explain how the intentional system succeeds in producing behaviour that is appropriate to conditions in the environment. In this section, I will argue that R is a causal relation of some kind. In the next section, I will argue for the stronger claim that it is an informational relation. I will then conclude the chapter by attempting to defuse what I take to be a plausible objection to these claims.

Consider again the example of the arrow worm's sensory system. The devices produced by the system will normally be causally related to the presence of prey. What we need to find out is whether this will be a feature of all simple intentional systems. To answer this question we need to compare the arrow worm with an imaginary cousin, one that does not rely on the existence of a causal connection of this kind. Suppose that this cousin also possesses an organ that prompts darts, but that it does so purely at random, or in response to cues that have no connection with the presence of prey. In this situation, any correlation between darts and the presence of prey will be purely accidental. Nevertheless, suppose that this organism inhabits an environment in which prey is sufficiently common that producing darts at frequent intervals

---

[24] It is always important to remember that, when I say that there is some causal relation between two events, this should not be taken to imply that one of these events causally explains the other.

is enough to ensure that the organism stays fed. If so, we can say that the operation of the organ helps to explain the organism's survival just because it produces devices that (sometimes) coincide with prey.

We could describe a system of this kind as working by guessing when prey is present. Is a guessing system an intentional system? I think that there is (at least) one good reason to deny that this is the case. If we treat guessing systems as intentional systems, this will have the consequence that the content of simple signals will turn out to be very broad. This is because there will be a long list of conditions with which the devices produced by this system will sometimes coincide: not only the presence of prey, but also the presence of oxygen, the absence of a predator, a safe ambient temperature, sand on the seabed, and so on. Some of these conditions can be excluded on the grounds that devices produced by the system do not coincide with them often enough to help explain the survival of the system. Others will be ruled out by the fact that they are irrelevant to the success of the organism's behaviour. But there will remain a long list of conditions with which these devices often coincide, and which do conduce to the success of the organism's behaviour. We will have to accept that the guessing system signals not only the presence of prey, but also the presence of oxygen, the absence of predators, and a safe temperature.

It is important to remember that exactly the same conclusion will apply to the sensory system possessed by the real arrow worm. The arrow worm's sensory system is not a guessing system with respect to prey. But it is a guessing system with respect to oxygen, predators, temperature, and so forth. And yet it might be thought that, in the case of the real arrow worm, we have a very good reason to deny that the states produced by the sensory system are about anything other than prey: the visual system is not sensitive to whether any of these other conditions occur. But it is sensitive to whether there is prey ahead, because there is a causal connection between the presence of prey and the operation of the system.

My argument at this point is not meant to depend on the claim that it could not be the case that the content of simple signals is as inclusive as this. There will be a worry, of course, that the more inclusive we take the content of these signals to be, the more pressure we put on the idea that they are directed onto a specific chunk of the world. But I think that teleological considerations will be enough to ensure that the content of these signals will relate to some specifiable range of conditions, even if the list is very long. My point is rather that, if you share my intuition that the sensory organ of the genuine arrow worm signals the presence of prey, and not any of these other conditions, then a good explanation for this intuition is that intentionality requires causal sensitivity to the environment. If this is correct, it will explain why we feel that the content of a simple signal must be more specific than the example of the guessing systems would suggest.

However, it is important to note that Millikan (1990*a*: 155) has proposed a rather different reason to reject the claim that guessing systems are genuine intentional systems. Her reason is that, in the case of a guessing system, there is no single, unified explanation for how the system succeeds in ensuring that the organism's behaviour is appropriate to conditions in the environment. Hence there is no normal explanation for the operation of the system.

A reason that might be adduced in favour of this alternative diagnosis is that it leaves room for intentional systems that work by exploiting some brute, but stable contingency in the environment.[25] Imagine a population of night-flying moths, which inhabit an environment where the bats that prey on them have an innate propensity to stay near the ground. These moths tend to fly towards bright lights, a tendency that helps them to survive, because the most common source of bright light in their environment is the moon: flying towards a bright light will often guide the moth into an area where there are fewer bats. There is no explanatory connection, no matter how indirect, between the moon being in a certain direction and fewer bats being in that direction: the correlation is just the result of brute contingency. But, in the environment that these moths inhabit, the correlation is reliable enough to promote the moths' survival.

It certainly seems natural to characterize this system as an intentional system. This may well seem to undermine the claim that a signal must normally bear some causal relation to the condition that it is supposed to signal. According to the account of content that I sketched earlier on, the content of these signals will concern the direction of the bat-free zone.[26] But there is no obvious causal connection between the production of such a signal and the direction of the bat-free zone.[27] This could be taken to suggest that what is required for intentionality is that there is some unified explanation for the system's success, but not that a signal normally must bear some causal relation to the condition that it signals.

If this objection is to work, the objector needs to be able to maintain the distinction between systems like the moths' visual system and mere guessing systems. Perhaps the idea will be that the moths depend on one, persisting coincidence, whereas a guessing system relies on a series of separate, unrelated coincidences. However, it is not obvious that we are compelled to contrast the two systems in this way. We might say that the imaginary worm's guessing system

---

[25] Millikan suggested this worry to me some years ago (private communication). There is a hint of this in (Millikan 1993*a*: 99 n.). See also Dretske (1981: 73–5; 1988: 54–9; 1994: 202–3).

[26] A Low Church theorist would not have the same difficulty with this case. On a Low Church account, the content of the bat's visual signals would concern the direction of the moon; there will normally be a causal connection between the production of one of these devices and the moon being in a certain direction.

[27] There is, in fact, a (non-obvious) causal connection, as I will explain later on.

exploits a single statistical coincidence: it relies on the fact that, in its environment, a certain percentage of the cues that prompt the system to fire coincide with the presence of food. If so, we could offer a single, unified explanation of the system's success by saying that it exploits this statistical coincidence. On this way of looking at things, the only difference between the moths and an organism equipped with a guessing system is that the moths exploit a rather more reliable correlation. But this should not concern us, so long as the correlation exploited by the guessing system is reliable enough to ensure the organism's survival. If so, we could not distinguish between a system that exploits a stable correlation and a mere guessing system in the way that the objector suggests.

Nevertheless, I would agree that there is an important difference between mere guessing systems and systems that exploit some stable correlation in the organism's environment. However, I would like to argue that, once we see what this difference is, we will also be able to see that the devices produced by systems that exploit brute correlations will normally bear some causal, and indeed informational, relation to the condition that they signal. It will be easier to present this argument once we are clear about what notion of information is in play. For this reason, I will postpone my discussion of this case until the end of the chapter.

3.4. *Uninformative Causal Relations*

In the previous section, I considered the claim that intentionality is grounded in some kind of causal relation with the environment. However, as Dretske (1981: 27–31) has pointed out, the existence of a causal relation between two events does not guarantee the existence of an informational relation between them, because it need not have any bearing on the strength of the existing probabilities between them. In this section, I will argue that the intentional relation is not merely a causal relation, but an informational relation of some kind. In other words, we should not treat a device as signalling the occurrence of some condition in the environment, unless the occurrence of that condition is (at least) more probable, given the occurrence of the device.

As we have already seen, it must be the case that the fact that the signals produced by a signalling mechanism sometimes bear R to the environment must help to explain why the behaviour prompted by these signals sometimes succeeds. If this were not the case, then the fact that these signals sometimes bear R to the environment could not help to explain the continuing survival of the system that produces them. In this section, I will argue that the only relation that will meet this constraint is an informational one.

Consider the example of an organism, similar to the arrow worm, that would benefit from the ability to detect the presence of prey. The worm normally responds to the presence of prey by darting forward with open jaws.

Suppose that this worm sometimes produces a certain type of device that is sometimes caused by the presence of prey. In fact, one in three of these devices is caused in this way. But now suppose that the worm inhabits a rather benevolent environment, in which prey is present one-third of the time. In these circumstances, the occurrence of an instance of this device does not increase the probability that prey is present, even though there is often a causal connection between the production of this device and the presence of prey.

What we need to consider is whether the operation of the worm's sensory system helps to explain why it sometimes succeeds in producing a forward dart that captures prey. What is strange about this case is that the fact that the worm's behaviour is controlled by this system does not make it any more likely to be successful than if it had not been prompted by the sensory system at all, but had been produced by a guessing system of the kind described in the previous section. In this situation, it is hard to argue that the fact that the worm's behaviour was controlled by states that are sometimes causally related to the presence of prey helps to explain its success: the fact that this causal relation sometimes held seems to be redundant in this explanation.

Of course, this is not to deny that the operation of the sensory system has some role to play in explaining the success of the worm's behaviour. It is important that it triggers darts often enough to ensure that the worm obtains a sufficient quantity of food. It is the frequency with which the mechanism operates, rather than the fact that it is often triggered off by prey, that provides the most immediate explanation for the success of the behaviour that it prompts. In other words, the mechanism is operating as a guessing system, rather than an intentional mechanism.

If this is right, we must conclude that the fact that the devices produced by some system bear a certain causal relation to the environment will help to explain the success of the organism's behaviour only in certain cases: that is, cases in which the occurrence of some favourable condition is more probable, given that the system has fired. In other words, the only systems that are *supposed* to produce devices that have some causal connection to the environment are systems that exploit information. If so, the teleologist ought to accept that R will be not only a causal relation, but also an informational one.

3.5. The Informational Relation

If R is indeed an informational relation, then we will need to get much clearer about what we should take this informational relation to be. We have already encountered two different analyses of the informational relation. On Dretske's strong analysis, an event will carry the information that a certain condition occurs if and only if the occurrence of an event of that type is a sufficient condition (*ceteris paribus*) for the occurrence of that condition. On Lloyd's weaker analysis, an event will carry the information that a certain condition occurs if and only if the probability of that condition, given an event of that type, is higher than its probability *tout court*.

In this section, I would like to argue in favour of Lloyd's weaker analysis. My primary reason for preferring this weaker analysis is that it is far from clear why organisms should need to rely on Dretske's stronger relation. All that the organism requires is that the relationship between I_C and C should be reliable enough to explain why the behaviour normally prompted by I_C is sometimes successful. This is not enough to show that the relationship between I_C and C needs to be as strong as Dretske's formulation suggests. Indeed, Godfrey-Smith (1991, 1992) has suggested that there are situations in which an organism would be better off exploiting a weaker relationship: this can occur, for example, where the occurrence of a false alarm is not very costly but where failure to register C may be a disaster. This may hold of systems that are concerned with predator avoidance: better to cry 'Wolf!' too often than to miss a wolf that is really there. If so, there is no reason to suppose that a successful intentional system will be a system that is highly accurate: in certain circumstances, sensitivity is more important than accuracy.

Nevertheless, Jacob (1997: 129) has suggested an answer to Godfrey-Smith. Jacob, like me, would like to develop a theory of content that combines an appeal to function with an appeal to information. Unlike me, however, he prefers a Low Church version of the teleological account. In other words, Jacob would deny that the devices produced by Godfrey-Smith's predator avoidance system signal the presence of a predator: rather they signal the presence of the features that the system treats as signs that a predator is present. For example, suppose that the system normally works by producing signals in response to large, striped items: on the Low Church view we should take the system to signal the presence of something large and striped.

Given that he takes this line, Jacob is able to redescribe the case of the predator avoidance system in a way that avoids Godfrey-Smith's objection. This is because he can characterize the system as combining a high degree of sensitivity with respect to the production of predator avoidance behaviour with a high degree of accuracy in detecting large, striped items in the organism's environment. Indeed, it is because the system is able to detect large, striped items with this degree of accuracy that it succeeds in being sufficiently sensitive to the presence of predators nearby. So there does not need to be the kind of conflict between sensitivity and accuracy that Godfrey-Smith describes.

I think that this is a good response as far as it goes. But it suffers from two limitations. The first limitation is that it is not available to a proponent of a High Church account of intentional content. In the next chapter, I hope to show that there are good reasons for preferring a High Church version of the teleological theory. Secondly, it is not obvious to me that Jacob's response goes far enough, even for a Low Church theorist. There remains the possibility that an organism might benefit from the possession of a visual system that is not particularly accurate at detecting even the cues that it uses. For example, suppose that the predator detecting system described above is so sensitive that it sometimes produces signals in response to shifting patterns of light and shade in the surrounding vegetation. And suppose, moreover, that it is a normal feature of this system that it should be as sensitive as this: in this environment, a less sensitive system would produce too many false negatives. If so, Jacob must claim that this system functions to detect nothing more than a perhaps very disparate set of patterns of light and shade. The alternative is to accept Godfrey-Smith's recommendation, and to adopt a weak informational constraint.

For this reason, I would prefer to adopt Lloyd's weaker analysis of the informational relation. Lloyd's formulation allows that the probability of C given I_C might be vanishingly small. For this reason, it applies equally well to highly sensitive and to highly cautious signalling systems, enabling us to accommodate Godfrey-Smith's point, even given a High Church view of content.

I have argued that minimally intentional systems are systems that exploit information, in the weak sense suggested by Lloyd. As we have already seen, this has important implications for the content that we will ascribe to simple intentional devices. According to the preliminary account of content that I sketched earlier on, the content of a signal will concern some condition or set of conditions to which it normally bears a certain relation. We are now in a position to make this claim more precise. Consider the frog's visual system. As we saw earlier, there are a number of conditions that favour the success of fly snaps, including the absence of a predator, and the presence of sticky slime on the frog's tongue. We can now give a more precise explanation of why the visual signals that trigger fly snaps do not signal these conditions: these signals do not normally carry the information that these conditions obtain. The same point will also apply to the spatio-temporal aspect of a signal's content. For example, suppose that it benefits the arrow worm to dart forwards whenever prey is present up to 60 centimetres away, but that the arrow worm's sensory system is sensitive to the presence of prey only up to 30 centimetres away. If so, the content of these sensory signals will concern the presence of prey up to 30 centimetres away, because the sensory mechanism is not competent to detect prey further away.

I have argued that intentional systems are systems that use information. Nevertheless it would be unreasonable to claim that all, or even most, intentional devices are supposed to carry information about the condition that they represent. Intentional devices that are supposed to represent goals, for example, will not function in this way. Nor will devices that are used in very sophisticated processes of reasoning that require the subject to speculate about what might occur under certain circumstances.[28] In neither of these cases would it be very

---

[28] This point is made by Rebecca Kukla (1992: 220–1). For discussion of intentional phenomena of these kinds, see Chapters 6 and 10.

plausible to suggest that there will be a direct connection between the content of the intentional state and information that it carries. But it does not seem so implausible to suggest that all intentional systems will make use of information at some level, or that the content of all intentional states will be grounded, perhaps in some very indirect way, in causal connections with the environment.

3.6. Identifying Information

We still have one debt to pay. In an earlier section, I suggested that one of Millikan's reasons for rejecting the idea that the function of a signalling mechanism is to produce an informational relation between the response of the cooperating device and the world is that she wishes to allow for situations in which an intentional mechanism exploits a long-standing, stable correlation in the environment. In response, I suggested that we can allow for such cases even if we insist that the relation that is supposed to hold between a simple signal and the environment is an informational one. But I have yet to offer any justification for that claim.

I will end this chapter by arguing that systems that exploit stable correlations can be described as exploiting *identifying information* about a particular object or place. The notion of identifying information will be important later on, when we consider how an intentional mechanism could come to represent particular objects or places. So it is helpful to introduce it early on.

Recall the example of the moths that are able to fly into an area that is free of bats by flying towards the moon. Given that there is no explanatory connection between the direction of the moon and the direction of the bat-free zone, we will not be able to say that one carries information about the other. Nevertheless, I will try to show that the occurrence of the visual state that is normally caused by the moon being directly ahead does carry the information that there are fewer bats directly ahead. This is because this visual state—call it I_M—carries the information not only that there is some moonlike object straight ahead, but that a particular object—the moon—is straight ahead.

At first glance this might seem a rather curious claim. Certainly, I_M carries some information about the night sky: it carries the information that there is a bright source of light straight ahead. But this is not to say that I_M carries the information that the bright source of light is the moon. The identity of an object does not seem to be a causally relevant feature of it: the moon does not cause anything in virtue of being the celestial object that it is.

On the other hand, it does not seem right to say that the identity of an object can have no relevance in explaining how one event caused another. This is particularly obvious where relational features are involved. For example, the laws of gravity will help to determine how the distance between two individual bodies will change over time: someone might calculate that, if two interplanetary bodies, Odin and Thor, are *n* metres from each other at t, then, given all the relevant variables, *those very same* bodies will be *n+m* metres from each other at t+1. In this case we can say that, because it was *Odin* that was *n* metres away from Thor at t, then it was *Odin* that was *n+m* metres away from Thor at t+1.

The first thing we need to show is that the success of the moth's visual system is normally explained by the fact that I_M carries the information that the light source ahead is the moon. In other words, I_M will carry identifying information about the moon. The idea will be that an intentional device will carry identifying information about some particular object if it is a normal feature of that type of device that it carries two pieces of information about the *same* object. It is easy to see how this might come about in the case of systems that engage in processes of inference in which information about a single source is combined in order to produce some conclusion about that source. What I need to show here is that this can also happen where a simple signalling system exploits information from a single source over many generations. The idea will be that a token of I_M produced on a particular occasion will benefit the moth in a normal way only if the object that is currently ahead of the moth is the *same* object as the object that triggered tokens of I_M in other, earlier moths.

The causal connections involved are a little complicated, so it might help to begin by getting an intuitive feel for what is going on. Imagine the moth reasoning as follows. 'That is the moon over there. When my ancestors flew to the moon before, they arrived in an area that was free of bats. Now, the moon I am seeing is the *same* moon as they encountered before and the bats around here now are the *same* low-flying bats that were here before. Given that the moon is in a stable orbit, and given that the genetic make-up of these bats is fairly stable, it is likely that there are still no bats in that direction. So I will fly over there.'

Needless to say, the moths do not reason in this way. What I need to show is that the causal connections mirror the connections in this imaginary process of reasoning. To show this we need to consider in some detail the causal history of a particular token of I_M that has been produced in response to light from the moon.

There are two different facts about the history of I_M that are important. The first is that a full explanation for the production of I_M on any occasion will include the fact that the moon was beyond the bat-free zone in the past. If this had not been the case, then the fact that earlier moths produced I_M in response to the moon would not have helped them to avoid bats, and so moths having that kind of visual system would not have survived. So the fact that the moon was beyond the bat-free zone in the past is more probable, given that the system has produced an instance of I_M in the normal way: instances of I_M produced in the normal way carry this information.

The second point is as follows. We cannot offer a causal explanation of how it came about that the moon is beyond the bat-free zone: it is just a coincidence. Nevertheless, we can give a causal explanation of why the moon *continued* to be there, and why it continues to be there still. This explanation will include the gravitational facts that have ensured that the moon remains in a stable orbit, and the genetic and developmental facts that have ensured that the local bats have never started to fly higher. Moreover, the explanation for why that spatial relation continued to hold in the past will be the same explanation for why it continues to hold now: the fact that the moon continued to be there in the past and the fact that the moon continues to be there now have a common causal ancestor.

Note how important it is that we are dealing with the same moon, and the same population of bats. Suppose that the moths had inhabited a planet on which a series of causally unconnected moonlike objects had, quite fortuitously, appeared in the sky each night. If so, the continuing correlation between the direction of these moonlike objects and the direction of the bat-free zone would have been merely accidental, and so the moths' visual system would have been acting as a guessing system.

So, the production of I_M on this occasion is a causal descendant of the fact that the moon was beyond the bat-free zone in the past. Moreover, the fact that the moon was there then and the fact that it is there now have a common causal ancestor. It follows that the production of I_M on this occasion and the fact that the moon is there now will also have a common causal ancestor. So the production of I_M carries the information that the moon is beyond the bat-free zone now.

We can represent the situation so far with a diagram (Figure 2). The arrows represent the flow of information, rather than the direction of causation.

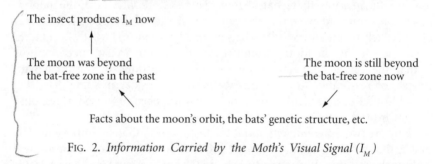

The insect produces I_M now

The moon was beyond   The moon is still beyond
the bat-free zone in the past   the bat-free zone now

Facts about the moon's orbit, the bats' genetic structure, etc.

FIG. 2. *Information Carried by the Moth's Visual Signal (I_M)*

The rest of the story is much easier to tell. We know that I_M carries the information that the moon is beyond the bat-free zone now. We also know that I_M will carry the information that the moon is straight ahead now, because that is the condition that has triggered its production. If this token of I_M carries these two pieces of information, it will also carry the information that the bat-free zone is straight ahead now, and hence that there are no bats straight ahead now. This is the information that is needed to guide the moth's behaviour. So, this is the piece of information that constitutes the content of I_M.

Note that, although this production of I_M carries information about the position of the moon, and about the position of the bat-free zone, and about the absence of bats, it signals only the last of these. When we explain why the behaviour prompted by I_M is successful, we need only to mention the fact that there were no bats present up ahead. There is nothing in the moth's behaviour that requires that it should be directed towards the moon, or even towards that particular area in the moth's environment. What is important is a feature of that area—its freedom from bats. So the moths' visual system exploits identifying information, but it does not signal it. Later, in Chapter 7, we will encounter systems that can be described as representing identifying information.

3.7. Intentionality and Information: Summary

In the first half of this chapter, I argued that a minimally intentional system must possess a certain kind of function: that is, the function to ensure that the behaviour of some cooperating device coincides with some condition or conditions in the environment. In the second half of the chapter, I have added the requirement that an intentional mechanism must perform this function in a certain way: it must do so by producing devices that carry the information that such a condition occurs. I have adopted a relatively weak notion of information: on this account, an event of type X will carry the information that an event of type Y occurs if Y is more probable, given X. Finally, I have argued that systems that exploit a brute, but stable correlation in the environment can be characterized as making use of information.

During the course of this chapter I have made use of some preliminary assumptions about how we should go about assigning content to the devices produced by a signalling system. In the next chapter, I will attempt to turn this rough sketch into a properly developed account.

5

Minimal Truth?

1. Introduction

The account of minimally intentional systems presented in the previous chapter suggests that the content of a simple signal will concern some condition in the environment provided that (1) the signal normally carries the information that the condition occurs; and (2) the signal has the function or derived function to ensure that the behaviour that it prompts coincides with that condition. In the previous chapter, I suggested that the content of the signals produced by the frog's visual system can be rendered roughly as 'Fly within range now!'[1]

There are two things to note about this ascription of content. First, the content that is ascribed to the arrow worm's sensory system is what Millikan terms *indicative* content: the sensory device is taken to signal the occurrence of some state of affairs. Indicative content can be contrasted with imperative content—content that concerns some state of affairs that is to be brought about. It would be possible to dispute this claim: Millikan (1984: 99), for example, would suggest that the signal has both indicative and imperative content: 'Prey ahead now!' *and* 'Dart forward now!' In the next chapter, I will explain why I think it would be inappropriate to ascribe imperative content to a device of this kind.

Secondly, the device is taken to be concerned with the presence of some feature in the worm's vicinity at the time that the signal is produced, and not with a particular object, place, or date. Again, it would be possible to object to this claim: not everyone is impressed by the distinction between feature-placing systems and systems that represent particulars. In the previous chapter, I suggested that a device could only be described as representing some item if the success of the behaviour that it prompts normally depends on the presence of that item. The success of the arrow worm's behaviour requires

---

[1] Remember that I am using the term 'fly' to pick out those items that have the biochemical properties that make flies nutritious to frogs.

only the presence of items of a certain kind—that is, prey. In Chapter 7, I will say more about what I take this distinction to be. For the time being I will assume only that the capacity to represent particular objects requires more than a simple signaller can achieve: 'Prey ahead now!' is the best the arrow worm can manage.

In this chapter, I will examine two crucial objections to the teleological theory. The first objection is that the teleologist is unable to ascribe determinate content to intentional devices. The second is the objection that the teleologist is unable to allow for the possibility that the content of intentional devices is marked by a certain kind of objectivity. These two objections are crucial because they throw into doubt the teleologist's ability to provide a complete account of intentional norms. This is because there is an important connection between the notions of determinacy and objectivity and the notion of truth.

It is far from obvious what is required of an intentional device if it is to be described as having truth conditions. The answer to this question will depend to a large extent on what we take truth to be. This is an issue that would take me well beyond the scope of this book. Nevertheless, I take it that the following two assumptions are relatively uncontroversial. First, if we are to ascribe a truth condition to an intentional device, we must be able to specify determinate conditions under which that device will be true or false. Hence, if the content that the teleologist attributes to intentional devices is indeterminate, she will be unable to ascribe truth conditions to these devices. Secondly, human beings are able to represent the world as extending beyond their behavioural reach: to do so they must produce representations whose truth does not depend on their actual or potential biological utility. To accept this second assumption is to adopt a certain kind of realism: the items and properties that we represent are there independently of our capacity to make use of them. This second assumption is the more controversial of the two, and I will say a little more about it later on.

The teleologist, then, cannot claim to have offered an account of the truth conditions of intentional devices until she has answered the determinacy objection. Nor can she claim that the notion of truth that emerges from a teleological theory of content is one that is compatible with realism until she has answered the objectivity objection.

Nevertheless, it is not clear that we need to answer these objections at this stage of our account. After all, simple signals are extremely primitive devices. Indeed, it has sometimes been claimed that the primitive perceptual and executive devices possessed by simpler organisms such as frogs or rats exhibit a form of content that is far less determinate or fine-grained than the content possessed by the representations produced by human beings (Davidson 1982: 322; Dennett 1987: 20–1, 115). On this view, it might be thought, we should not expect to find a solution to the determinacy problem when we are considering these less sophisticated devices. It is only when we begin to investigate more sophisticated intentional phenomena that we should begin to look for a solution to the problem.

Again, it not unreasonable to suppose that the move from simpler to more complex forms of representation will involve an increase in objectivity. It should not worry us if the teleological theory has the consequence that frogs and rats cannot be described as conceiving of their environment as independent of them. What is important is that we should be able to solve the objectivity problem for more sophisticated kinds of representation.

In this chapter I will argue that we can, in fact, solve the determinacy problem even for the simplest intentional devices. To do so, we will need to draw on the theory of functions developed in Chapters 2 and 3. In contrast, I will argue that the objectivity objection cannot be answered at this point. I will accept the claim that the teleologist cannot ascribe truth conditions, as the realist conceives them, to the devices produced by minimally intentional systems. I take it that this is not a disturbing result in itself. Nevertheless, until we have put this objection to rest, the suspicion will remain that the difficulty derives, not from the simplicity of these intentional system, but from limitations in the teleological account itself. This suspicion will haunt us until the final chapter of the book.

2. The Determinacy Objection

2.1. *Four Problems about Determinacy*

There are a number of different reasons for supposing that the teleological account will fail to ascribe determinate content to intentional devices. To make things clearer, I will set them out using the now familiar example of the frog's fly-detecting system.

Whenever a small, dark object passes in front of the frog's eyes, its visual system produces a signal of a certain kind, which I will label I_F. The production of I_F normally gives rise to a stereotypical snapping response. Our question is: what is the content of I_F? I suggested earlier that, according to the preliminary account of content, I_F signals the presence of a fly. I will introduce four different objections to this claim.

(1) *The distality problem (close-up version)*: the teleologist cannot decide between the claim that I_F signals the presence of a fly and the claim that I_F signals the properties of the light that reaches the frog's eyes.

(2) *The distality problem (far-out version)*: the teleologist cannot decide between the claim that I_F signals the presence of a fly and the claim that I_F signals the presence of the fly some distance away a few seconds ago.

(3) *The description problem (input version)*: the teleologist cannot decide between the claim that I_F signals the presence of a fly and the claim that I_F signals the presence of something small and dark.

(4) *The description problem (output version)*: the teleologist cannot decide between the claim that I_F signals the presence of a fly and the claim that I_F signals the presence of a fly that is less than 1 centimetre across and moves at less than 50 kilometres per hour (say).

The two versions of the distality problem are concerned with events earlier and later on the causal chain than the presence of a fly. The two versions of the description problem have to do with which features of the fly I_F is supposed to register.

The first and third of these objections should be familiar to anyone who has followed the literature on this issue. Both Dretske (1986) and Fodor (1990: 64–82) have presented arguments to show that the teleologist, or at least a teleologist who begins with innate functions, will be unable to rule out rival content ascriptions of these kinds.[2] In my discussion here I will be concerned primarily with Dretske's version of these objections. The other two problems, as far as I know, have not been discussed in detail by other commentators.[3]

I suggested earlier that we might try to respond to these objections by accepting that relatively primitive devices, such as I_F, cannot be ascribed determinate content. However, I do not believe that this move would provide us with an adequate response to the problem posed by Dretske and Fodor. The problem is not simply that the teleologist, once she has identified the function of a primitive intentional system, cannot ascribe determinate content to the devices that it produces. Their point is that there is no principled way of saying what the function of an intentional system is. The teleologist can hardly accept that *functions* of intentional mechanisms are indeterminate: for, if that were true, she would not be able to solve the indeterminacy problem for any intentional system, no matter how sophisticated. In Chapter 3, I argued that it is possible to ascribe determinate functions to biological devices. So we should expect that discussion to be important here.

Another preliminary question is whether we need to view this issue as an

---

[2] See also Sullivan (1993).
[3] Fodor has also suggested a fifth problem:

(5) The disjunction problem: the teleologist cannot decide between the claim that I_F signals the presence of a fly and the claim that I_F signals the occurrence of a disjunctive state of affairs, for example, the presence of a fly *or* a berry.

It is far from clear whether this is really a separate problem: certainly on one interpretation it is simply equivalent to the input version of the description problem. In other words, the suggestion will be that I_F should be regarded as signalling the presence of a fly or a berry *or any other small, dark object*. For this reason, I will not give the disjunction problem any direct consideration here.

issue about indeterminacy. Perhaps the conclusion we should draw from the existence of these alternative content ascriptions is simply that the content of I_F covers a range of different conditions, all of which must obtain if a particular token of I_F is to present the environment correctly. Nicholas Agar (1993) has suggested that the content of the frog's visual device should be rendered as 'small, dark, non-dangerous food', thereby indicating a way of sidestepping the description problem.[4]

Once again, this approach has its dangers. If the content of I_F is as thickly sliced as Agar suggests, it must be because the teleological facts slice equally thickly; and, if this is the case, it is unclear how we could ever get more fine-grained ascriptions of content out of a purely teleological account. Moreover, I take it that Agar will agree that we still need to solve the distality problem: he does not suggest that I_F is concerned with the light reaching the frog's eyes, or the presence of a fly nearby a few minutes earlier.

In what follows, I will consider all four problems. I will suggest why each rival function ascription might seem plausible, and I will try to show how the account that I have been developing over the last four chapters will rule it out. I will pay most attention to the input version of the description problem, since this is the problem that has provoked most discussion in the literature. For the same reason, this is the problem with which I shall begin.

2.2. The Description Problem (Input Version)

The objection is that the teleologist cannot decide between the claim that the content of I_F concerns the presence of a fly and the claim that the content of I_F has to do with the presence of a small, dark thing. Dretske's argument runs as follows. According to the teleologist, the content of an intentional device will be determined by the function of the visual system that produced it. The claim that the function of the frog's visual system is to detect flies rests on the claim that the presence of the system can be *explained* by the fact that earlier systems responded to flies. But this is not the only way of explaining the success of those earlier systems. We could also say that the earlier systems were successful because they responded to small, dark things: after all, it was *just because* they were sensitive to small, dark things that those earlier systems were sensitive to flies.

Dretske points out that, even though we may accept that the function of the frog's snapping mechanism relates to flies, we cannot move straight to the claim that the function of the frog's visual system also relates to flies. Perhaps what we should say is that the function of the frog's visual system is to detect small, dark things; it is facts about the frog's environment that ensure that, by responding to small, dark things, the frog's visual system helps the snapping

[4] See Griffiths and Goode (1995) for a similar suggestion.

mechanism to catch flies. If both function ascriptions can be defended, the function of the frog's visual mechanism will be indeterminate, and the content of the devices that it produces will be indeterminate as well.

A natural reaction to Dretske's argument is to appeal to what would have happened had the frog been equipped with one of these capacities, but not the other. Surely, we might protest, if the frog's visual system had been sensitive to small, dark things but not to flies, it would not have survived; but if it had been sensitive to flies, though not to small, dark things, it would have done just as well. This shows that it is its sensitivity to flies, and not its sensitivity to small, dark things, that explains its survival.

Unfortunately, this response fails. It fails because the second of these counterfactuals is false: it is not true that, if *this* kind of system had been sensitive to flies, but not to small, dark things, it would have survived. As Dretske points out, *this* kind of system is sensitive to flies only *because* it is sensitive to small, dark things. Of course, if the *frog* had been sensitive to flies but not to small, dark things, it might have survived; this is just to say that the frog might have possessed a different kind of sensory system. But this possibility is quite irrelevant to our problem: what we need to know is what explains the survival of the visual system that the frog actually possesses. This system survived because it was sensitive to flies; and it was sensitive to flies because it was sensitive to small, dark things. Either feature is sufficient to explain the survival of the system given the environment in which it normally operates.

However, the theory of content that I sketched earlier centred, not only on the workings of the intentional mechanism, but also on the workings of the cooperating mechanism. Can we appeal to this aspect of the account to solve the difficulty? It seems reasonably clear, that, on the account of functions offered in Part I, the function of the frog's snapping mechanism is to ensure that the frog swallows flies, not to ensure that the frog swallows small, dark things. Of course, in the frog's environment there is a correlation between snapping at flies and snapping at small, dark things. But it is the flies' nutritional qualities, not their appearance, that explain why directing snaps at flies helps the mechanism to survive. If this is right, a successful snap will be a snap that succeeds in capturing a fly; and it will be the presence of a fly, not the presence of a small, dark thing, that will explain the success of the snap. If so, we can rule out the claim that the content of I_F concerns the presence of a small, dark thing, according to the account of content that I sketched earlier on: this is not a condition that has any role in explaining the success of the cooperating device.[5]

---

[5] This is essentially Millikan's response to the problem. See Millikan (1990*a*: 153–4; 1991: 160–1; 1993*a*: 101). Dretske's solution (1986) has the same structure, but he suggests that it is the process of learning that creates the connection between the content of the signal and the success of the organism's behaviour.

Essentially, I think that this is the correct solution to the problem. However, I think that it requires some further defence. This is because it is not obvious that the account of content that I have proposed is the only promising account. Someone might think that Dretske has offered a rather convincing alternative characterization of how we should assign content to simple intentional devices. We need to explain why it is right to say that the content of I_F must be fixed in the way that I have suggested. I can think of no better way for a teleologist to do this than by showing that, on an acceptable theory of functions, the *function* of I_F will be determined in this way. Once again, we need to appeal to our theory of functions to solve the problem.

Karen Neander (1995) also argues that we need to appeal to a developed theory of functions to solve this kind of problem. She appeals to her preferred theory of functions, which I discussed in Chapter 3, in order to defend the claim that the content of I_F relates, determinately, to small, dark things. This is because, as we saw earlier, Neander believes that the privileged level of description is the *lowest* level of description we can give of the operation of a mechanism as a whole. The claim that the frog's visual system is sensitive to small, dark things characterizes the workings of the system at the lowest possible level because it is *by* responding to small dark things that the system responds to flies, guides the snapping mechanism, helps the frog to survive, and so on.

In Chapter 3, I argued that Neander's account of function ascription gives rise to implausible function ascriptions. In this chapter, I would like to argue for a different account of content ascription: I would like to argue for the claim that the content of I_F relates, determinately, to flies. The support for this claim will come from the abstractness condition. This should not be surprising, since it was precisely at this point that my account of functions and Neander's account of functions came apart.

My suggestion is this: Dretske's claim that the function of the frog's visual system might be to signal the presence of a small, dark thing breaches the first clause of the abstractness condition. In other words, it fails to abstract away from the design of the frog's visual system. As a result, Dretske's proposal confuses what the system is supposed to do with how it is supposed to do it.

I believe that Dretske's argument would work very well if we were to suppose that the function of a signalling mechanism is to produce a certain type of device whenever a certain condition occurs. It is certainly true that the survival of the frog's visual mechanism can be explained by the fact that it produces I_F whenever there is a fly nearby. But, as we have seen, it can also be explained by the fact that it produces I_F whenever there is something small and dark nearby. So, if we were to characterize the function of the device in this way, we would not be able to decide which of these states of affairs it functioned to detect.

The first clause of the abstractness condition, however, required that the function of a device must be characterized in terms of some *effect* that it brings about. The function of an intentional mechanism is not simply to produce an intentional device that has certain relational properties, but to bring about some effect by doing so. This is why I have described signalling systems as functioning to produce some relation between the response of the cooperating device and the environment. And this is why it is correct to say that the content of I_F is determined by the normal operation of the snapping mechanism. This will be true because the function of the visual mechanism is to bring it about that the response of the snapping mechanism occurs when a particular condition, favourable to its success, obtains.

The function of the frog's visual system, then, is to ensure that the frog's snap coincides with some condition in the environment, thereby helping to explain why it succeeds in capturing a fly. Does the fact that the snap occurred when a small, dark thing was present *explain* the fact that the snap successfully snared a fly? Again, there is certainly a correlation between these two conditions. But the first does not *explain* the second. The fact that the item that was in the vicinity at the time that the frog launched its snap was small and dark has no role to play in the explanation for the snap's success. However, the fact that the item in question was a fly certainly does have a role to play in this explanation. So it could very well be the function of the frog's visual system to ensure that the snap occurs in the presence of a fly.

2.3. The Description Problem (Output Version)

I will now turn to the output version of the description problem. This objection is that the teleologist is committed to the claim that I_F signals the presence of an object that is that is less than 1 centimetre across and moves at less than 50 kilometres per hour. Why should anyone suppose that this is a plausible ascription of content to I_F?

The frog, let us assume, is not capable of catching every insect that crosses its path: there are insects that are too big or too fast for it to catch. Fortunately for the frog, flies are not too large or too fast to be caught. So, another feature that explains the success of the frog's visual system is that it is sensitive to things that have these properties. Had it responded only to insects that were more than 1 centimetre across or that moved faster than 50 kilometres per hour, it would not have helped the frog. Moreover, I_F will normally carry the information that there is an object that is less than a centimetre across and that moves at less than 50 kilometres per hour in the vicinity. This could be taken to suggest that the function of the visual mechanism is to detect objects of a specific size and speed.

The solution to this problem is to appeal once more to the abstractness condition. This time it is the second clause that needs to be invoked. The suggestion that the content of I_F concerns flies of a specific size and speed fails to abstract away from the workings of the visual system's fellow components, including the frog's tongue.

In this case, it is quite true that the success of the frog's snap can be explained by the fact that it was aimed at something less than a centimetre across that moves at less than 50 kilometres per hour. But that this is so depends on facts about the design of the frog's tongue: if the frog's tongue had been able to move more quickly, the frog would have been able to catch speedier insects; if it had been longer or stronger, it would have been able to cope with larger prey. Hence the output version of the description problem fails to abstract away from the design of the frog's tongue. If so, the abstractness condition will rule out the claim that I_F signals the presence of something small and not too fast because this ascription of content is far too specific.

2.4. *The Distality Problem (Close-up Version)*

I shall now turn to the distality problem, beginning with the close-up version. The objection is that the teleologist cannot exclude the possibility that the content of I_F concerns the pattern of light reaching the frog's eyes. Once again, the objector will argue that the function of the frog's visual system is to produce I_F whenever a certain pattern of light reaches the frog's eyes. This will be an appropriate function to ascribe to the visual system, because it was just because the system was sensitive to the light reaching the frog's eyes that it survived.

We can answer this objection just as we answered the input version of the description problem: the objection appears to succeed only because it ignores the first clause of the abstractness condition. To assign content to I_F, we have to determine how the visual system helps to ensure the success of the frog's snap: in this case, we need to ask whether the most immediate explanation for the success of the snap is that it occurred just after a certain pattern of light reached the frog's eyes. Once again, the answer to this question will be negative: even though there will normally be a correlation between these two conditions, the one does not explain the other. So the close-up version of the distality problem also falls foul of the abstractness condition.

2.5. *The Distality Problem (Far-out Version)*

This leaves only the far-out version. This is the objection that the teleologist cannot exclude the possibility that I_F signals the presence of a fly in the area a few seconds ago. As we have seen, the success of the frog's snap can be explained by the fact that it coincides with the presence of a fly. But the presence of a fly at the time the snap occurs can be explained by the fact that a fly was in the area a few seconds earlier; and, therefore, the success of the snap will be explained by the presence of a fly in the area a few seconds ago.

It should be reasonably obvious that this rival ascription of content will be ruled out by the extended immediacy condition: the fact that the frog's visual system normally ensures that the frog's snap coincides with the presence of a fly in the area a few seconds earlier fails to provide the most immediate explanation of the snap's success. So it is not the function of the frog's visual system to signal this state of affairs.

2.6. In Defence of the High Church

Earlier in this chapter, I mentioned that Neander rejects the claim that I_F should be taken to signal the presence of a fly, and instead argues that it should be taken to signal the presence of a small, dark, moving thing. As we saw in the previous chapter, Neander uses the term 'Low Church' teleology to describe this approach to a teleological theory of content. She contrasts her approach to one that she terms 'High Church' teleology. High Church teleology is the faith of Millikan and myself.

Neander, as we have seen, embraces the Low Church approach on the basis of an account of functions that I have rejected. But she also argues that Low Church ascriptions of content are far more plausible than those that would be justified by a High Church approach (Neander 1995). In taking this line, she hopes to defend a teleological theory of content from the objections of Paul Pietroski (1992), who has argued that the teleological theory produces implausible results. In this section I would like to give some indication of how I would go about defending the High Church approach from this charge of implausibility.

Pietroski's example concerns some imaginary creatures, called kimus, which inhabit an environment in which they are hunted by dangerous predators, known as snorfs. The kimus manage to avoid snorfs because they are attracted by red light. As a result, they have a tendency to congregate at the top of a westerly hill every evening, a time when the snorfs are prowling lower ground to the east. The High Church teleologist will want to say that kimus migrate to the top of the hill because they recognize that there are no snorfs in that direction. And yet, Pietroski protests, it is quite counter-intuitive to suppose that kimus are able to represent snorfs: perhaps kimus cannot even recognize snorfs when they see them. Indeed, as Pietroski points out, if snorfs turned out to be red, the hapless kimus would tend to approach any snorf that happened by.

Before assessing Pietroski's objection, we need to get clear about the content that may be ascribed to the kimus' visual devices, according to the theory of content that I have developed here. The story of the kimus is almost identical to the case of the moths described in the previous chapter. In that discussion I suggested that the moths should be described as producing signals with the content 'bat-free zone that way!' Similarly, we could take the kimus' visual system to signal 'snorf-free zone that way!' In other words, on the account that I have presented, we should take the content of the kimus' visual devices to relate to a certain feature of their environment—namely, the absence of snorfs. Pietroski's objection needs to be phrased, then, as the claim that it is implausible to suppose that the kimus should have the capacity to signal the absence of snorfs.

The objection turns on a distinction between two different sets of properties. The properties in the first set are those that feature in the most immediate explanation of the success of the organism's behaviour: I will call these *target properties*. The absence of snorfs will count as a target property for the kimus. The properties in the second set are those to which the sensory system is immediately sensitive and which it exploits in order to register the presence of the target properties that it is supposed to detect. I will refer to these properties as *auxiliary properties.*[6] Redness is an auxiliary property exploited by the kimus' visual systems. Pietroski's objection is that it is implausible to claim that a system as simple as the kimus' visual system should be characterized as signalling the presence of target, as opposed to auxiliary, properties. Neander (1995: 132–5) agrees. She argues that only a system that is capable of engaging in some form of inference can be said to represent target features: such a system will use intentional devices that register the presence of some auxiliary property in order to infer the presence of a target property.

My main reason for rejecting this objection to High Church teleology has to do with the explanatory role of intentional content. In the previous chapter, I suggested that, when we appeal to the content of a simple signal in order to explain the organism's behaviour, we are trying to make sense of that behaviour in the light of the information that the signal is supposed to carry. To make sense of a piece of behaviour in this sense is to show how it is appropriate, given the content of the intentional device that triggered it. To say that the kimus migrate to the top of the hill each evening because they recognize that there are no snorfs in that direction is indeed to make sense of their behaviour: given that there are no snorfs there, it is appropriate for them to

---

[6] The distinction between target and auxiliary features has a connection with the familiar distinction between primary and secondary qualities, in that secondary qualities will be auxiliary rather than target features for almost all intentional systems, though, of course, not all auxiliary features will be secondary qualities. It is possible to invent cases where a secondary quality might act as a target feature for a system: for example, where an organism could be blinded by seeing a particular shade of red. But for us, at any rate, colours, smells, and sounds will act as auxiliary features.

head off in that direction. But to say that they migrate up the hill because they sense that there is red light in that direction does not make their behaviour intelligible in the same way. An explanation of this kind would succeed as a regularizing explanation of their behaviour, but not as a normalizing explanation.

Pietroski suggests that to make sense of the kimus' behaviour in the way in which I have described is to give an ethological, not an intentional, explanation of their behaviour. But what I would like to suggest is that it is precisely in the case of simple organisms like the kimus—organisms that rely on signals whose content is innately fixed—that intentional and ethological explanations coincide. It is only in the case of organisms that are capable of developing their own goals and interests through learning or reasoning that this distinction emerges.

A moral that might be drawn from this discussion is that proponents of different theories of content may have different views of what counts as a more or less sophisticated capacity. The High Church teleologist, because she attempts to account for the content of an intentional device by appealing to its biological utility, will naturally regard the capacity to detect target properties as the fundamental capacity.

Nevertheless, this might be taken to prompt a further objection: the worry will be that the High Church theorist, having tied intentional content to biological utility, will be unable to allow that any intentional mechanism, no matter how sophisticated, is able to represent auxiliary properties. This is a serious objection, since human beings, at least, are clearly capable of representing such properties. In the next chapter, I will answer this objection.

2.7. The Determinacy Objection: Summary

By the end of the previous chapter, I had worked my way to the following account of the content of simple signals such as the frog's visual signal: where S is a signalling mechanism and I_c is a type of device produced by S and C is some type of condition; I_c will signal the occurrence of C if and only if there is some informational relation R such that:

(S.1) In the past, instances of I_c sometimes bore R to instances of C.

(S.2) The fact that instances of I_c bore R to instances of C sometimes helped to explain the fact that the behaviour normally prompted by I_c coincided with an instance of C.

(S.3) On some of those occasions, the fact that that behaviour coincided with an instance of C helped to ensure its success.

The discussion in this chapter suggests that we need to modify (S.2) to something like the following:

(S.2*) The fact that instances of I_C bore R to instances of C sometimes helped to provide *a suitably abstract and immediate* explanation of the fact that the behaviour normally prompted by I_C coincided with an instance of C.[7]

I have argued that an approach of this kind offers a more attractive account of the force of intentional explanations involving simple intentional devices than accounts that centre on the actual discriminatory capacities of the intentional system.

My claims here stand in contrast with the view mentioned earlier, according to which the content of more primitive intentional devices is taken to be less determinate or fine-grained than the content of human beliefs and desires. On this account, the content of I_F is extremely fine-grained. Indeed, as I hope to show in Part III, there is a sense in which the move from simple intentional devices such as I_F to more sophisticated representations is a move towards a much *less* fine-grained—a much richer—form of content.

I have now completed my discussion of the determinacy objection in this chapter. Nevertheless, I will return to issues about determinacy in Chapters 6 and 11. In the next section, I will turn to the objectivity objection.

3. The Objectivity Objection

3.1. *Teleology, Objectivity, and Realism*

Both Ruth Millikan (1984, 1990*b*) and David Papineau (1987, 1993) have presented the teleological theory as going hand in hand with a forthright metaphysical realism. Millikan argues that the naturalist, externalist theory of content that she offers both complements and is complemented by an ontological theory that presents the environment as comprised of what she terms 'objective selfsames': that is, substances and properties whose identity is determined quite independently of our capacity to pick them out. Teleology and realism go together, she suggests, because a theorist who holds that the contents of our thoughts are determined by the causal relations that they bear to substances and properties in the environment cannot also suppose that what substances or properties there are in the environment depends on the thoughts that we have. She writes: 'the theory of intentionality that I have offered depends upon the assumption that there is such a thing as a real Normal explanation for the

---

[7] And of course we will need to make the same adjustment to the corresponding clause (SS.2) in the version of the account that is intended to cover signalling mechanisms that can produce novel devices.

proper function of any intentional icon or representation—a kind of explanation that is, as it were, out there in the world supporting rather than being supported by our ways of thinking and speaking' (Millikan 1984: 263).

More recently, however, Christopher Peacocke (1992: 129–32) has questioned the teleologist's credentials as a friend of realism. He argues that the teleologist cannot account for the possibility that an organism might represent items on which it could never usefully act. This objection, if successful, would imply that the content that the teleologist attributes to a thought will depend in part on the behavioural *reach* of the organism. If so, it will follow that the teleologist can no longer take herself to be capable of representing items that are behaviourally inaccessible to her. She would have to suppose that the thought that there are such substances or properties is incoherent. If metaphysical realism is the view that what substances and properties there are in the world is quite independent of our own epistemic or practical capacities, she will have to accept that metaphysical realism is incoherent too. If we wish to maintain metaphysical realism, then, we will have to abandon any attempt to give a teleological theory of content.

3.2. Peacocke's Challenge

Peacocke presents his objection as a problem about universal quantification. I will transpose his objection into a different key: I will illustrate it using the example of the bee dance mechanism. I will begin by running through the example again.

Before we can assign content to the dances produced by the mechanism, we need to determine the mechanism's function. We can say that the function of the mechanism is to guide the watching bees to nectar because its presence is explained, in part, by the fact that earlier mechanisms of the same type sometimes had that effect (Millikan 1984: 19–38; 1989*b*). As we have seen, a device cannot be assigned a function unless devices of that type are *competent* to perform it: for example, we cannot regard the bee dance mechanism as being competent to indicate the location of nectar unless the bees have some way of ensuring that the dances they produce correlate with sources of nectar; for example, by exploiting olfactory information of the right kind (Millikan 1990*a*: 127; 1990*b*: 219).

As always, it is important to emphasize that the notion of competence that is needed on this account is a quite minimal notion: what is important is that the bees are *sometimes* sensitive to the presence of nectar. It is not important that they should be able to detect it with any great sensitivity or accuracy. What matters is that the success of earlier mechanisms should be explained by the fact that the bees did at least sometimes produce dances that correlated with the presence of nectar close to the hive (Millikan 1984: 34; 1990*b*: 223).

Having determined the function of the mechanism, we now need to consider how to assign content to the dances that it produces. To do this, as we have seen, we must look at the way in which the mechanism normally works. The mechanism normally works by producing dances that correlate with particular locations in the area around the hive. It is able to do this because it produces dances in accordance with a set of *rules*, rules that associate certain variable features of the dance, such as its speed, with variable features of the location of the nectar source, such as its distance from the hive (Millikan 1984: 107–8). For example, we could characterize the mechanism as operating in accordance with the following rule:

D The further away the nectar source is, the slower the dance.

How should we identify the rules that the mechanism normally follows? An intentional mechanism will count as normally following a certain rule if the fact that such mechanisms have followed that rule in the past helps to explain how they sometimes succeeded in performing their functions. This is what distinguishes D from a rule such as:

C The colder the ambient temperature, the slower the dance.

It may be that the workings of the bee dance mechanism commonly satisfy both D and C; but, when it comes to explaining why earlier mechanisms succeeded in guiding the bees to nectar, we will need to mention only D. So D, but not C, is a rule that the mechanism normally follows.

In characterizing the rules by which a system normally operates, we need to balance two desiderata. First, we need to characterize the rules with a sufficient degree of *generality*: sufficient, that is, to provide the most unified possible account of the operation of the system. Secondly, we need to characterize the rules with a sufficient degree of *specificity*: sufficient, that is, to avoid any redundancy in our account of the system's success (Millikan 1990b: 221). It is this second desideratum that is going to cause the trouble.

Peacocke's point is that, if we take the bee dance mechanism to operate in accordance with D, we will violate the specificity requirement. This is because we can find a tighter characterization of the way in which the mechanism normally operates. Suppose that there is some distance that is the furthest that a bee laden with nectar can fly. We can replace D with:

D* The further away the nectar source is, the slower the dance should be, down to the speed that correlates with the presence of nectar at the furthest distance from which a bee laden with nectar can normally return to the hive.

The suggestion will be that D* provides a more accurate characterization of the way in which the mechanism normally behaves than D. This is because the ability to locate nectar further away from the hive is normally of no use to the bees. These locations are behaviourally inaccessible to the bees, at least with respect to nectar gathering. But it is no part of the normal explanation for the success of the bee dance mechanism that it should sometimes produce dances that correlate with locations that are behaviourally inaccessible to the bees. And so we cannot suppose that the mechanism sometimes produces dances whose content concerns such locations.

Assuming that a similar argument can be applied to all intentional systems, the teleologist will have to concede that she cannot allow for the possibility that an organism might be able to represent some location that lies beyond its behavioural reach. Moreover, it is not difficult to see how the objection might be extended to cover representations, not only of places, but of objects, times, events, properties, and so on. The teleologist, it seems, cannot be a realist.

3.3. The Nature of the Challenge

I would like to pause at this point to say a little more about the nature and implications of the objection that Peacocke has raised. An important feature of Peacocke's objection is that it rests on the assumption that metaphysical realism is correct. One move that a teleologist might make at this point would be to reject the realist assumption on which the objection is based, and to accept that the notion of a place (or an item of any other kind) that is inaccessible has turned out to be incoherent. To adopt this view would be to adopt a form of pragmatism, understanding truth partly in terms of potential biological utility.

We might wonder whether a teleologist could consistently hold a view of this kind. I began this discussion by citing Millikan's reason for supposing that a teleologist will be committed to realism. But now it looks as if things may not be so simple. The reason seems to be that we do not have to suppose that explanation for the success of intentional systems will mention only the intrinsic, non-relational properties of items and features in the environment; it may mention only their relational features. After all, it is because these items bore certain *relations* to us—spatial, temporal, and so on—that they were able to affect us and our ancestors in the way that they did. So it might be suggested that, if the content of our thoughts relates to items and features in the environment in so far as they are causally related to them, it will relate to items-in-relation-to-us and to properties-in-relation-to-us, not to items and properties characterized as independent of us.

But, even if it were possible to formulate a view of this kind, it is not a view that I would wish to hold. I regard the challenge of giving a theory of content as equivalent, in part, to the challenge of explaining how we come to conceive of items and properties in the world as independent of us, in the sense that would be espoused by a thoroughgoing metaphysical realist. The discovery that the teleological theory had failed to answer Peacocke's challenge would, for me, be the discovery that the teleological theory had failed to provide us with a convincing account of doxastic content. I have nothing but uncultured intuition to justify this assumption, and there may be others who do not share it. But, since I hold this, I need to take Peacocke's challenge very seriously indeed.

3.4. Millikan's Response

In this section I will set out Millikan's response to Peacocke's challenge.[8] I will argue that it fails to answer at least one version of the objection.

Millikan responds to Peacocke's argument by suggesting that he has paid insufficient attention to two important features of her account (Millikan 1995). The first point is that the normal explanation for the workings of an intentional system must be pitched at a level general enough to capture how that system has benefited its possessors over a long period of history. To say that the system is working normally is not to say that it is capable of benefiting its possessor in the particular circumstances that prevail at the time. It is to say that it is working in the way in which its ancestors worked on earlier occasions when they successfully performed their functions.

Secondly, in order to count as producing dances that correlate with a range of conditions in the environment, an intentional system must have some way of *ensuring* that the devices that it produces correlate with those conditions. There must be some way of characterizing the rules with which the system normally operates that makes it clear how the system is sometimes able to bring this about.

She goes on to argue that there can be no normal explanation, formulated with the appropriate degree of generality, that would explain how the bee dance mechanism ensured that the representations that it produced correlated with conditions that were in fact destined to have some causal impact on the bees. In other words, bee dance mechanisms are not, in general, competent to ensure that the devices that they produce correlate only with locations that are accessible to the bees. And so we cannot ascribe to them the capacity to represent only accessible locations.

At this point, it might be objected that the bee dance mechanism is not competent to ensure that bee dances correlate only with nectar sources either, given that the bees are unable to distinguish between nectar and nectar-scented poison. Millikan's point depends on the idea that, in producing a dance that correlates with a source of nectar-scented poison, the mechanism is operating in

---

[8] Papineau (1996) presents a rather different response to Peacocke's challenge. However, since his response relates primarily to the content of beliefs and desires, I will postpone my discussion of his response until a later chapter.

a way that differs from the way in which it operated on earlier occasions when the operation of the mechanism benefited the bees; whereas, when the mechanism produces a dance that correlates with an inaccessible location, it is behaving in the same way as it did on those earlier occasions. I think that Millikan is entitled to make this distinction in some cases, but not in others.

To see this, we need to consider two different circumstances under which a location might turn out to be inaccessible to the bees. The first situation is one in which the site is inaccessible as a result of circumstances that apply to a particular population of bees: for example, a certain location might be out of range of a certain group of bees because their hive is sited in an area where there are particularly strong northerly winds that blow more or less constantly, limiting the bees' flying range north of the hive. The bees' ancestors, we will suppose, did not have to contend with these conditions. We could describe the locations north of this particular hive as being *fortuitously* inaccessible to this population of bees.

We can contrast this situation with one in which a location is inaccessible because it is outside the normal flying range of any laden bee. We could describe a location of this kind as being *normally* inaccessible to the bees. What I would like to suggest is that Millikan is right to reject the claim that we should take the bee dance mechanism to be capable of representing only fortuitously accessible locations; but that we cannot rule out the suggestion that it represents only normally accessible locations.

Millikan is right to insist that the bee dance mechanism can produce dances that represent locations that are fortuitously inaccessible to the bees. It may be true that the production of a dance of that type is futile on this occasion. Nevertheless, the dance has been produced in accordance with a rule that has benefited the bees on many occasions in the past. Nevertheless, it is not clear that we can say the same thing about dances that correlate with a location that is normally inaccessible to the bees. In this case it *is* possible to offer a general and unified explanation of the way in which these mechanisms have operated in the past that makes no mention of their capacity to produce dances of this kind: we can do this by describing the bee dance mechanism as normally operating in accordance with D*.

Nevertheless, it might be asked whether we have paid sufficient attention to Millikan's second point: this was the point that we cannot regard an intentional system as representing a certain set of conditions unless the system has some way of ensuring that the devices that it produces correlate with those conditions. It might be claimed that we cannot treat the bee dance mechanism as normally operating in accordance with D*, because it is simply not competent to do so. The system has no way of ensuring that the dances that it produces correlate only with locations that are accessible to the bees: to do this, it would have to distinguish between locations that are normally accessible to the bees and locations that are normally inaccessible to them.

Unfortunately, this response rests on a misunderstanding of what is required for a system to be competent to operate in accordance with a certain rule. Earlier in the book, I argued that a system cannot be described as normally operating in a certain way unless it is minimally competent to operate in that way. But a system may be *minimally* competent to follow a certain rule, even though the system does not typically or characteristically operate in a way that satisfies the rule. All that is required is that *there are some occasions* on which the behaviour of the system satisfies the rule. Even if the behaviour of the bee dance mechanism were not in general captured by D*—because the mechanism sometimes produces dances that, in fact, correlate with inaccessible locations—it does *sometimes* behave in a way that fits the rule. Moreover, these are precisely the occasions on which the mechanism has succeeded in performing its function.

Perhaps it is worth reiterating why we need to operate with such a minimal notion of competence. Consider the claim that the bee dance mechanism generally operates in a way that satisfies D. It is quite possible that this claim is false. For example, suppose that it is true that the bees' dances slow down when the temperature drops. The rule that would best characterize the workings of the bee dance mechanism would be:

— CD The further away the dance and the colder the ambient temperature, the slower the dance should be.

It might look as if we ought to accept that it is CD, and not D, that normally governs the workings of the system. We could support this claim by arguing that the mechanism is not competent to operate in accordance with D: it is not competent to operate in accordance with D because it does not discriminate between situations in which a nectar source is very far away and situations in which the temperature is very low.

But, although the mechanism's behaviour does *in fact* typically satisfy CD, we would not want to say that this is the rule that the mechanism normally follows: we do not need to mention the fact that very low temperatures produce very slow dances in order to explain the system's success. To avoid this kind of redundancy in our explanation of the mechanism's success, we need to disregard the way in which the system typically operates, and instead focus on how it operates on just those occasions on which it succeeds in performing its function. We can explain the mechanism's success on these occasions without mentioning the fact that it was operating in accordance with CD. So, we do not need to suppose that CD characterizes the way in which the mechanism normally operates.

But, equally, it is possible to explain the mechanism's success without mentioning that its workings satisfy D. The most precise explanation of its success will mention only that it sometimes operates in accordance with D*. If this is right, it will be D*, and not CD or D, that characterizes the normal workings of the system.

For this reason, I believe that Millikan's response fails to answer at least one version of the objection: this is the objection that the teleological account is unable to explain how an intentional system can come to represent places (or items of some other kind) that are normally inaccessible to the organism.

There is one last line of response that we could try: it might be thought that we have been operating with an oversimplified account of functions. Once we factor in the additional constraints on the ascription of functions that I set out in Chapter 3, we will see that Peacocke's argument fails. The thought will be that Peacocke's argument succeeds only if we ignore the second clause of the abstractness condition. This was the condition that stated that in ascribing a function to an item we should not take into account the design of other components of the same system. It might be suggested that Peacocke's argument relies on treating the function of the bee dance mechanism as answerable to features of other components of the system—such as the size and strength of the bees' wings. It is these factors that determine which locations are accessible to the bees. Hence we should not take the function of the mechanism to be to direct the bees to accessible locations, since this would contravene the abstractness condition.

But this response fails. This is because the abstractness condition introduced in Chapter 3 does not prevent us from taking the function of the bee dance mechanism to be to direct the bees to accessible sources of nectar. All it ruled out was our saying that the function of the mechanism is to direct the bees to nectar sources within some *specified* distance of the hive.[9] The abstractness condition will not rule out the claim that the function of the bee dance mechanism concerns normally accessible nectar sources. Nor will it rule out the claim that the function of the arrow worm's sensory system is to ensure that the worm's darts are directed towards normally catchable prey; or that the function of the frog's visual system is to prompt the frog to snap at normally catchable flies. If this is correct, we have not found a way to answer Peacocke's challenge with respect to any of these systems.

3.5. A Different Hymn Sheet?

It might be thought that the problem lies, not with the teleological approach itself, but with the details of the account that I have attributed to Millikan, and in particular the notion of competence suggested by this account. In

[9] The abstractness condition ruled out our saying that the function of the sinoatrial node is to cause the heart to beat in some specifiable way; but not our saying that the function of the node is to cause the heart to beat in the right way (whatever that might be). Similarly, the abstractness condition does not preclude us from saying that the function of the bee dance mechanism is to guide the bees to nectar sources of a kind the bees are able to use (whatever that might be).

particular, it might be suggested that Neander's Low Church version of the teleological theory would be able to provide an answer to Peacocke's objection.

This is because a Low Church teleologist will operate with a much more
demanding standard of competence than a High Church theorist. Call this
more demanding form of competence 'maximal competence': a system will be
maximally competent to signal the presence of some feature F only if systems
of that type are actually capable of discriminating cases of F from other features that occur in the organism's environment. The Low Church theorist will
be able to argue that, since the bees are unable to discriminate between accessible and inaccessible locations, it is D, not D*, that captures the way in which
they normally operate.

Unfortunately, this move will not defuse the objection. The worry will now be
that the bees are maximally competent to detect sweet-smelling stuff only at
locations that are *perceptually* accessible to them. The dances produced by the
bees will normally correlate only with the presence of sweet-smelling substances
at locations within the bees' perceptual range: and so it can be argued that the
Low Church teleologist is unable to allow that the bees are able to represent the
world as extending beyond their perceptual reach. We seem to have jumped out
of the frying pan of pragmatism straight into the fire of verificationism. For this
reason, I do not believe that a Low Church teleological theory will be more successful in securing a realist conception of truth than a High Church account.[10]

Nevertheless, it is important to reiterate that it has not yet been shown that
the objectivity problem is insoluble even for the most sophisticated intentional systems. It may yet turn out that the journey from simple to more
sophisticated intentional systems is a journey from subjective to objective
forms of representation. Peacocke has presented us with a challenge that needs
to be answered by the end of the book.

3.6. The Objectivity Objection: Summary

My second task in this chapter has been to introduce Peacocke's claim that the
teleologist is unable to account for the possibility that intentional systems might
be able to represent the environment as extending beyond the organism's behavioural reach. In this chapter, I have failed to find an answer to Peacocke's claim,
at least as it applies to simple intentional devices. Nevertheless, in a later chapter,
I will argue that the move from simple intentional devices to more sophisticated
representations is a move towards a more objective form of representation.

[10] Indeed, it is not only teleologists who ought to be worried by Peacocke's objection.
Anyone who would like to offer an account of intentionality that takes the content of
intentional states to be determined by causal relations that those states bear to items or
properties in the environment risks being open to a challenge of this kind.

6

Learning and Wanting

1. Introduction

In this chapter, I would like to consider two ways in which it is possible to advance beyond the minimal intentional systems described in the last two chapters. I will begin by investigating systems that are capable of simple forms of learning, I will consider how the learning process generates intentional content, and I will argue that a good account of learned content will need to take account of the innate function of the mechanism that controls the process of learning. I will then return to an issue raised in the previous chapter: how will the teleologist account for the possibility that an intentional system might be capable of signalling or representing the presence of some auxiliary feature in the environment? I will argue that only systems that are capable of learning are able to represent auxiliary, as well as target, properties.

I will go on to consider what is required of a system if it is to be characterized as representing goals—as having what Millikan terms 'imperative content'. I will argue that the ability to represent goals is a more sophisticated capacity than the ability to signal the occurrence of some state of affairs. I will end by considering systems that are capable of acquiring new goals through learning.

imperative content

2. Learning Systems

2.1. Learning to Recognize

I would like to begin by considering how the teleologist should characterize intentional systems that are capable of learning. In this discussion, I will focus on the development of new recognitional capacities through learning, rather than the development of new behavioural routines. By developing new representational capacities, the organism will become able to recognize a situation as possessing a feature that it was not able to recognize in that situation before.[1] When learning of this type occurs, the connections between the indicative devices produced by the organism's sensory mechanisms and the executive devices that control its behaviour are altered: a new connection may be formed or an old one strengthened or destroyed. In this process, some of the organism's sensory devices will acquire a new content: for example, a sensory device that is normally triggered by the presence of a certain odour may come to signal the presence of poison.

How should we go about ascribing learned content to these sensory devices? On one view, the nature of the content that these devices acquire will depend on the innate design functions of the mechanisms that control the process of learning, together with the rules by which they normally operate. The learned content of these sensory devices will be determined by the content that they derive from the innate functions of these learning mechanisms. This is the position that I am going to endorse.[2]

But there is another possible view. A number of writers have pointed out that the process of associative learning operates in a way that is analogous to the process of natural selection: a tendency to produce a certain kind of behaviour under conditions where that behaviour benefits the organism will be confirmed; while a tendency to produce the same kind of behaviour in circumstances under which that behaviour is harmful will be dropped. A learning process of this kind is one that is capable of conferring new *use functions* on intentional devices, functions that might be quite independent of any function that they might derive from the innate design functions of the mechanisms that produced them.

If we view the process of learning in this way, we will be able to treat the process of learning as generating content in a way that is quite independent of the processes that generate the content of devices whose content is fixed innately. On this view, the learned content of a device is determined by the use function that it develops during the course of learning.[3]

This second suggestion starts to look attractive when we consider how we are able to make sense of an organism's behaviour by invoking the content of states that have acquired their significance for that organism through a process of learning. Any organism that possesses intentional mechanisms represents the world from its own point of view, a point of view that is determined by its needs: for a frog, small black things are flies, while for another

---

[1] I will not be considering systems that are capable of developing completely novel recognitional capacities at this stage. We will not encounter systems that are capable of these types of learning until Part III.

[2] This is Millikan's view. See Millikan (1984: 46–7; 1989*b*: 292; 1990*a*: 161; 1990*b*: 337–8).

[3] This is the account of learned content that is proposed by Dretske (1986: 35–6; 1988: 95–6) and by Papineau (1987: 66; 1993: 59).

kind of organism they might be berries or eggs. But an organism that is capable of learning is able to develop its own unique view of the world in a way that is determined, not only by its needs, but also by its history as an individual, as different events gain their own significance for the organism. To make sense of such an organism's behaviour from its own point of view is not necessarily to invoke its needs alone. It may also be to invoke the organism's past experiences and what it has learned from them. To give a teleological explanation of the organism's behaviour is to display it as the result of a process that has taken place in the course of these past experiences. Hence, the force of this explanation might seem to derive, not from the design functions of the organism's intentional states, but from the use functions that they have acquired during its lifetime.

In what follows, I would like to explain why this alternative account of learned content is unsatisfactory. Before considering the objections to this alternative account, we need to be clear about how it is supposed to work: we need to investigate how an intentional device might develop a use function via the process of learning.[4]

Consider the case of a rat, Frederica, who has become sick after eating a baneberry that contains harmful toxins. As a result she has learned to avoid baneberries. There is now a link between the olfactory device triggered by the baneberries (call it I_B) and Frederica's avoidance response. The fact that Frederica's learning mechanism sets up this link can be explained by the fact that, on an earlier occasion, I_B was triggered by feeding behaviour that was followed by a bout of sickness. The fact that Frederica became sick can be explained by the fact that her feeding behaviour involved the ingestion of poison. Her ingestion of poison can be explained in turn by the fact that her behaviour was triggered by a device that bears a certain informational relation to poison. So, the fact that I_B carries information about poison helps to explain why it is now hooked up to Frederica's avoidance response. As a result, I_B has developed the use function of carrying this information.[5] According to the alternative account, the learned content of the sensory device I_B will

---

[4] Any intentional system can develop a new use function in an individual organism, by contributing to the organism's survival in some novel way. For example, a phototropic mechanism that functions to keep its possessor away from oxygen rich surface water might work to protect an individual organism from a new type of predator equipped with a luminescent lure. But this method of acquiring a new use function does not involve any form of learning.

[5] It might be suggested that Frederica has learned a new behavioural response—avoiding baneberries—rather than a new recognitional capacity. But I take it that the function of Frederica's behaviour remains the same—to enable her to avoid poison. The function of her sensory devices, on the other hand, has changed, because they have now been given a job that they did not have before—that is, to prompt Frederica to produce poison avoidance behaviour.

be determined by this acquired use function: the role of this device will now be to signal the presence of poison.

One problem with this account is that it fails to accommodate the possibility that an organism can make a mistake in learning. As a result, the learned content of an intentional device will not always coincide with the way in which it actually benefits the organism. Consider the case of Frederica's cousin Freddie, who becomes sick after eating some dewberries, and now refuses to eat anything that smells like those berries. But now suppose that the berries were not poisonous at all: perhaps Freddie got sick, not because the berries were poisonous, but because they grow near an area contaminated with radioactive waste. If so, the olfactory device that the berries normally trigger (call it I_D) will have developed the use function of carrying the information that radioactive waste is present. And yet it does not seem correct to say that Freddie has come to recognize the berries as growing near a radioactive area. It seems far more natural to say that, for Freddie, I_D conveys the message that those berries are poisonous: when he avoids the berries, he avoids them *as if* they contained poison. It is his need to avoid ingesting poison, rather than his need to avoid exposure to radiation, that makes sense of his behaviour in avoiding these berries.[6]

If this intuition is correct, we need to find another way of characterizing the learning process. The view we have been considering centres on the idea that we can explain the fact that the learning mechanism links devices such as I_B and I_D to the rats' avoidance response because of the information that they carry. But there is another feature of these devices that is relevant to this explanation: the production of one of these devices on an earlier occasion triggered feeding behaviour that was followed by a bout of sickness. This feature is one that will frequently be exhibited by devices that carry the information that poison is present. Hence, it is a property that the learning mechanism can use to recognize devices that carry this information; though, as we saw in the case of Freddie, it is not an infallible sign. We might say that the learning mechanism normally operates by linking the rats' avoidance response to devices that *seem* to carry the information that poison is present. We can make sense of the fact that the learning mechanism operates in this way only if we take into account the fact that its function is concerned with the rats' need to avoid ingesting poison. If we look at the process of learning in this way, we will conclude that the content that I_B and I_D acquire through learning will be determined by the function that they derive from the innate function of the learning mechanism.

How should we characterize the function of the learning mechanism? The mechanism operates by creating links between the signals produced by the

---

[6] Millikan (1990*b*: 340) describes a similar case in which an organism dies as the result of exercising a learned capacity.

rat's sensory mechanisms and behaviour that has the function to protect the rat from poison. If we put things in this way, we can leave room for a gap between the use function that a device actually has and the use function that it is supposed to have, and so allow for the possibility of erroneous learning: for, although I_D does not *actually* have the use function to protect Freddie from poison, nevertheless, thanks to the function of the learning mechanism that linked it to his avoidance behaviour, this is the use function that it is *supposed* to have.

The distinction between the use function that a sensory device actually has and the use function that it is supposed to have can help us to deal with other cases that involve a change in the content of a sensory device. For example, when a newly hatched duckling imprints on an object, a set of sensory devices comes to represent that object as the parent duck. Ducklings can be induced to imprint on all kinds of objects, including human beings. Suppose that a duckling imprints on a human researcher who resolves to keep it out of trouble: in this case, the duckling's sensory devices will develop the use function of representing that human being. However, it still seems natural to say that the duckling has mistaken the researcher for its parent. The use function that its sensory devices actually develop concerns the researcher, but the use function that they were supposed to develop concerns the parent duck.

There is a second reason why it would be unwise to identify learned content with the use function actually acquired by the intentional device during the process of learning. Not all learning takes place while the organism is actually engaged in useful behaviour; learning may take place through observation. For example, a young predator may learn which animals to hunt by watching older members of the same species. This may occur before the young predator is ready to hunt for itself, so that what it has learned has no use function for the individual organism at the time of learning. Again, rats learn to find their way around their environment before they are able to use this information to satisfy needs such as hunger or thirst (O'Keefe 1993: 53).

The most plausible response to cases of this kind is to insist that these devices can be ascribed intentional content, even before they give rise to useful behaviour, and that their content is fixed by the design function of the mechanisms that govern the process of learning. It is just because the organism's tendency to hunt prey favoured by its parents makes it a more successful hunter that the organism is able to benefit from this tendency when it begins to hunt for itself; and it is in virtue of this fact that the devices produced by the organism's sensory mechanisms function to signal the presence of prey. Once again, we need to take seriously the history of the mechanisms that govern the process of learning if we are to give a plausible account of the content of learned devices.

2.2. Auxiliary Features

In the previous chapter, I made a distinction between two different sets of conditions that are relevant to the normal workings of an intentional system. The first set consists of those conditions that are directly relevant to the success of the organism's behaviour. I referred to these conditions as *target* conditions for that intentional system. For example, the presence of prey will be a target condition for the arrow worm's sensory mechanism; while the presence of a male stickleback will be a target condition for the female stickleback's visual system. The second set of conditions consists of states of affairs to which the organism's sensory system is sensitive and which it normally uses as a sign that some target condition occurs. I referred to these conditions as conditions that are *auxiliary* for a particular sensory system. The occurrence of a certain kind of vibration will be an auxiliary condition for the arrow worm; the presence of the colour red will be an auxiliary condition for the female stickleback's visual system.

In the previous chapter, I argued that a simple signalling system will be able to signal the occurrence only of features that are target features for that system: the arrow worm's sensory mechanism can signal the presence of prey but not the occurrence of a particular kind of vibration. Indeed, it might be argued that a High Church teleological theory cannot allow for the possibility that any intentional system might be able to represent an auxiliary feature. Intentional devices will be ascribed content on the basis of their contribution to the workings of a system whose function is to satisfy a particular need. It seems to follow that the devices produced by the system will represent only features that are directly relevant to the need that the system is supposed to satisfy. If this were correct, it would follow that no sensory system would be able to represent the auxiliary features that it uses as signs of the target features that it is supposed to detect. If we were to extend this claim to all sensory systems, including our own, then this would certainly be a counter-intuitive consequence of the theory.

In this section I would like to investigate this issue. I will argue that a system will be capable of representing auxiliary properties if it is a system that is capable of developing new recognitional capacities through learning. Nevertheless, I would like to begin by considering an alternative suggestion.

It might be suggested that a system will be able to represent auxiliary features if it is able to engage in simple inference. As we saw in the previous chapter, Neander (1995: 132–5) suggests that a system that is capable of engaging in inference may combine a number of sensory devices representing auxiliary features in order to draw the conclusion that some target feature is present.

I will start by considering a system that is able to infer the presence of a target feature by combining information about two or more auxiliary features. When they are first hatched, ducklings use a number of different cues to identify their parents: for example, the parents produce a species-specific 'exodus' call as they move away from their brood, and they walk with a distinctive waddling motion. Let us assume the sensory devices triggered by these cues belong to a distinct recognitional system that functions to ensure that the ducklings imprint onto their parents soon after hatching. What is the content of the auditory device that is normally triggered by the parent's 'exodus' call? Is this device supposed to indicate the occurrence of a particular kind of sound, or is it supposed to signal the presence of the parent duck?

On Neander's view, we should take it that the device is supposed to indicate the occurrence of an 'exodus' call. This might seem plausible, given that the occurrence of this device by itself is not enough to prompt the duckling to behave as if its parent were present. However, we need not view matters in this way. An alternative picture might be that the duckling's representational system is more cautious than the signalling systems that we have encountered so far: it requires two 'Parent!' signals before it takes action. On this view, what is different about this system is not the nature of the information that the devices convey to the cooperating mechanism, but the nature of the cooperating mechanism's normal response to that information. If so, we cannot conclude that the more cautious system produces devices that represent auxiliary features.

According to the version of the teleological theory that I have developed here, the answer will depend on how the occurrence of this auditory device has, in the past, helped to ensure the success of the duckling's attempts to follow its parent. The answer to this question is that the occurrence of this device helps to ensure that the duckling follows its parent, and not some other object. And, of course, we can say exactly the same about the visual device that is triggered by the parent's waddling motions. In other words, both these devices have the same function, although they will perform it in different ways. It follows that we should not treat the duckling's parent-recognition system as inferring the presence of a parent from the presence of certain auxiliary features, but rather as double-checking the parent's presence.

Another plausible suggestion is that an intentional system will be able to represent auxiliary features if it is able to use information about an auxiliary feature to help it to detect two or more target features. Birds have good colour vision, and use colour cues in a variety of contexts. Imagine that there is a species of birds in which the presence of a particular colour—red, say—might help to elicit either feeding behaviour or courtship behaviour, depending on the nature of the other cues that occur at the same time. In this system, visual devices that are normally triggered by red objects will be used by two different representational systems, one that functions to identify food and another that functions to identify potential mates. As a result, we will not be able to interpret the content of these devices in a way that is tied to their role in just one of these systems. This might suggest that we should take them to signal the presence of a red object. If so, we will have found a sensory mechanism that is able to signal the presence of an auxiliary feature.

The problem with this suggestion is that there is no reason why we should not assign a disjunctive content to these devices. Just the same argument will apply as before: the production of this kind of device contributes to the success of the birds' visual system just because it is normally triggered by the presence of food *or* by the presence of a potential mate. There is no reason why we should not view this kind of device as signalling this very disjunction.

Clearly, there are many more complications that we could add to the inferential procedures of an intentional system. But I suspect that, as long as we confine our attention to devices whose content is fixed innately, we will always find ourselves assigning content that concerns target features. What I would like to suggest is that we will do better if we appeal to systems that are capable of developing new recognitional capacities through learning in the way I described earlier on. A system that is capable of this kind of learning *must* be able to represent auxiliary features as well as target features. This is because the process of learning that I have described just *is* the process of coming to associate the presence of an auxiliary feature with a target feature—in associating a particular odour with the presence of poison, for example.

Consider the rats' olfactory mechanism. In the past, rats have used information about the odours of things to help them to avoid poison, to identify food, and to evade predators. But if I were to ask for a precise account of how this mechanism has helped its possessors to avoid poison or find food, the answer will vary, depending on the learning history of each individual. The same can be said of each type of device produced by the mechanism. For this reason we cannot simply say that the function of the rats' olfactory mechanism is to signal the presence of poison, or food, or predators. Nor can we say that it is the function of any of the devices that it produces to do one or more of these things. Indeed, in advance of some process of learning, these devices are not normally competent to help to satisfy any of the needs that they have helped to satisfy in earlier rats. This is because they are not yet connected to any particular behavioural response. A complete and unified account of the way in which this mechanism has contributed to the rats' survival will make essential reference to its role in discriminating between objects in a way that enables the rats to *learn* about poison, food, and predators. It does this by distinguishing between different odours.

For this reason, it would be incorrect to assign a disjunctive content to the devices produced by these mechanisms: for this would be to ignore the fact that they have helped their possessors to survive only by contributing to processes of learning. The innate function of these devices will be to signal the presence of distinctive odours—auxiliary features. It is only when the individual rat has learned that a certain odour signifies poison that a particular device will acquire an additional content that concerns a feature that is directly relevant to the organism's needs.

2.3. Auxiliary Features and the Distality Problem

At this point, however, we are confronted with a familiar problem. Consider the case of an organism, such as a quail, that is capable of learning and that distinguishes between different types of objects by exploiting information about colour and shape. And now consider the sensory device—call it I_R— that will normally be produced by the quail's visual system in response to the presence of a small, red, round object just ahead. The causal chain that leads to the production of I_R will be made up of a series of events that will include the advent of a small, red, round object just ahead of the quail. But it will also include the arrival of an array of light of a certain kind just in front of the quail's eyes. We need to determine which of these conditions we should take I_R to represent. In other words, we need to explain how we are to solve the distality problem for devices such as I_R.

The difficulty arises because we cannot use the same solution for devices that signal auxiliary properties as we employed when we were dealing with devices whose content relates to target properties. Our earlier solution depended on the claim that the content of a simple signal must relate to some feature whose presence provides an immediate explanation for the success of the organism's behaviour. But auxiliary features are, by definition, not features on which the success of the organism's behaviour directly depends.

In fact, it might be argued that we were simply wrong to assume that the content of I_R relates to the colour and shape of some distal object. It is the fact that the quails' visual systems are sensitive to features of the light reaching their eyes that provides the most direct explanation for their success in learning to recognize significant features in their environment. The fact that these features vary with the colours of objects in the distal environment is not essential to this explanation. But, if we were to take this line, we would be left with no explanation of how any organism, including ourselves, could come to represent colours, or shapes, or odours as auxiliary features belonging to distal objects.

A natural thought is that humans are able to represent the colours and shapes of distal objects because we are also capable of representing the spatial location of those objects: very crudely, it is because the spatial content of our representations puts those objects 'out there' that we can be said to represent colours and shapes 'out there'. Perhaps we could try to make use of this idea in explaining how sensory systems are able to represent distal auxiliary features.

Suppose that I_R is normally prompted by the presence of a certain type of light array, Φ, just in front of the quail's eyes. Φ carries the information that there is some red, round object just ahead of the quail: we can divide Φ into two elements: Γ, the element that carries the information that there is something red and round in the area, and Λ, the spatial element. Does I_R signal that an instance of Φ is occurring, or does it signal that there is something red and round just ahead of the quail?

We can assume that, whenever behaviour prompted by I_R has led to some successful outcome in the past, this is because it has had certain spatial features. In particular, it is because it has been directed at some feature or object just ahead of the quail. If this is the case, this spatial property will be a target, not an auxiliary feature for the quails' visual system: it will feature in an immediate explanation for the success of the quails' behaviour. If this is the case, we are entitled to conclude that part of the content of I_R will concern that distal spatial property: the quails' visual system treats Λ as a sign that there is something happening just ahead of the quail.

It is tempting to think that it is just because Γ is so closely associated with Λ, together with the fact that Λ is used by the visual system as a source of information about a distal spatial property, that it is right to claim that the system uses Γ to indicate the presence of distal auxiliary features. But how exactly does this work? To get clear about this we need to consider how the production of I_R on past occasions has helped the quails to learn to recognize target features, such as food or poison.

Suppose that on a number of occasions a quail responds to an instance of Φ by producing feeding behaviour, and on each occasion succeeds in eating a berry that contains useful nutrients. As a result, the quail's tendency to respond to Φ by producing feeding behaviour is strengthened. The success of the quail's behaviour will be explained by the fact that it was directed towards some object that possessed some non-spatial target feature—in this case, some feature that makes the object nutritious. The quail has come to treat Γ as a sign of this target feature. But the success of the quail's behaviour will also be explained by the fact that it was directed towards an object that was just ahead of the quail—the spatial relation that the quail associates with Λ. Moreover, the success of this behaviour depends on the fact that the object that was good to eat was the *same* object as the object that was just ahead of the quail. In other words, when we come to explain how I_R has contributed to successful processes of learning, we will have to mention the fact that Γ and Λ normally derive from the same source.

It will follow that the content of I_R cannot be concerned with Γ. Rather, the function of I_R will be to carry the information that an instance of Γ has occurred that originates from a source just ahead of the quail. But this information will normally be equivalent to the information that there is something red and round just ahead of the quail. Hence the content of I_R will concern the presence of something red and round, and not the occurrence of Γ.

Contrast this with an organism that is incapable of producing devices with a spatial component. In this case the causal origin of the proximal cue need have no relevance to the success of the resulting behavioural response. All that will matter in this case is that there should be some causal connection between the target feature that the organism learns to recognize and *some* auxiliary condition in the environment that the organism is able to detect. But, if there is a causal connection between the occurrence of that target feature and the occurrence of some distal auxiliary feature, there will also be a connection between the presence of that target feature and the occurrence of more proximal cues to which that distal auxiliary feature gives rise. In this case, we should take the organism's sensory states to represent those proximal cues: its sensitivity to those proximal cues will provide a more immediate explanation for its success.

Γ, then, is able to act as a source of information about the colour and shape of a distal object in virtue of its close association with Λ in giving rise to behaviour that is appropriate both to the spatial and to the non-spatial properties of distal objects in the quail's environment. But what if Γ had been associated with a proximal cue that carried information about some other form of target feature? Suppose, for example, that there was an organism that was able to adapt its behaviour to the temperature of the objects in its environment—responding cautiously to hot objects, boldly to cool ones, for example. Now suppose that Γ were accompanied not by Λ but by Θ, a proximal cue that carries information about the temperature of its source. The situation appears to be just the same as before: it will be causally relevant to the success of the system that Γ and Θ derive from the same source. It is just because this is so that the system gives rise to behaviour that is appropriate to both the thermal and the non-thermal features of objects in the environment. What is important, then, is that Γ should be accompanied by some further element that is normally used as a source of information about some target feature in the environment.

If this is right, an organism will be capable of representing auxiliary features in the distal environment only if it is equipped with a sensory system that relies on information not only about auxiliary features but also about distal target features to which the organism's behaviour is sensitive, in the way that I have described. This will include organisms whose behaviour is adapted to the spatial features of objects and features in the environment, but may include others, such as the temperature-sensitive organism described above.[7]

---

[7] Note that this solution is parasitic on the solution to the indeterminacy problem suggested in the previous chapter: it is only because we have already solved the distality problem for target features that we can appeal to the target features to help us to solve the problem for auxiliary features.

2.4. Learning Systems: Summary

The content of the devices produced by an intentional mechanism that is capable of developing new recognitional capacities through learning will be determined, not by the use function that those devices actually come to play, but by the use function that they are supposed to serve. This, in turn, will be determined by the innate design function of the mechanism that controls the process of learning and by the rules that normally govern its operation.

An intentional system that is capable of this kind of learning will be able to represent or signal the presence of auxiliary properties as well as target properties. Hence, the ability to represent auxiliary properties turns out to be a more sophisticated capacity than the ability to represent target properties. But a system will be able to detect distal auxiliary properties only if it produces devices that signal the presence of some conjunction of auxiliary and target features possessed by a single source. This will occur, for example, if the system normally detects not only the presence of some auxiliary feature but also its location.

3. Representing Goals

3.1. The Function of an Imperative Device

So far, we have confined our attention to systems that function to ensure that the responses of their cooperating mechanisms bear an appropriate informational relation to the environment. The signals produced by these simple systems can be ascribed what Millikan terms *indicative content*: in other words, these devices can be characterized as signalling that some condition in the environment occurs. We have yet to consider how an intentional device might come to have what Millikan calls *imperative content*; in other words, how an intentional device might come to represent some condition as something *to be produced*. As we saw in the previous chapter, it is possible to justify the ascription of indicative content to very simple systems, such as the arrow worm's sensory mechanism. These were systems that we characterized as minimally intentional systems. We might wonder whether a minimally intentional system will be capable of generating imperative, as well as indicative, content, or whether the ability to represent goals will turn out to be a more sophisticated capacity than the ability to signal occurrences.

We might start with the thought that the function of an imperative device is to bring about a certain state of affairs. Unfortunately, this will not get us very far, since this will be true of any device that possesses a function: as we saw in Chapter 3, the function of a device will always be to effect some further state of affairs. In Chapter 4, however, we saw that one distinguishing mark of an intentional device is that it is supposed to be used by some cooperating mechanism. This might suggest that a device will count as an imperative device if it is supposed to cause some second device to produce some further state of affairs. Indeed, this is not too far away from Millikan's own view (Millikan 1984: 99–100).

On this picture, then, the capacity to represent a goal will be extremely easy to come by. We will be able to ascribe imperative content to the most primitive intentional devices. The simple signals that I introduced in Chapter 4 will possess both indicative and imperative content: the frog's visual signal, for example, will possess both the imperative content 'Snap now!' and the indicative content 'Fly within range now!': this is because the function of this signal will be both to prompt the frog to snap, and to ensure that its doing so coincides with the presence of a fly. It is only when we encounter a very sophisticated intentional system that we will meet devices that may be ascribed content that is either exclusively indicative or exclusively imperative (Millikan 1986: 71–2).

I will call this view *the straightforward view*. I believe that the straightforward view is too simple to account for the distinction between intentional mechanisms that represent goals and other, non-intentional mechanisms. Instead, I would like to suggest that the simplest intentional devices should not be regarded as representing goals. As we shall see, the systems that produce imperative devices need not be very sophisticated: they will, for example, include the bee dance system. Systems of this kind will produce intentional devices that combine indicative and imperative content, just as Millikan suggests. Nevertheless, there will be some intentional systems that are too simple to generate imperative content. Systems of this kind will produce devices that possess indicative, but not imperative, content. On this alternative view, the capacity to represent goals will constitute an advance, albeit a small one, on the capabilities of a minimally intentional system.

According to the straightforward view, any device that normally prompts some cooperating mechanism to produce some further state of affairs will possess imperative content. But this suggestion is far too weak: it will underwrite the ascription of imperative content to a great many devices that we would not usually regard as intentional devices at all. For example, the squeezing motions produced by the heart will normally cause the blood to bring it about that oxygen and nutrients are distributed around the body. But it would seem very unnatural to describe the heart as *telling* the blood to distribute oxygen and nutrients.

A proponent of the straightforward view might appeal to a further feature of Millikan's account—the idea that imperative devices *map onto* the states of affairs that they represent. This was an aspect of her account that I rejected in

Chapter 4. But this element in her account is not relevant here. This is because, as we saw in Chapter 4, Millikan wishes to allow that even unstructured devices map onto states of affairs in the environment, in virtue of the fact that they may be produced at different times. Since the heart makes squeezing motions over and over again, we could treat the heart's making a squeezing motion at a certain time as mapping onto the blood's distributing oxygen and nutrients at that time. Moreover, even if we were to reject this feature of Millikan's account, and insist that only structured devices will count as mapping onto states of affairs, we might still be able to treat the heart's squeezing motions as having some kind of structure: for example, the heart beats at different speeds at different times. Variations in the heart's speed will correlate with variations in the rate at which the blood delivers oxygen and nutrients to the organs of the body. This aspect of Millikan's account, therefore, is not relevant here.

Again, a proponent of the straightforward view might respond to the objection by suggesting that the squeezing motions produced by the heart do not possess imperative content, because neither they, nor any other device produced by the heart, possess indicative content. On this view, imperative content would be seen as parasitic on indicative content: no intentional system could be ascribed imperative content unless it could already be ascribed indicative content. But this seems a rather *ad hoc* way of dealing with the objection. It may well be true that imperative content presupposes indicative content. But, if so, there ought to be some reason for it: it should not just be true by stipulation.

I would like to suggest an alternative to the straightforward account. My proposal is very similar to an account offered by Angsar Beckermann (1988). Beckermann's account differs from mine primarily in that it is couched in causal, rather than teleological, terms.

Why does it seem so strange to describe the heart as telling the blood to distribute oxygen and nutrients? In Chapter 4, we accepted a principle that we should not ascribe a form of intentional content to a device unless we can see how the possession of that kind of content might help to explain the behaviour to which the device gives rise. I also suggested that the kind of explanation that will interest the teleologist will be an explanation that shows how that behaviour is appropriate, given the content of the intentional device that caused it.

How will an appeal to the content of an imperative device help to make sense of the behaviour that it prompts? The point of an explanation of this kind will be to present the behaviour as appropriate, given the goal represented by the imperative device that caused it. In other words, the point of the explanation will be to make sense of that behaviour by showing that it was produced in order to achieve that goal.

We are now in a position to see why it is inappropriate to ascribe imperative content to the squeezing motions of the heart. The problem lies with the fact that the movement of the blood has a function of its own—to distribute oxygen and nutrients around the body. This function is derived from the function of the blood itself, in just the same way as the function of the frog's snaps derives from the function of the mechanism that produces them. The functions of these activities are the same on every occasion—the movement of the blood has the function to distribute oxygen and nutrients whenever it occurs. Moreover, we can explain the movement of the blood by appealing to this function. So, there is no need to refer to the functional properties of the heart to make sense of this activity.

Not all the activities produced by biological devices and systems have their own stable function in the way that the movement of the blood does. Many of the bodily movements produced by human beings, for example, cannot be ascribed stable functions of their own. The raising of an arm, for example, may be employed to serve virtually any function. If we want to know how the raising of an arm was appropriate on any particular occasion, we need to look at the desires and intentions that caused it. It is those desires and intentions that determine what its function was on that occasion. In this case, we can only make sense of the movement by appealing to the imperative content of the intentional devices that caused it to occur.

So, if we are to ascribe imperative content to a system, it must be the case that the system is able to trigger movements whose function varies from occasion to occasion, depending on its causal origin. This requirement can be separated into two criteria. First, the cooperating mechanism must be a mechanism that is capable of selecting which physical movements the organism will produce in order to perform a certain kind of behaviour. Consider the example of the bee dance mechanism. The information provided by the bee dance is used by the mechanism that controls the bees' foraging flights. The role of this executive mechanism is not simply to prompt the bees to fly off in a particular direction and to keep flying for a certain amount of time. Rather, it causes them to fly towards a particular location, taking account of environmental factors, such as the direction and speed of the wind. For this reason, the physical movements produced by this system do not have their own, stable functions—on different occasions the same set of physical movements might be used to take the bee to quite different locations around the hive. Hence, if we are to explain why a particular bee produced a particular flight on a certain occasion, we cannot appeal to some function that is shared by all flights of the same type: we will have to consider the content of the intentional devices that led to its being selected on that occasion.

Contrast this with a simple signalling mechanism, such as the arrow worm's sensory mechanism, which, when it fires, simply triggers the production of a stereotypical physical response—in this case, a forward dart. If we wish to know the function of this response, we do not need to know anything about the content of the signal that prompted it: the worm's darts all share the same, unchanging function.

The bee dance mechanism, then, differs from a simple signalling mechanism in that bee dances trigger a process of inference in which physical movements are selected to realize a certain kind of behaviour, on the basis of information about how things are in the environment. But this alone is not sufficient for the representation of goals. To see this, consider the example of a navigational system that functions to guide the organism back to its birthplace so that it can mate. The behaviour prompted by this system might display a high degree of flexibility and sensitivity to changing conditions along the way, in just the same way as the behaviour prompted by the bee dance mechanism. Nevertheless, this navigational system differs from the bee dance mechanism in one important respect. Although the system functions to ensure that the physical movements that the organism produces vary with changing circumstances, the function of these movements always remains the same—to take the organism back to its birthplace. Hence, although the behaviour produced by this system might be described as goal-oriented, it is not oriented towards a goal that needs to be represented by the system. It is only when the goals of the system vary from occasion to occasion that they need to be represented by imperative devices.[8]

In contrast, the bees' flights take the bees to a range of different locations, and so serve a range of functions. As a result, this mechanism not only has the task of selecting movements that will take the bee to a particular location, given the prevailing conditions. It needs this process of selection to be guided by an intentional device that represents the goal of this process of selection—in other words, it needs a device that represents the location to which the bee is supposed to go. The bee dance, together with the perceptual device that the dance generates in the watching bees, will perform this task.

Of course, there is an important distinction between the bee dance system and the representational system that controls the movements of the human arm. Our own representational system is directed towards the satisfaction of a range of different needs. The flights produced by the bee dance system, on the other hand, are directed towards the satisfaction of a single need—the bees' need for nectar. But this does not affect the point that the specific function of each flight—to take the bee to a particular location—will vary from occasion to occasion.

---

[8] It might be tempting to make a distinction between implicit and explicit representation at this point, and to say that a system of this kind represents its goal only implicitly. But it seems to me that it is only when a representation is explicit that its content is doing any explanatory work, so it is only when a representation is explicit that we need to talk about representation at all.

We can sum up the difference between the two kinds of system by saying that the purely indicative system works by using information about its environment to ensure that a certain kind of behaviour, having a particular function, is produced in the right circumstances or in the right manner; whereas a system with imperative content is one that works by selecting a sequence of movements, which have no stable function of their own, in the light of a goal represented by an imperative device, together with information about conditions in the environment.

In order to select the correct sequence of movements, a system that represents goals must rely on some process of simple inference that takes into account both the content of the imperative device, and the content of indicative devices that inform the system about conditions in the environment. In order to possess this level of complexity, a system need not be very sophisticated, as the example of the bee dance shows. But it must at least be more complex than the minimally intentional system. In this sense, imperative content is a more sophisticated kind of content than indicative content.

3.2. Imperative Content

How should we ascribe content to imperative devices? At this point, I will confine my attention to the simplest possible imperative system: one that is dedicated to a particular need and engages in only the simplest possible forms of inference. I will continue to use the bee dance system as an example.

The bee dance system, together with the bees' internal flight controller, is a component of a larger system whose function is to guide the bees to sources of nectar. In order to determine the function of the bee dance mechanism as an imperative system, we need to differentiate its function from the function of the flight controller that it directs. The bee dance mechanism functions by issuing bee dances in response to information about the location of nectar sources close to the hive. In response, the flight controller produces a flight, making use of information about the speed and direction of the wind, say.

The function of the bee dance mechanism is to ensure that the behaviour produced by the flight controller takes the bees to nectar. It does this by operating in accordance with a set of rules that normally ensure that each type of dance will cause the flight controller to produce behaviour that would normally take the bee to nectar, if the information that normally triggers the dance were correct. It is this behaviour that this type of dance may be said to represent. In response, the flight controller is supposed to produce a flight that, if its information about the prevailing meteorological conditions is correct, will normally be an instance of the kind of behaviour that the bee dance mechanism has 'told' it to produce.

For example, consider the bee dance that is normally produced in response to the information that there is nectar at position p. The behaviour normally prompted by this bee dance will be behaviour that, given that there is nectar at p, would normally take the bee to a nectar source. In other words, the dance will normally cause the bee to go to p. It is this behaviour that the dance represents. In response, the flight controller will produce a flight that, given that it has the right information about meteorological conditions, will normally take the bee to position p. In this way, the whole system ensures that the bee goes to a nectar source.

We can set this out more formally using the following set of schematic letters:

- S   an intentional system capable of producing imperative devices (for example, the bee dance mechanism);

- K   S's cooperating mechanism (for example, the flight controller);

- V   the type of behaviour that the whole system functions to produce (for example, going to a nectar source);

- C   a range of conditions $C_1 \ldots C_n$ the resource or threat to which B is normally a response (for example, the presence of nectar at a certain location);

- B   a range of behaviours $B_1 \ldots B_n$, each of which under some member of C normally constitutes an instance of V (for example, going to a certain location);

- Q   a range of conditions $Q_1 \ldots Q_n$ involving the organism and/or the environment (for example, meteorological conditions);

- M   a range of movement sequences $M_1 \ldots M_n$, each of which under some member of Q normally constitutes a member of B (for example, flights).

Suppose that S is in receipt of the information that C_1 obtains and K is in receipt of the information that Q_1 obtains. In these circumstances, the function of S is to ensure that K produces an instance of some member of M that, given Q_1, constitutes an instance of just that member of B that, given C_1, normally constitutes an instance of V. The imperative content of the device issued by S on this occasion will concern that member of B.

The bee dance mechanism is a 'one-step' imperative system: that is, it generates goals that are then put into execution by the flight controller. But it is easy to see how a series of 'one-step' mechanisms could be strung together to form 'two-step', 'three-step', or even 'four-step' systems—systems capable of generating a hierarchy of goals, taking into account information about a wide range of conditions in the environment. In accounting for the working of these more complicated systems we would have to add further layers to our analysis, but the basic principles would remain the same.

In determining the membership of *B* we may be faced by problems of indeterminacy, similar to those we met in the previous chapter. Once again we will have to appeal to the four additional constraints on function ascription in order to rule out rival ascriptions of function. For example, someone might suggest that the function of the bee dance is to tell the flight controller to make the bees *fly* to a certain position. We will be able to rule out this suggestion by appealing to the second clause of the abstractness condition: the fact that the bees must reach nectar sources by flying is dependent on the design of the bee's locomotory system. If this had been different, the bees might have walked or hopped to their destination. Only the content 'go to position p' covers all these possibilities. Again, someone might suggest that the function of the bee dances is to tell the bees to *gather nectar* at a particular location: but, clearly, the bee dance mechanism cannot do this on its own—the bee's visual and olfactory systems are needed to trigger the gathering of nectar once the bees have flown to the right location. Hence this suggestion will breach the independence condition.

It is when we have a system that possesses imperative content that we are first able to provide intentional explanations of its behaviour that are analogous to the explanations we give of human actions. In the case of the arrow worm, we can appeal to the informational content of the sensory signal to explain why the worm darted off when it did. But, if we want to explain the point of the worm's darting motions, we have to appeal to the function of its response—and this does not depend on the content of the sensory signals that prompted it. When we give the agent's reason for performing a particular action, we are usually concerned, not with her timing, but with explaining what kind of action it was that she produced, what its goal was: and to discover this, we must look at her desires and intentions, states that represent her goal in acting. It is only when the system represents its goals that we can appeal to its intentional states to explain its purpose in behaving in a certain way, as we do when we rationalize the actions of an agent.

3.3. Learning Goals

There will be another situation in which an organism will normally produce behaviour that has no innate function. This is where the organism is capable of developing new forms of behaviour by the process of trial and error learning. For example, a small bird that has found a nut may manipulate it in all sorts of different ways, until something it does causes the nut to break, allowing the bird to eat the kernel inside. Next time the bird encounters a similar-looking nut, it will try the same behaviour again: the bird's behaviour has now acquired a new function that it did not have before. The difference between this process and the processes of inference used by the systems described in the previous section is that the selection of this piece of behaviour is not guided by information—the bird hits on the right solution to the problem by chance.

An organism that is capable of this kind of learning may acquire a new conative capacity—the capacity to represent a new goal—as a result. This will be the case if what the organism learns is not a stereotypical response (two shakes of the beak and then a twist) but an objective, which can be brought about in a number of different ways (break the nut against a stone). In the second case, whenever the organism puts what it has learned into practice, it will engage in a process of inference to select the correct bodily movements, just as the bees do when they respond to a bee dance.

Just as before, we will not be able to identify the functions acquired by these new behavioural schemes with the use functions that they actually serve, for once again we will be able to imagine cases in which a lucky mistake in learning has occurred. For example, it might turn out that the kernel that the bird learns to extract is devoid of nutritional value; and yet the act of breaking the shell makes a noise that frightens the local cats. The bird's behaviour will develop the use function of protecting it from the cats; but the behaviour is reinforced by feedback from the bird's alimentary system. The function that the behaviour acquires through learning is not its actual use function, but the use function that it is supposed to have, given the function of the learning mechanism and the rules that normally govern its operation.

3.4. *Representing Goals: Summary*

I have argued that the devices produced by signalling systems will not possess imperative content. The capacity to represent goals is more sophisticated than the capacity to signal the occurrence of a certain state of affairs because it requires that the intentional system should be able to engage in a certain form of inference—one that involves the selection of a physical response that, in the circumstances, will realize one of a range of possible behaviours. It is only when this is the case that we can appeal to the fact that the system is supposed to produce a certain kind of behaviour in order to make sense of the response that the organism has produced.

Conative capacities, like recognitional capacities, may be acquired through learning. Once again, the learned content of an imperative device will be fixed, not by the use function that it actually plays, but by the use function that it is supposed to play. This will be determined by the innate function of the mechanism that controls the process of learning.

The capacity to learn and the capacity to represent goals are two modest advances beyond minimal intentionality. In the next chapter, I will consider a third advance: the capacity to represent particular items. This will give me the opportunity to introduce a notion that will play an important role in Part III—the notion of an ontological category.

7

Keeping Track

1. Introduction

The intentional systems that we have considered up to now have been systems that function to register the presence of certain *features* or *type of condition* in the environment. In this chapter, I would like to consider what is required of a system that is able to represent particular items of some kind.

I take it that there are many different categories of particular that an intentional system might be capable of representing. Some belong to familiar ontological categories, such as *object, time, place,* or *event*; others might belong to less familiar categories, such as *time slice, lineage,* or *trope.* The aim of this chapter is to find a system that can be characterized as representing spatio-temporal particulars, such as objects or places, to set out the minimal competence conditions that such a system must meet, and to make it clear how we should go about ascribing content to the devices produced by such a system.

In addressing this issue, I am going to take certain things for granted. One assumption that I shall make is that we should begin our search by looking for a system that is able to pick out particulars by identifying them in the course of some perceptual encounter, rather than by forming some descriptive representation of them. This is a reasonable assumption for a teleologist to make, since it is hard to see how an organism could ever make use of a descriptive identification of a particular to guide its behaviour unless it already had some capacity to recognize particulars perceptually.[1] In contrast, there is no obvious reason to rule out the possibility that an organism might have the capacity to represent a particular perceptually, and yet lack the capacity to produce some non-perceptual, descriptive representation of it. But, if the capacity to represent particulars perceptually is both independent

---

[1] Strawson (1959: 20–1) argues, plausibly in my view, that the capacity to identify particular objects descriptively is parasitic on the capacity to represent particular objects and places in perception.

of and prior to the capacity to represent them by description, then an account that aims to set out *minimal* conditions for the representation of particulars had better begin with organisms that can be described as perceiving particulars of some kind.[2]

The discussion in this chapter touches on two long-standing philosophical debates. The first of these concerns the relationship between the capacity to represent objects and the capacity to represent places. A number of philosophers have argued that the capacity to represent objects is somehow dependent on the capacity to represent places, while others have taken up the opposite position, arguing that the capacity to represent places is dependent on the capacity to represent objects. A third position might be that these two capacities are interdependent—that neither can exist without the other.[3] In this chapter, I will argue that these two capacities are quite independent of each other: a system might have the capacity to represent particulars of one sort without being able to represent particulars of any other kind.

There is a dialectical problem here: the philosophers who have written on this issue have generally been concerned with the capacities of conscious, thinking subjects. In this chapter, however, I am concerned with the capacities of relatively unsophisticated organisms. In what follows, I hope to make it clear that, while we might well concede that only the most sophisticated intentional systems can be ascribed *thoughts* about particulars, there is no need to restrict the capacity to *represent* particulars to such sophisticated systems. For this reason, much of what I say here will not be relevant to the concerns of these writers.

Nevertheless, it would be odd to suppose that there is no connection between what I do when I make a perceptual judgement about a particular and what a simpler organism does when it perceives a particular. There is plenty of room for disagreement about how strong we should take the connection to be;[4] but, even on a relatively cautious view, we might at least expect that our account of perception will put some constraints on any account we might give of perceptual judgements. At the very least, we need to distinguish between constraints that emerge from our account of perceptual representation and constraints that could be justified only by considerations relating to the possibility of thought about particulars.[5]

The second long-standing debate with which we will make contact in this

[2] In the next chapter I will describe a system that is capable of identifying particular items by description.

[3] See especially Strawson (1959). Evans (1982: 170 ff.) argues that a subject who demonstratively identifies a particular object must locate it at a particular place; Wiggins (1963) puzzles over the relationship between the two capacities.

[4] Evans (1982: 143–4) explicitly distinguishes between the capacity to perceive an object and the capacity to make a perceptual demonstrative judgement about an object.

[5] I will offer an account of the content of perceptual judgements in Chapter 10.

chapter concerns the nature of the causal relationship between the perceiver and the object that she perceives. The literature contains an array of notorious puzzles about the causal chain that links the object to the perceiver. In particular, there are puzzles about what constitutes a causal chain of the right kind, and puzzles about where the causal chain should be thought to start. I will propose a teleological solution to these puzzles.[6]

2. Systems that Represent Particulars

2.1. Keeping Track of an Object

My first task is to find a system that can be described as representing particulars of some kind. For the time being, I will concentrate on finding a system that is able to represent particular *objects*. I will argue that a system will be able to represent particular objects if it meets two independent requirements: it must make use of *identifying information*; and it must function to control behaviour that is *directed onto* particular objects, in a sense to be explained.

For an intentional system to count as representing particular objects, it is not sufficient that devices produced by the system are triggered by particular objects. It will be true even of simple signalling systems that the signals they produce are triggered by objects in the environment. The signals produced by the arrow worm's sensory system, for example, are produced in response to small organisms. Indeed, we could equally well say that these signals are prompted by prey-infested *places* or by *events* involving prey. But there seems to be no reason to mention particulars of any kind when we characterize the way in which this system normally helps the arrow worm to feed. It is enough to say that the system is sensitive to the presence of a certain feature—that is, there being prey.

Why would it seem so extravagant to suppose that the arrow worm's sensory mechanism presents the organisms on which the worm preys as particular objects? A particular object is, in essence, a spatio-temporal entity: a particular object persists through time; at any one moment, it occupies a unique position in space; and it may move through space in certain ways. Moreover, a number of writers—most recently, John Campbell (1994: 27–9)—have argued that the spatio-temporal structure of objects is underpinned by their causal structure. The unity of particular objects depends on what Campbell terms their *internal causal connectedness*: the state of an object

---

[6] For a more detailed discussion, see Price (1998).

at one time will be causally dependent, in part, on its state at some earlier
time; and a single object may be a common cause of two distinct effects.[7]

There is no reason to treat the worm's sensory mechanism as functioning to
detect entities of this kind. It makes no difference to the success of the mechanism whether it is responding to one large prey organism or to ten small
ones; it does not matter whether the organism that it detects at one moment
has any causal or spatio-temporal connection with the organism that it detects
a moment later. This suggests that a system that is able to represent particular
objects will be a system whose success somehow depends on the distinct and
continuing *identity* of a particular object. What kind of system might this be?

We have already encountered systems that can be described as making use
of identifying information deriving from particular objects in their environment. A system will count as using identifying information if some of the
devices that it produces are such that each device normally carries more than
one piece of information about a single item.

To give a fresh example: suppose that a female cricket normally registers the
presence of a male cricket only if she hears the sequence of sounds that is normally produced by a male cricket when he is looking for a mate. The male's
song, we will suppose, consists of a chirp followed by a chirrup. When a male
cricket is singing nearby, the female's auditory system responds by producing
a pair of auditory devices corresponding to the two stages of the song. Suppose, too, that the auditory device that corresponds to the 'chirrup' is not normally produced unless the system has already recognized the occurrence of a
chirp immediately before.

When all is going normally, the 'chirrup' device will carry a number of different pieces of information. First of all, it will carry the information that a
chirrup is occurring: this is one of the conditions that trigger the production
of the device. Secondly, it will carry the information that a chirp has just
occurred: this is because it has also been triggered by the production of a
'chirp' device. Putting these two pieces of information together, we can say
that this device carries the information that a chirp–chirrup sequence is
occurring. Finally, the occurrence of this device will carry the information
that the male that produced the chirrup is the same individual as the male that
produced the chirp. This is because, when all is going normally, the fact that
the chirp and the chirrup occurred one after another is explained by the fact
that they formed part of the song produced by an individual male; moreover,
the fact that they were temporally related in this way explains the fact that the
'chirp' device helped to trigger the 'chirrup' device. So the 'chirrup' device carries the information that the chirp–chirrup sequence has been produced by a
single male. Moreover, the success of the system in recognizing that a male
cricket is present will normally depend on the fact that the sounds that the

---

[7] See also Slote (1979) and Shoemaker (1984).

female can hear emanate from a single male cricket. Hence we can say that the 'chirrup' device will *normally* carry this information. For this reason, then, the system can be described as using identifying information, in the sense defined.

This can be made clearer with a diagram (Figure 3). The arrows represent the direction of the flow of information.

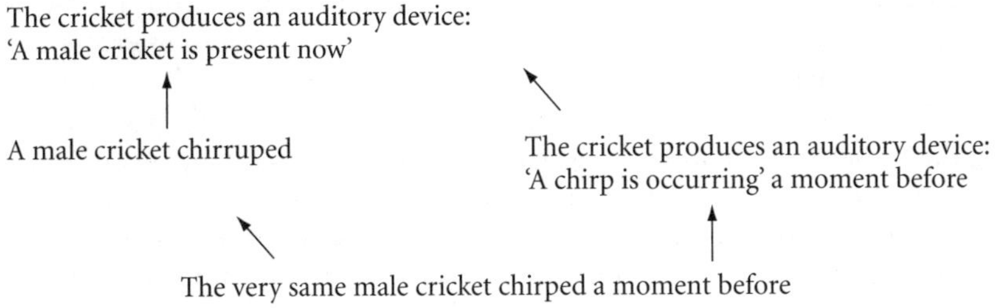

The cricket produces an auditory device:
'A male cricket is present now'

A male cricket chirruped

The cricket produces an auditory device:
'A chirp is occurring' a moment before

The very same male cricket chirped a moment before

FIG. 3. *Information Carried by the Male Cricket's 'Chirrup' Device*

The use of identifying information certainly presupposes the internal causal connectedness of particular objects: the possibility of using identifying information presupposes both that the current state of the object is causally dependent on its state at an earlier time and that a single object may be a common cause of two distinct perceptual devices. In the light of this, it might be suggested that we should characterize the female cricket's auditory system as *identifying* the source of the song as the same male cricket, and so conclude that it is able to represent particular objects.

In Chapter 4, however, I suggested that a system can make use of identifying information without representing it. The reason I gave was that the content of a perceptual device will depend, not only on the information that it normally carries, but also on the nature of the behaviour that it triggers. The success of the female cricket's behaviour does not depend on the presence of a particular male cricket. It does not matter, for example, whether the male that is present when she lays her eggs is identical with the male whose song she heard. To explain the success of her behaviour, it is enough to say that it occurred in the presence of some male cricket or other. The function of her auditory system, then, will be to ensure that her behaviour coincides with this feature, and so it is the presence of this feature that the devices produced by the system must be taken to signal.

We can get closer to what we need by introducing the notion of a tracking system. The kind of system that I have in mind is one that has the capacity to keep track of particular objects through changes in their spatial position, and perhaps also through alterations in their appearance;[8] in order to be able to

[8] See Strawson (1961: 100), Wiggins (1963: 181 ff.), and Evans (1982: 174).

track particular objects in this way, a perceptual system must be able to discriminate between two distinct objects presented at the same time and to re-identify a particular object from moment to moment. A cheetah, for example, is able to keep track of a particular antelope, even as it crosses the paths of other antelopes in the same herd. By keeping track of a particular antelope, the cheetah is able to anticipate where the antelope will be from moment to moment, so enabling the cheetah to follow and, eventually, to intercept it.

Like the female cricket, the cheetah will make use of identifying information. Once the cheetah's visual system has produced a visual device registering the presence of an antelope at a particular location, further visual devices produced in response to the same antelope as it moves about will not only carry information about the antelope's current location; they will also normally carry the information that this is the very same antelope as the one that the cheetah originally spotted and has since been tracking. This is because any subsequent visual device will normally be produced both in response to the presence of the antelope at a particular location, and in response to the production of earlier visual devices triggered by the antelope; moreover, the fact that this particular sequence of visual devices occurred will normally be explained by the movements of a single antelope. So these subsequent visual devices will normally carry identifying information about that particular antelope.

Once again, this can be made clearer with a diagram (Figure 4). Again, the arrows represent the direction of the flow of information.

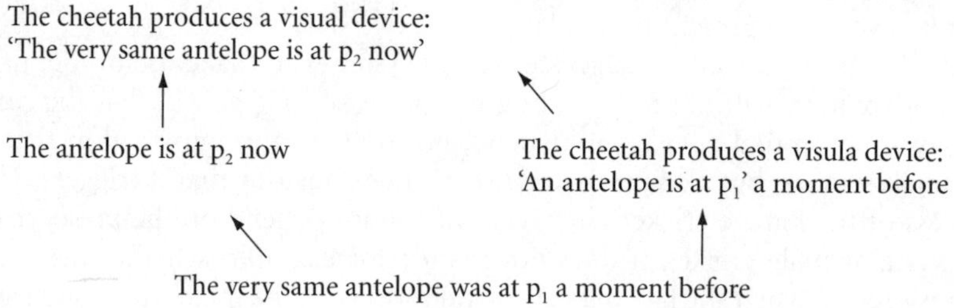

The cheetah produces a visual device:
'The very same antelope is at p_2 now'

The antelope is at p_2 now

The cheetah produces a visula device:
'An antelope is at p_1' a moment before

The very same antelope was at p_1 a moment before

FIG. 4. *Information Carried by the Cheetah's Visual Device as the Cheetah Keeps Track of an Antelope that has moved from one place (p_1) to another (p_2)*

I have already argued that the fact that a system uses identifying information about particular objects is not enough to show that it may be said to represent particular objects: a tracking system will only count as representing particular objects if the success of the behaviour that the system controls is somehow dependent on the identity of objects in the environment. Even in the case of a tracking system, this is not necessarily the case. Consider the case of a frog that possesses a tracking system that helps it to target snaps at flies by predicting their location. There is no difference between the behaviour produced by this frog and a frog that simply reacts to the arrival of something small and dark in a certain direction by snapping in that direction. The success of the frog's snap may be explained in just the same way in each case: that is, by the fact that the frog's snap coincided with the presence of some feature: *there being a fly in that direction*. A tracking system of this kind, then, cannot be characterized as representing particular objects, but only as predicting the location of features in the frog's environment.

Nevertheless, what I would like to suggest is that, although a tracking system need not possess the function to represent particular objects, it is at least *competent* to perform that function. This is because a tracking system is the right sort of system to control the kind of behaviour we are looking for. To see this, we need to see what kind of behaviour this is.

The activities I have in mind are ones in which the organism interacts with a single object over a period of time. Activities such as stalking a particular prey animal, rolling an object along, or making a tool might be behaviours of this kind. An activity of this type may be described as directed onto a particular object because its success depends on the fact that it continues to be directed towards the same object over time. For example, consider the behaviour of a chimpanzee that is fashioning a termite sticker by pulling the leaves off a twig and sharpening the point. This activity will not normally produce a useful tool unless the twig that the chimpanzee strips of leaves is the *same twig* as the one that he then goes on to sharpen. Again, a cheetah's success in running down an antelope will be explained in part by the fact that he continues to chase the same antelope for a period of time.

An organism that engages in behaviour of this kind will be more likely to succeed if it possesses a perceptual system that is able to keep track of particular objects as they move around. The cheetah's success in pursuing an antelope through a milling herd is, I presume, explained partly by the fact that the cheetah's visual system is competent to keep track of that antelope as it moves about. For this reason, we can claim that the cheetah's visual system does not only make use of identifying information about particular antelopes: it can also be said to represent that information.

Note that the requirement that the system should control this type of behaviour is a necessary, not a sufficient, condition. An arrow worm might be able to chase its prey by continually moving in the direction in which it senses that prey is present; at any moment, the fact that it sensed prey ahead a moment before would help it to continue its chase by directing its sensory receptors in that direction. But the worm's sensory system could do nothing to ensure that the organism that it is chasing at any one moment is the same organism as the one that it was chasing a moment before. The system works by prompting the worm to approach, and to go on approaching prey, not by keeping track of a particular target. Unlike a tracking system, the worm's sensory system is not competent to represent particular objects.

A system will count as representing particular objects if it uses identifying information in order to guide some form of sustained, object-directed activity. The cheetah's visual tracking system is a system of this kind. Note that I have not claimed that it is only tracking systems that are able to represent particulars perceptually. In the next chapter, for example, I will argue that the perceptual devices used by certain types of mapping system will also represent particulars. As we shall see, the two kinds of system have much in common, but it does not seem that the capacity to map particulars *depends* on the capacity to keep track of them. So we cannot claim that the capacity to keep track of particulars is fundamental, in the sense that any system that is able to represent particulars perceptually must have the capacity to track them. Nevertheless, I suspect that tracking systems are the simplest systems capable of representing particulars; for, unlike mapping systems, they rely on perceptual capacities alone.

2.2. Minimal Tracking

In this section, I shall suggest three conditions that must be satisfied by a perceptual system that is competent to track particular objects. The first two constraints must be met by a perceptual system if it is to be competent to track spatio-temporal particulars of any kind. The role of the third condition is to ensure that the particulars represented by the system are particular *objects*, rather than particulars of some other kind.

First, the perceptual system must be sensitive to certain features possessed by particular items in the environment. If this were not the case, the system could not have enabled the organism to respond appropriately to the presence of particulars of that kind.

Secondly, the perceptual system must be competent to discriminate between particular items, and to reidentify an item through changes in its spatio-temporal position. To do this, it seems, requires the ability to represent particular items as located in space and time. It is only by exploiting information about their spatio-temporal properties that the tracking system will be able to discriminate between different items of the same type and to reidentify a particular item from moment to moment.

This brings us to our third condition: a tracking system will normally operate in accordance with a certain set of rules, which characterize the way in which the system normally reidentifies a particular item, or distinguishes between two different items. The rules that characterize the workings of a tracking system determine which kind of particular the system is competent to track. A tracking system can be said to track particular objects only if the rules that characterize its normal workings reflect the way in which objects are actually able to move through space. It is only by following rules of this kind that the system is able to ensure that the entities that it reidentifies from moment to moment possess the spatio-temporal and causal connectedness characteristic of particular objects.

The kind of rules I have in mind are described by Elizabeth Spelke and Gretchen Van de Valle (1993) in a study of the workings of the perceptual systems of human infants. Spelke and Van de Valle identify a number of different principles that constrain the way in which these systems individuate particular objects. For example, the parts of a single object must not be separated by a spatial gap and must move together (the principle of *cohesion*); the parts of two distinct objects must either be separated or fail to move together (the principle of *boundedness*); a single object follows a continuous path through space (the principle of *continuity*); the paths traced by two distinct objects must not permit both objects to occupy the same position at the same time (the principle of *solidity*). Spelke and Van de Valle's study is an empirical one; but the suggestion here is constitutive: a system that fails to meet constraints of this kind might still be competent to represent particulars of some kind, but it will not be competent to represent particular objects.[9]

A system that is characterized by rules of this kind need not rely on simply recognizing incoming sensory information as conforming to some predetermined pattern. Rather, the system will be able to track a particular object through an indefinite number of possible changes in spatial position in a way that reflects the way in which objects, as particulars, are actually able to move. These conditions are the minimal requirements that must be met by a perceptual system if it is to be described as representing particular objects. In order to succeed in identifying an object on a particular occasion, the system must meet these conditions with respect to that object.

2.3. The Phoenix Fly Case

It is important to bear in mind that I am claiming only that a system that meets these three conditions will be *competent* to represent particulars of some kind. A system may be competent to exercise a capacity without this being its function. To discover the function of the system, we must also consider how the fact that it met those conditions helped to explain its survival. In particular, the fact that a tracking system normally operates with a certain

---

[9] Exactly which principles ought to constrain the workings of a system that functions to represent particular objects is a matter of some controversy. It is certainly possible to dispute even the rather vague constraints that I have mentioned here. But I will not pursue this here. For some different views, see Strawson (1959: 39–40), Ayers (1974), Wiggins (1980), and Peacocke (1993).

set of rules is not by itself sufficient to determine what kind of particular the system functions to track. In this section, I will illustrate this point with the case of the phoenix flies.[10]

Imagine two lizards, which live in different environments. Lucy inhabits an environment that is infested with flies, on which she feeds. She possesses a tracking system that helps her to stalk and capture her prey. The operation of this tracking system is characterized by a set of rules (call it Ω) that reflects their status as particular objects.

Lizzy is identical to Lucy in every respect, except that she inhabits an environment infested with phoenix flies. Phoenix flies are (imaginary) flylike organisms that have a rather unusual lifecycle. They reproduce asexually: the young fly grows inside its parent and devours it from the inside.[11] By the time the young fly emerges, its parent has all but disappeared. The process occurs frequently and rapidly, and cannot be detected by Lizzy. As a result, Lizzy has no way of telling whether the item that she is stalking consists of a single phoenix fly or a series of phoenix flies, each replaced by its offspring. But Lizzy's inability to distinguish individual phoenix flies from phoenix fly lineages makes no difference to her ability to capture her prey: a phoenix fly lineage moves in just the same way as an individual fly. So a tracking system that is competent to track individual flies will be equally competent to track phoenix fly lineages.

Ordinarily, it should be easy to distinguish between an object-tracking system and a lineage-tracking system. As we have seen, it is a constitutive feature of objects that each part of an object must be contiguous with at least one other part. But this is not a constitutive feature of lineages, which may at any time possess members that are spatially separated. The problem posed by phoenix fly lineages is that their members cannot be separated in this way. They have this feature, not in virtue of their status as lineages, but because of the way in which phoenix flies happen to reproduce: as long as the parent and its offspring coexist, they are contiguous—one is inside the other. But, because phoenix fly lineages have this feature, we will have to concede that it is a normal feature of Lizzy's tracking system that it operates in accordance with Ω: Ω is the set of rules that would normally be used by an object-tracking system. But it is *also* the set of rules that would normally be used by a lineage-tracking system that assumes that members of lineages cannot be spatially separated. We must conclude that, in order to determine what kind of particular a tracking system functions to track, we need to ascertain, not only which

[10] I owe this gruesome tale to Mike Martin.
[11] If this was the only way in which phoenix flies reproduced, the species would, of course, soon disappear. Perhaps we should assume that phoenix flies engage in this form of reproduction when conditions are harsh, but lay eggs in large numbers whenever conditions are favourable.

rules it normally follows, but also how following those rules has helped to ensure its survival.

Nevertheless, the third minimal competence condition does constitute a necessary condition that a tracking system must meet before it can be ascribed the function to track particulars of some kind. A tracking system will not be competent to track particulars of a certain kind, unless the rules that characterize its normal workings are strong enough to capture the features essential to particulars of that kind. Lizzy's tracking system differs from other lineage-tracking systems in that it normally operates in accordance with an *additional* assumption, an assumption that reflects a special feature of the lineages that it functions to track. But the situation would be different if the system had *discarded* some other relevant assumption—for example, the assumption that lineages exist continuously through time. If a tracking system discarded this assumption, it would not be competent to track particular lineages, and so this could not be its function.

2.4. Tracking Objects and Tracking Places

In this section, I would like to consider how we might distinguish between a system that is competent to track particular objects and a system that is competent to track particular places. We have already seen how an organism might benefit from the capacity to track particular objects. It is perhaps less obvious how an organism could benefit from the capacity to track a place. Nevertheless, it is possible to imagine circumstances in which this would be the case. For example, consider the case of a mouse that preys on beetles. The beetles respond to the presence of the mouse by burrowing a little way into the soil. If the mouse can find the spot where it saw a beetle disappear, it can dig it up. But this may not be easy: the ground may be relatively uniform, making it necessary for the mouse to keep its eyes on the spot where the beetle disappeared.

It might be objected that we do not need to characterize the mouse as keeping track of the *place* where the beetle is buried. Instead, we could describe it as tracking a particular *object*, namely the chunk of soil that now conceals the beetle. To decide between these two hypotheses, we need to start by getting clear about what differentiates a system that is competent to track objects from a system that is competent to track places.

As we have seen, it is the rules that characterize the way in which the system identifies particulars from moment to moment that determine what kind of particular it is competent to track. If so, we can expect that the set of rules (Π) that must characterize the normal operation of a system that is competent to track places will differ in some way from the set of rules (Ω) that must characterize the normal operation of a system that is competent to track objects. In this section, I would like to consider what this difference might be.

I would like to suggest that the difference has to do with whether the system differentiates between two different ways in which the location of an item relative to the organism may change. First, its location may change because the *organism* has moved relative to the environment. Secondly, its position may change because the *item* has moved relative to the environment. In the case of a system that is competent to track particular places, the difference between the two kinds of change will be crucial. This is because the only way in which a place can change its spatial location relative to the organism is if the organism itself moves in relation to the environment: places cannot move about by themselves. So Π must respect the assumption that the relative location of a place may change if and only if the change can be explained by the way in which the organism has itself moved. A system that operates in accordance with Π must have some way of telling how the organism is moving.

This is not true of Ω. Flies, for example, have no access to information about their own movements. But it does not seem to follow from this that a fly could not keep track of a particular object through changes in its relative spatial position. To do this, all the fly would need to do is to work out how the relative spatial position of the object is changing over time. To perform this calculation, the fly does not need to decide whether it is gliding past the object or whether the object is gliding past it.

It is certainly true that the fly suffers from certain limitations. For example, it is unable to distinguish between an object getting nearer and an object getting larger: it treats both these situations as instances of the former. But all this amounts to is a limitation on the fly's ability to detect what is going on around it. The teleologist does not have to insist that a tracking system has to be infallible. What is important is that the system should be able *sometimes* to determine how objects are moving in relation to the organism.

If this is right, we can distinguish between systems that are competent to track places and systems that are competent to track objects as follows: a place-tracking system will normally reidentify a target through a change in its relative position if and only if that change can be explained by the way in which the organism has moved. An object-tracking system does not need to take account of the organism's movements when it reidentifies a target through a change in its relative position. A place-tracking system requires access to information about the organism's movements; an object-tracking system does not. In this sense, Π is a stronger set of rules than Ω.

So, if the mouse's tracking system functions to track places, it must normally operate in accordance with Π, with or without any additional assumptions. As we saw in the previous section, this is a necessary, not a sufficient condition. We still need to consider the possibility that the mouse's tracking system is an object-tracking system that operates in accordance with Π; or, to be precise, one that operates in accordance with Ω, together with an additional assumption that objects are immobile in relation to the environment. How could we distinguish between the hypothesis that the mouse's tracking system functions to track the beetle's hiding place and the hypothesis that it functions to track the lump of earth, but assumes that the lump of earth is immobile?

To solve this problem, we need to consider how the tracking system helps the mouse to find food. This, to some extent, will depend on the policy normally adopted by the beetle: is it the beetle's normal policy to burrow downwards and then stay still, or is it to get under an object, such as a clod of earth or a rock, and stay under that object? If the former, it makes sense to describe the mouse as tracking the place where the beetle is hiding; if the latter, we should describe it as tracking the object under which the beetle hides.

The account given in this section suggests that a system may be able to track objects without being able to represent particular places. Earlier, I argued that a tracking system can track a particular object without being able to ascertain how the object is moving relative to the environment. It is enough for the system to determine how the object is moving relative to the organism. To determine this, the tracking system does not need to identify which place the object occupies at any one time. The only information that it needs to use is information about the object's spatial *properties*—that is, its location relative to the organism. The cheetah's tracking system does not need to use the information that the antelope is at the waterhole (say), or even that it is at that place over there, but only that it is ten paces away to the left.

Conversely, there is nothing in the workings of the place-tracking system that suggests that the capacity to track places requires an ability to represent particular objects. The place-tracking system may reidentify a place from moment to moment using only information about the relative spatial location of that place, together with information about significant features that it possesses. The two capacities, it seems, are quite independent of each other.

Writers, such as David Wiggins (1963) and Gareth Evans (1982), who have suggested that the capacity to make judgements of certain kinds about particular objects might depend on the ability to identify particular places, or vice versa, have been concerned with epistemological issues. They start from the idea that, in order to think about a particular place or object, the subject must *know* which place or object she is thinking about. And then the thought is that the individuation of particular objects depends on their location in space; or, alternatively, that the individuation of places depends on the spatial relations between objects. But the only sense in which a tracking system needs to know which object or place it is tracking is that it must be able to discriminate that object or place from other objects and places, and to reidentify an object or place presented at different times. To do this, as we have seen, it does not need to represent particulars of any other kind.

2.5. Ontological Categories and Objectivity

I will end this part of the chapter by returning to the problem of objectivity discussed in Chapter 5. In that discussion, I could find no way to defend the claim that signalling systems are capable of representing the world as extending beyond the organism's behavioural reach. We might wonder whether systems that possess the capacity to represent particular objects or places should be treated in the same way.

It might be thought that they should not. I have argued that the workings of a place-tracking system, say, will normally be governed by rules that reflect the status of places as spatio-temporal particulars of a certain kind. There need be nothing in these rules that embodies the requirement that the objects tracked by the system are accessible to the organism. For example, it need not be the case that the system would normally refrain from tracking a place that the organism is able to see but unable to reach. As long as the system normally operates in this way, it could be argued, the teleologist is entitled to claim that the system represents places *tout court*, and not just accessible places.

However, it is easy to see that this response will fail, for just the same reason that Millikan's response was seen to fail in Chapter 5. As we saw when we considered the case of the phoenix flies, we cannot simply move from the claim that a system is competent to keep track of places *tout court* to the claim that the system represents places *tout court*. We also need to show that the system benefits the organism by exercising that competence. Nothing I have said in this chapter suggests a way in which an organism might benefit from the capacity to represent inaccessible places or inaccessible objects. The tracking systems that I have described benefit the organism by controlling place- or object-directed behaviour, such as stalking, chasing, or manipulating; the success of these behaviours will always be dependent on the accessibility of the place or object towards which they are directed. The particulars represented by the tracking systems considered here, therefore, must be regarded as representing *accessible* particulars, just as the bee dance mechanism represents accessible sources of nectar. We have not yet found an answer to Peacocke's challenge.

2.6. Systems that Represent Particulars: Summary

In this chapter, I have presented the following picture: a system will function to represent particulars of some kind if it is a system that normally makes use of identifying information in order to control behaviour that is directed onto particular items of that kind. I take it that a perceptual tracking system that controls an activity such as stalking or tool-making is a system of this kind. For a system to be competent to track spatio-temporal particulars of some kind, it must be able to recognize particular items as possessing certain features and to determine their spatial location relative to the organism at different times. None of this implies that the capacity to track one kind of spatio-temporal particular is dependent on the capacity to track any other kind.

The nature of the particulars that the system is competent to track will be determined by the rules that it normally follows. A system will be competent to track objects, for example, only if the rules that it follows at least include Ω; it will be competent to track places only if the rules that it follows at least include Π. But, to determine the nature of the particulars that a system actually functions to track, we also need to consider how following those rules has, in the past, helped to explain its success. It is for this reason that we cannot treat tracking systems as capable of representing particulars that are behaviourally inaccessible to the organism.

3. The Information Link

3.1. Normal and Abnormal Information Links

Up to this point, I have been considering what is required of a system if it is to be characterized as representing particular objects. I would now like to consider how we should go about ascribing content to the devices produced by systems of this kind. A device produced by an object-tracking system will differ from a device issued by a feature-placing mechanism in that its content will depend on the identity of the object picked out by the device. An account of the content of such a device will need to answer two related questions. First, in any particular perceptual episode, which object does the system represent? And what is the nature of the information link linking the perceiver with the object perceived? These questions may look familiar: they concern the problems of distance and deviance that plague the causal theory of perception.[12]

I will illustrate these problems using the example of the cheetah's visual system. Suppose that the system is capable of producing a device (I_A) that would normally be prompted by the sight of an antelope drinking at a waterhole. We need to set out the circumstances under which an instance of I_A will represent a particular object in the cheetah's environment. A simple suggestion might be that an instance of I_A will represent whichever object is causally responsible for the production of that instance of I_A. The problems of distance and deviance demonstrate that this simple answer will not do.

The deviance problem concerns the nature of the causal chain that links the perceiver with the object perceived. Imagine that a cheetah, drowsy from a

---

[12] See especially Grice (1961), Goldman (1977), Lewis (1980), and Davies (1983).

tranquillizer dart, is facing an antelope that is drinking at a nearby waterhole. The cheetah catches the antelope's scent and hallucinates an antelope similar in appearance to the one standing nearby. Indeed, suppose that the hallucination occurs because the antelope's scent, in conjunction with the tranquillizer, prompts the cheetah's visual system to issue an instance of I_A. In this situation, it will be true that the antelope causes the production of an instance of I_A; but it will not be true that the cheetah is seeing the antelope.

The distance problem concerns the length of the causal chain linking the perceiver and the object perceived. Suppose that, on a different occasion, the presence of an antelope at the waterhole causes the cheetah's visual system to produce an instance of I_A; and suppose that the antelope is there partly because the heat of the sun has made it thirsty. In this case, both the antelope and the sun are causally responsible for the production of I_A. We need to explain why the cheetah should be described as seeing the antelope, but not the sun. The distance problem is, of course, just a special case of the distality problem considered in Chapter 5, and my response to it depends on the solution to the distality problem that I proposed there.

In order to solve these problems, we need to make an appeal to the normal workings of the cheetah's visual system. If we want to know just what kind of causal relation a particular perceptual mechanism is supposed to produce, we must determine exactly which causal features of the link help to explain the success of the mechanism's ancestors. This is because the system will be operating normally only when it produces states that are causally related to the world in just that way. In other words, the information link must be of the kind normally exploited by the system in producing perceptual states.

What we need to consider, then, is which features of the information link exploited by a perceptual system help to explain why earlier systems of the same kind survived. The obvious place to start is with the general physical form of the link. The fact that visual systems are sensitive to features of light reaching the organism, for example, will help to explain their success because the properties of light make it an appropriate source of information about certain properties of objects such as their location and size. The general physical form of the link will be an unvarying feature of any particular perceptual system.

But we can also make the explanation more detailed, by appealing to specific features of the link to explain how it succeeded in conveying a particular message to the perceiver. The link will have this capacity in virtue of physical features (for example, the wavelengths of the light) that may vary from occasion to occasion. These variations will depend in part on the properties of the objects in the perceiver's environment. It is in virtue of these dependencies that the link is able to carry information about those objects, and to convey that information to the perceiver. I will refer to these specific features of the link as its informative features.

In distinguishing between the general physical form of the link and its specific informative features, I do not wish to imply that there are two distinct kinds of explanation for the system's success. There is simply a vaguer and a more detailed version of the same explanation. But it is sometimes helpful to treat them as providing two distinct tests of normality, one easier and one more demanding. This is because the most obvious problem cases of distance and deviance fall at the first hurdle without getting anywhere near the second. For this reason, I will phrase my proposal as follows: what will count as a normal information link for a given system will be an information link that has *not only* the same general physical form *but also* the same informative features as the information links used by ancestors of that system. The suggestion will be that for a perceiver to perceive a given object she must be linked to that object by an information link that is normal in both these respects. How can we distinguish between a normal and an abnormal information link? I will attempt to get clearer about this question by considering some problem cases involving vision.

A group of conservationists have set up a cinema screen at the edge of a wildlife reserve, on which they are showing a group of tourists scenes of an antelope at a waterhole, via a live video link-up. Chester, a cheetah, is lurking nearby, watching the shapes on the screen. Nearer the waterhole, Chester's brother Chase is looking towards the same antelope through the newly cleaned windows of a jeep. The visual systems of both cheetahs, let us suppose, respond by producing an instance of I_A.

All these cases differ to some degree from what we might think of as a standard case of vision, where a cheetah is standing directly in front of an antelope. What we need to consider is whether these differences should lead us to conclude that any or all of these cases involve an abnormal information link. If so, we will be committed to the view that, in these cases, what the cheetah sees is not the antelope, but the image of an antelope on a cinema screen or on the surface of a sheet of glass.

It is easy to see why someone might suppose that the information links involved in all these cases should be classified as abnormal. It is a natural assumption that the cheetahs' evolutionary ancestors did not encounter cinema screens or clear plates of glass. It is important to remember, however, that normality is an explanatory, not a statistical, notion. What counts as normal or abnormal depends on the explanation for the success of the device, not the circumstances under which the device is usually successful.[13] So it would be illegitimate to argue that, because cases in which Chase's ancestors benefited from the operation of their visual systems did not usually involve plates of glass, such cases will not count as cases of vision on this account. What we

---

[13] For example, it may be a statistically normal feature of the workings of our visual systems that they exploit light that originally came from the sun. But this would count as a normal feature of our visual systems only if it helped to explain their success.

need to consider is how we should explain the success of Chase's visual system in producing a device that was appropriate to his environment: can this success be explained in the same way as the success of his ancestor's visual systems on those occasions on which they helped their possessors to survive?

In what follows, I will assume that the cheetahs' evolutionary ancestors did not benefit from the workings of their visual systems in encounters with cinema screens or windows; but that they did sometimes benefit in encounters with objects separated from them only by air or by water. I will also assume that, in these standard or rewarded cases, the successful operation of the visual system may be explained partly by the fact that the light reaching the cheetah's eyes conveyed accurate information to the cheetah's visual system about some object in the environment; and that this can be explained in turn by certain properties of light—for example, that it does not spontaneously vary in wavelength and that it travels by the quickest route.

This explanation will also depend on the fact that the air or water that separates the cheetah and the object is transparent to visible light. The fact that visible light passes through these substances has to do with the way in which it interacts with the electrons of which they are partly composed. When light in the visible range meets air or water, it causes the electrons to oscillate; because they are not able to absorb light in the visible range, they give out light at the same wavelength as the original light. The way in which the electrons are arranged ensures that only light travelling in the same direction as the original light continues on, so that the path of the light overall is straight.

It seems quite clear that, on this account, Chester should not be described as seeing the antelopes. Although the information link as it passes from the antelope to the film crew's camera, and from the screen to Chester's eyes, is perfectly normal, there is a significant stretch in between where this is not the case. On this stretch of the link, information about the antelope's appearance is carried by an electrical current and by radio waves. To explain how Chester recognizes the antelope, we will have to refer, not only to the properties of the light scattered by the antelopes, but also to the properties of the electrical current and the radio waves that travel from the photoelectric plate inside the camera to the cinema screen. This explanation will not approximate to a normal explanation for the operation of the cheetah's visual system, and so Chester's visual state will not be connected to the antelope by a normal information link.[14]

Many of the standard problems of deviance and distance in the literature may be treated in this way. Cases involving mad scientists, evocative odours,

---

[14] It is easy to see why we find it natural to extend our core conception of vision to cover this kind of case: after all, the information link is perfectly normal at the beginning and at the end, and the information carried by the television system concerns just the same features of the environment as the information that our visual system normally exploits.

or holograms centre on causal chains that introduce abnormal (that is, non-optic) forms of information transmission. Hence, the subjects in these cases cannot be said to see the object at the beginning of the causal chain.

We can apply the same principle to Chase, who sees the antelope through a window. In this situation, the information link connecting Chase and the antelope is perfectly normal. When we explain why the light reaching Chase's eyes had the properties that it had, we can tell just the same kind of story as in the rewarded case. Light passing through glass retains its properties for just the same reason as light passing through air or water: the electrons in the glass give out light at the same wavelength as the light that reaches them; and they are arranged in such a way that the light continues on through the glass. In this case, then, the route by which the light from the tree reaches Chase's eyes is perfectly normal, and we can conclude that Chase sees the antelope.

Both these cases turn on the requirement that the information link connecting the perceiver with the object should be normal in its general physical form. I have not yet considered a case in which an information link meets this requirement, but fails the requirement that the specific informative features of the link should also be preserved in the normal way. It is possible to find cases where the link meets the first requirement but fails the second.

Suppose that a third cheetah, Charlie, has wandered into an abandoned chapel built by some eccentric in the middle of the wildlife reserve. Charlie is looking in the direction of a young zebra. But interposed between Charlie and the zebra is a door made of small panels of rippled and multicoloured glass. As he looks towards the door, Charlie sees a pattern of colours and shapes. This pattern carries the information that there is a zebra beyond the door, but it does not convey this information to Charlie's visual system: none of the informative features that Charlie's visual system would normally exploit in recognizing the presence of a zebra (or even a solid, middle-sized object) is present. We cannot say, in this case, that Charlie is seeing the zebra but mistaking it for an insubstantial pattern of light. Even if the incoming light were to have an unusual effect on Charlie's visual system, causing it to register a zebra, we should not conclude that Charlie sees the zebra. Even though the information link is normal in general physical form (that is, it is made up of light in the visible spectrum), this is not true of the specific informative features of the link.

3.2. Getting it Wrong

In the previous section I argued that an organism can be said to perceive an object only if the information link between them is working normally. One question that might be raised at this point is whether this should be taken to imply that an organism will not be able to make a mistake about an object that it is perceiving, unless there is something abnormal about the operation of its perceptual system. As we have seen, a perceptual system will succeed in identifying an object on a particular occasion only if it locates that object and recognizes it as possessing certain features. In this section, I would like to investigate whether this implies that a perceptual device produced on a particular occasion will succeed in identifying a particular object only if it recognizes it and locates it *correctly*.

It might be thought that this will indeed follow from the account that I have proposed. This is because it could be argued that the information link connecting the perceptual system with some object in the environment will be working normally only if the perceptual devices that it triggers are able to benefit the organism in the normal way. But the perceptual system normally benefits the organism only by producing devices that are correct. If the perceptual system were to produce a device that was incorrect, the informational relation that it bears to the environment will be abnormal. Hence that device will fail to identify any particular object.

This argument is based on a misunderstanding. It is perfectly possible for a perceptual system to produce a device on the basis of a normal information link, even though that device fails to recognize or locate that object correctly. The mistake may arise, not from a failure in the information link, but from the fact that the system is itself lacking in discriminatory power. For example, consider a situation in which an object appears misplaced owing to the refraction of light by water. In this case, the device will carry information of a kind that has, in the past, enabled the system successfully to locate the object from which the information derives. And to this extent it will succeed in identifying that object: it is partly by providing information of just this kind that these devices characteristically contribute to the successful operation of tracking systems. But the locational information conveyed by the device will be misinformation for the system. Hence the device will fail to locate the object correctly.

What this suggests is that, when a perceptual system identifies a particular object, it must at least represent that object as spatially located; it must at least *mis*locate it. It is only when this is the case that the system exercises its capacity to provide spatial information about some object and so satisfies the second requirement. This requirement leaves it open that an organism might be able to pick out an object seen under water, say, that appears misplaced owing to the refraction of light. I think that this is a plausible result. As Peacocke (1983: 153, 170–1) points out, we are often unable to judge the distance of objects when they are far away. There certainly seems to be no temptation to conclude that we are unable to see the object in such cases.

The same point will apply to the non-spatial information carried by the device. All that is required is that the system should recognize the object as having some set of features or other, not that it should recognize the object correctly. The information on which the recognitional component of the device is based may not be adequate to discriminate the kind of object that the system represents from all other kinds of object. Hence, the device may succeed in conveying recognitional information to the system and yet be incorrect.[15]

But this is not the only situation in which an organism may make a mistake about an object that it is perceiving. Consider the case of a cheetah looking at a distant herd of animals through a heat haze. Through the haze, some of the information about the animals' colouring is lost, so, although the animals are in fact zebras, they look like wild asses to the cheetah. The light that reaches the cheetah's eyes carries the information that those are equine creatures; and this information reaches the cheetah in a perfectly normal way. But the information that those creatures are striped has been lost, so that the information that the cheetah does receive is misleading.

This prompts the following question: can we allow that a certain amount of information might be lost, or retained only in an abnormal way, along the information link? There are a number of different answers that might be given to this question. For example, someone might take a maximalist approach, and insist that all the information that the organism would normally need if it is to recognize and locate the object correctly must have been conveyed to it in the normal way. On this view, there will be very little room for the perceiver to be in error about the object that she perceives. In contrast, someone might take a minimalist approach, and require only that the organism must be able to get something right (the general shape or colour of the object, say, or its approximate location) on the basis of information that reaches it in the normal way.

The argument so far suggests that we should adopt neither of these approaches. Rather, we should adopt a *selective* approach. We should argue that an organism may perceive an object only when it has received, in the normal manner, a certain *kind* of information from that object: that is, the information that it requires to discriminate that object *as* a spatially located, stable object of some kind. This is a very weak condition. It certainly leaves ample room for an object to be misrecognized and mislocated owing to loss of information, or for a perceived object to be correctly recognized or located on the basis of information that has been transmitted in an abnormal way.

This can be made clearer by considering two contrasting examples.

(1) Chester is wandering near a lake in a heavy morning mist; nearby a flamingo is feeding. The light from the flamingo is so diffused by the mist that

---

[15] My position here can be contrasted with Evans's account (1982) of perceptual judgements. Evans allows that the subject may misrecognize the object she identifies; but he insists that she must locate it correctly. Once again, this requirement is prompted by Evans's epistemological concerns: the subject must know which object she is identifying— she must think of it as 'that object located there'. If there is no object at that location, there is no object that she has succeeded in identifying.

all Chester can make out is a shapeless pink glow. The light reaching Chester's eyes carries some information about the flamingo—that it is pink—in the normal way, but there is nothing in the features of the light reaching his eyes that would convey to him, in the normal way, the information that there is a bounded, stable, trackable object through the mist. On this account, Chester cannot be said to see the flamingo.

(2)   Chase is also wandering in the mist. He can make out, not a coloured glow, but a shadowy shape, whose outline changes as he moves. There may be enough information for Chase to recognize (rather than infer) that there is some object ahead of him in the mist, even though he is not in a position to recognize it as anything more specific than, say, a potential obstacle. In this case, the suggested conditions for perception do hold, though only just.

If this is correct, there are two ways in which a perceptual tracking system may make a mistake about a particular object without itself operating in an abnormal fashion. First, it may mislocate or misrecognize the object as a result of a lack of discriminatory power in the system itself. Secondly, some of the information reaching the system may be lost or carried in an abnormal way, so misleading the system. In order to count as identifying an object on a particular occasion, all that is required is that the system should at least *mis*locate and *mis*recognize that object and that it should do so on the basis of information that reaches it in the normal way.

3.3. *The Information Link: Summary*

In order to count as representing a particular object (say) on a certain occasion, the system must be linked to that object by an information channel of the kind normally exploited by the system. This normal information channel must carry information sufficient to allow the system to recognize its source as a bounded, stable object. This allows plenty of scope for the system to be wrong about the object that it is representing, even on occasions when the system is itself operating normally. The system may be misled by the information it receives, either because the system is lacking in discriminatory power, or because important information has been lost or distorted along the way.

8

Making Maps and Forming Plans

1. Introduction

In previous chapters, we have encountered a number of intentional systems to which some form of spatial content may be ascribed. These included systems that operate by registering the presence of some feature or object at some location relative to the organism's body; and systems that are capable of keeping perceptual track of particular places. In this chapter, I would like to consider a system that is capable of a rather more sophisticated form of spatial representation: that is, a system that enables the organism to find its way about by forming a *topographic map* of the surrounding environment.

I have two reasons for investigating the workings of a system of this kind. The first is that a topographic mapping system will possess a number of abilities that we have not encountered before. In particular, I will argue that it is able to identify particular places in a way that is quite distinct from the capacity to keep perceptual track of them. I will also consider what is involved in planning a route from one place to another; and I will examine Peacocke's claim that an organism that possesses a topographic mapping system must be able to represent itself.

My second reason for examining the operation of a topographic mapping system is that a number of the issues raised by such systems will be important in the next part of the book. One of the purposes of this chapter is to introduce some ideas and to raise some questions that will be explored in more detail later on.

2. Making Maps

2.1. *Frames of Reference*

To talk about a space is to talk about a set of locations relative to a frame of reference. This is why I can truthfully say that I have stayed in the same place for the last five minutes, even though the chunk of Planet Earth on which I am sitting is moving through space at the rate of 30 kilometres per second. My statement is true because, by 'the same place', I mean the same place, relative to the surface of the earth. A great deal has been said about frames of reference in the recent literature on spatial representation, and a number of writers have stressed the need to clarify the terminology we use to classify different kinds of frame. In this section, I would like to explain the terminology that I intend to use here.

One type of frame of reference that we commonly use is one that is centred on our bodies, or some part of the body such as the head or the hand. For example, we identify a location in this way when we identify it as 'just to my left' or 'a few inches in front of my nose'. I will refer to this type of frame of reference as a *body-centred frame*. Sometimes this kind of frame is called an *egocentric frame*; but recently John Campbell (1994: 8–16) has suggested that we ought to distinguish between the notion of a body-centred frame and the notion of an egocentric frame. He suggests that it would be more helpful to reserve the term 'egocentric' for a frame of reference that has an immediate connection with the organism's behaviour. What is important about an egocentric frame of reference is that the organism does not have to orient itself with respect to such a frame in order to act: for example, I do not have to find out which way is straight ahead before I reach out for something that I can see ahead of me. My understanding of what it is for something to be at a certain egocentric location is inextricably linked with my knowledge of how to reach it. Campbell points out that, although an egocentric frame of reference will tend to be a body-centred one, the two do not always coincide. It might be suggested that an experienced car driver operates with an egocentric frame of reference centred on her car rather than her own body. Conversely, a woman who is trying to trim her fringe while looking in a mirror could be described as using a frame of reference that is body-centred, but not egocentric. To describe a frame of reference as body-centred is to say something about which spatial properties are being represented; to describe a frame as egocentric is to say something about the role of those spatial representations in the subject's psychology.

A body-centred frame of reference individuates locations in relation to some privileged object—namely, the organism's body. It is also possible to individuate locations by their relation to some other privileged item. For example, it would be possible to have a frame of reference that centred on some salient object, such as the organism's nest. The term 'allocentric' has sometimes been used to describe this kind of frame, but Campbell (1994: 20) suggests that we should reserve this term for a rather more sophisticated form of spatial representation, one that underpins an objective conception of the world. For this reason, I will call this kind of frame a *landmark-centred frame*.

Finally, it is possible to have a frame of reference that is not centred on any particular object or point: within a frame of this kind, the identity of each location is determined by its spatial relations to every other location. A frame of this kind provides a space that is independent of the objects and features located in it: any object may move around within the space, and any object located there may be removed without changing the nature of the space. We would expect a space of this kind to be made up of locations that are static relative to each other, such as points on the surface of a planet, or inside a car. The frame of reference will be relative to the planet or the car, but it will not be centred on something. For this reason, I will refer to a frame of this kind as a *centreless frame*. In a centreless frame, locations are individuated by their position in a network of locations, and not by their relation to some privileged object.

2.2. *Navigational Systems*

It is possible to envisage many different types of navigational system. One way in which navigational systems may differ from each other is with regard to the frames of reference they employ. In this section, I will introduce a number of navigational systems that operate with different frames of reference. By contrasting the topographic mapper with these other navigational systems we will get a clearer idea of what is distinctive about a system that employs a topographic map.

The perceptual tracking system discussed in the previous chapter enabled the organism to find its way to a place by locating it within a body-centred frame of reference. At this point, however it will be more helpful to contrast the topographic mapping system with two systems that operate with a landmark-centred frame: a *route mapper* and a *vector mapper*.

A route mapper operates by learning a route from one location in the environment to another, using a series of landmarks along the way. The route map will record the appearance of each landmark, together with the direction, and perhaps the distance of the next landmark along the route. Hence, we may characterize the system as operating with a landmark-centred frame of reference; or, to be more precise, a series of landmark-centred frames, one for each landmark on its journey.[1]

---

[1] There may be systems that represent routes, not as a sequence of landmarks and goals, but as a series of landmarks and bodily movements. Such a system would operate

Route maps are simple and easy to use, but they also have serious limitations: a route map tells you how to get from one place to another, along a particular route. If the route is blocked, a route map will not help you to get around the obstacle. Route maps are not reversible: a route map tells you how to get from A to B; it does not tell you how to get from B to A. If I were to give you a second route map that specified how to get from A to C, the two routes might overlap for some of the way. But there would be no way to record this fact on the maps that I had given you. Nor would possession of the two maps tell you how to get from B to C.

In this respect, a route map may be contrasted with a vector map. A vector mapping system is a system that locates significant items or features by recording their spatial position relative to some landmark or configuration of landmarks. O'Keefe (1993) has suggested that rats locate significant features of their environment in relation, not to an object, but to a geometrical point— the geometrical centre, or *centroid*—of the distribution of landmarks in their environment. As long as the rats are able to estimate their own position relative to the centroid, they will be able to calculate a direct route to any of these features.

The vector mapper, then, will exhibit a kind of flexibility that the route mapper lacks: it will be able to reach any location represented on its map from any starting point. Nevertheless, it still suffers from a significant limitation. As Campbell (1994: 81) points out, when a vector mapper calculates a route to any given location, the only information that it is able to exploit is information about the position of that location; it is not able to call on information about the area through which its route will lie. For example, it will not be able to select a more indirect route in order to avoid an obstacle or a predator. The space represented by the vector mapper consists of a collection of discrete locations, rather than a continuous expanse within which those locations lie.

A topographic mapping system differs from the vector mapper and the route mapper in two ways. First, it operates with a centreless frame of reference. On a topographic map, no one point has a privileged position: the identity of each point is dependent on its relations to all the others. Secondly, a topographic mapping system will create its map by fitting features and objects into a preconfigured representational space. As a result, the topographic mapping system will be able to represent not only the locations it has visited, but also the locations in between. It will be open to the topographic mapper to make inferences about how things are at those locations, or to plan a route that would take the organism to a place that it has not visited before. The

by learning a series of conditional responses of the form 'When condition C obtains, move in way W'. A system of this kind does not need to represent the spatial relations between the landmarks that it uses: hence, although it can be described as learning a route, we could not describe it as using a route *map*.

space represented by a topographic map is continuous in a way that the space represented by other navigational systems is not.

Of course, it would be possible for a navigational system to operate with a centreless frame of reference without representing space as a continuous expanse. A system of this kind would operate by recording the relative spatial relations of the places that it visited without possessing the ability to represent the places in between. The system would not treat any of these locations as having a privileged status. But it would be able to represent only a limited set of locations and the spatial relations between them. In what follows, I will refer to this kind of map as a *network map.*

It is clear that a topographic mapping system will constitute a very powerful and flexible navigational system. Once the system has recorded the locations of significant features and objects on its map and determined the organism's current position, it will be able to compute the most efficient route to any of those features or objects. It will be able to record routes that it learned while building up its map. But, once its map is complete, it will be able to reverse a route, modify a route that has been blocked, or use information about the spatial relations between different routes to plan an efficient journey between a number of different resources. The system will be able to design a route that takes account of information about hazards or obstacles encountered on previous occasions.

Adrian Cussins (1990, 1992) characterizes the kind of flexibility exhibited by a topographic mapper as involving a form of *perspective-independence.* According to Cussins, a navigational system will operate in a maximally perspective-independent way if it is able to reach any location in the environment from any starting position. A route mapping system will operate in a relatively perspective-dependent way, because it is capable of guiding the organism only to a particular goal and from a particular starting point. A system that uses a vector map or a network map will exhibit a greater degree of perspective-independence, because it is able to guide the organism from any starting point in the environment to any location represented on its map. But not all locations in the environment will be represented on its map: it will represent only locations that it has located relative to the landmark or landmarks on which the map is centred.

A topographic mapping system, on the other hand, will be a maximally perspective-independent system. Because the topographic mapper operates by fitting locations into a preconfigured representational space, any location in the environment will correspond to a point on the map, whether the organism has visited that location or not. Moreover, there are no locations to which the system gives privileged status: any point on the map may be treated as a starting point, as a goal, or as a landmark.

2.3. *Locating the Organism*

Any mapping system that uses a frame of reference that is distinct from its egocentric frame must have some way of translating information about locations on its map into information about locations within its egocentric frame. Otherwise it will not be able to use its map to guide the organism's behaviour. Usually, this will mean that the system will need to determine the location of the points that it has recorded on its map in relation to the organism's body; or, to put it another way round, it will need to discover where the organism is located on its map. And, of course, the system will also need to do this if it is to make use of perceptual or kinaesthetic information to determine the spatial relations between the locations on the map.

There are three different ways in which a topographic mapping system might try to determine the organism's position on its map: it might try to keep track of some landmark that it can currently perceive; it might use dead reckoning to estimate the organism's location relative to some point that it has visited; or it might recognize some location by its appearance. There are situations in which the system will have nothing more to go on than the appearance of the organism's surroundings: situations in which the system's tracking or dead reckoning systems have malfunctioned, or in which the organism has been displaced by some external force, such as a strong wind.

Whenever a topographic mapping system recognizes a location in this way, its identification will answer not only to information about the appearance of the organism's surroundings, but also to information about the spatial relations that the location bears to other locations on the map. This is because a topographic mapping system will normally operate by building up a consistent and stable map of the organism's environment. To do this, it needs to be able to distinguish between different places that have the same appearance; and it must allow for the possibility that the appearance of a place may alter over time. It follows that, when a topographic mapping system recognizes a location as a location that the organism has visited before, it would not be appropriate to describe the system as simply registering that the organism is at a certain *type* of place—for example, a place that has a certain type of appearance. The system must be described as reidentifying a particular place.

Of course, a topographic mapping system will not always need to make use of spatial information when it reidentifies a place. In a situation in which the organism has lost its way, it will have to rely entirely on information about the place's appearance, at least in making an initial reidentification of a familiar-looking place. What is important is that the reidentifications made by the system should normally be answerable to information about the spatial relations that the place bears to other recognizable places—that the system should normally reassess any reidentification thrown into doubt by recalcitrant spatial information. To this extent, any such system must work by forming hypotheses about the identities of places that it encounters that can be confirmed or disconfirmed by subsequent encounters.

The capacity to reidentify places from encounter to encounter distinguishes the topographic mapper from the vector mapper. This is because the vector mapper operates by locating resources or hazards relative to a single, privileged landmark or point. There is nothing the system can do to record the spatial position of the landmark itself, and so there is no information that the vector mapper can use to distinguish its landmark from an item of similar appearance. For this reason, a system of this kind will represent its landmark as an item of a certain type.

However, the topographic mapping system will not be the only mapping system that will be able to reidentify particular places. A network mapper will also be able to call on information about the spatial position that a place bears to other locations on its map in order to distinguish two places that have a similar appearance, or to reidentify a place that has altered its appearance. Indeed, a route mapping system might also be able to make use of spatial information in this way.

It is important to bear in mind that the capacity to reidentify places from encounter to encounter is quite independent of the capacity to keep perceptual track of a particular place during a single encounter: these are two quite different ways of representing particular places. One important distinction between these two capacities is that a topographic mapping system will be able to represent a place that it has encountered in the past but that it cannot currently perceive. It will do so whenever it remembers that there is some resource or hazard located at that place or plans how best to reach or avoid it. The capacity to represent a particular item in its absence is a capacity that we have not encountered before. I will refer to this form of representation as *mnemic identification*.

It is tempting to compare mnemic identification with Evans's notion (1982: 268–98) of *recognition-based identification*. Evans suggests that we would be willing to describe a subject as thinking about a particular object if that subject would be able to recognize that object again, using information acquired in a previous perceptual encounter. He gives the example of a man thinking about a particular sheep in a flock. Even though the man is no longer looking at the sheep, his thought will succeed in picking out that sheep provided it carries a certain kind of information about it—that is, information that would enable the man to recognize the sheep if he saw it again. Similarly, the topographic mapper's ability to represent a particular place in its absence is grounded in a capacity to recognize places that it has encountered before. I will bear Evans's discussion of recognition-based identification in mind in giving an account of mnemic identification.

2.4. *Mnemic Identification*

As we have seen, the capacity of a topographic mapping system to mnemically
identify a particular place will be grounded (in some way) in a capacity to reidentify that place when it encounters it again. This suggests that we should
begin by considering what will normally be required of a topographic mapping system when it reidentifies a particular place.

In the previous chapter, I characterized a number of requirements that a
tracking system must meet if it is to succeed in identifying a particular object
or place. Although I have emphasized that the capacity to reidentify a place
from encounter to encounter is independent of the capacity to keep perceptual track of a place, I take it that the exercise of this capacity will answer to
the same kinds of constraint. For this reason, my discussion at this point will
draw heavily on two principles established in the previous chapter.

The first principle could be expressed as follows: if an intentional system
is to count as perceiving a particular item of some kind, it must bear some
informational relation to that item. Moreover, this informational relation
must have the following property: the fact that devices produced by earlier
systems bore that relation to items of that kind helps to explain their success
in guiding the organism's behaviour. The second principle concerns the
nature of the rules that normally govern the way in which the system reidentifies particular places. We saw in the previous chapter that these rules
will have a crucial role to play in determining what kind of particular the
system may be said to represent.

When the system reidentifies a particular place as a place that it has encountered before, it will normally be relying on two different sources of information about that place: the information that it is currently receiving through the
organism's perceptual mechanisms and the information that it has recorded
during its earlier encounters with that place.

I will begin by considering the nature of the perceptual information on
which the system will normally rely. As we have seen, there are a number of
different kinds of information that a mapping system needs if it is to build
a map and use it to navigate: the system needs information about the
appearance of a place, which will help it to recognize a place when it encounters it again; and it must record information about resources, obstacles or
hazards to be found there. In other words it must be able to recognize particular places as having certain features. Finally, it must gather information
about the spatial relations that each place bears to other places in the environment. To do this, as we have seen, it must be able to determine where that
place is in relation to the organism. The perceptual information on which
earlier mapping systems relied, then, was information that enabled them to
recognize places and to locate them in within some frame of reference—
perhaps a body-centred frame.

As we saw in the previous chapter, it does not follow from this that a system will be able to perceive a place only if it succeeds in recognizing and locating that place. But it does imply that it must be receiving information that would at least allow it to misrecognize and mislocate that place. Moreover, this information must reach the system via an information link of the kind normally exploited by systems of this kind.[2] It is just because earlier mapping systems exploited information of this kind that they sometimes succeeded in guiding the organism through its environment.

Exactly the same principles will apply when we consider what will be required by the system if it is to remember a particular place. Once again, a system will succeed in remembering a particular place only if it is connected to that place by an information link of the kind that was exploited by earlier systems. The fact that earlier systems succeeded in guiding the organism's movements is explained by the fact that they stored information both about the features of particular places and about the spatial relations between places in the environment. Again, we can conclude that a mapping system will succeed in remembering a particular place only if it has stored, in the normal way, information that would allow the system to recognize (or misrecognize) the place and to locate it (or mislocate it) in relation to other places. It is possession of information of this kind that will sustain the system's capacity both to reidentify a place when it comes across it again and to represent that place in its absence.

We can now consider the nature of the rules that will normally govern the operation of the system. In the previous chapter, I argued that a tracking system will be competent to represent particular places only if the rules in accordance with which it normally operates reflect the spatio-temporal properties characteristic of particular places: they must embody the assumption, for example, that a place may alter its appearance over time, that each place will occupy a unique position in relation to other places, and that places will alter their position in relation to the organism only if the organism has moved. Exactly the same principle will apply to the workings of a topographic mapping system: such a system will be competent to map particular places only if the rules that characterize the way in which it builds and uses its map reflect assumptions of this kind.

If we compare this account with Evans's account of recognition-based identification, we will see that there is one important issue on which the two accounts will agree. But there is also a second issue on which my account of mnemic identification will diverge from Evans's account of recognition-based identification.

---

[2] In other words, the perceptual link on which the topographic mapper normally relies will be no different from the perceptual link on which a tracking system will normally depend.

The first issue—the issue on which the two accounts agree—concerns the utility of the system's memories about a particular place. I have already suggested that a topographic mapping system may succeed in remembering a place even though the information that it has recorded about that place is misleading for the system. This may occur if the perceptual information originally recorded by the system was misleading. But, as Evans points out, there is a second possibility: a system's memories about a particular place may become misleading as time passes, because the place itself has altered.

In his discussion of recognition-based identification, Evans (1982: 272–3) suggests that a subject's capacity to produce a recognition-based identification of an object may persist even after the object has changed so much that the subject would no longer be able to recognize it. Of course, the mapping system will usually be able to make use of information about the spatial relations that a place bears to other places in order to identify it, even when all the features previously found there have disappeared. But we can imagine situations in which the system is no longer able to locate a place in relation to the other places around it—perhaps because the whole area has changed. Nevertheless, the system's capacity to identify a particular place does not depend on its being able to recognize it again. As we have seen, what is required for a successful identification is that the information that the device carries about that place should be information of just the kind the system normally uses to re-identify particular places. This may be true, even though, on this occasion, the system will not be able to use that information to reidentify a place.

The second issue—the issue on which the two accounts diverge—concerns the ability of the topographic mapper to discriminate between different places in its environment. As we have seen, some of the information about a particular place stored by the mapping system will be information that would normally allow the system to reidentify that place if it encountered it again. But the teleologist should not insist that the system should be able to discriminate that place from all other places in its environment. What is important is that the information stored by the system is the kind of information that might sometimes enable the system to reidentify a particular place, not that there should be any guarantee of success. In this respect, the mapping system's capacity to mnemically identify a particular place is not equivalent to the capacity that Evans describes. According to Evans (1982: 283), a system that is able to identify a particular object in a recognition-based way must be able to discriminate that object from all other objects in the subject's environment.[3]

---

[3] This suggestion is closely related to Evans's strong location requirement on demonstrative identification. Both suggestions are motivated by the idea that, if a subject is to understand a thought, that thought must identify its object uniquely. This kind of consideration is not relevant to our purposes here.

Of course, given that the topographic mapping system will normally be able to reidentify a particular place, not only on the basis of its appearance, but also by taking account of its spatial position in relation to other places the organism has visited, such a system will usually be able to discriminate between all the places that it can mnemically identify. But consider a mapping system belonging to an organism that has been trapped inside a maze that is made up of two qualitatively identical areas, symmetrically arranged: any place p in either area will have a counterpart in the opposite area, that is qualitatively identical to p, and that is surrounded by places that are qualitatively identical to the places around p. As soon as the system loses track of which area the organism is in, it will cease to be able to distinguish between any particular place and its counterpart.

Suppose that the organism has only just lost its way: this assumption allows us to discount the possibility that information from a particular place and information from its counterpart have become confused. Suppose that the organism, having lost its bearings, comes to a place that it recognizes, correctly as it happens, as place p. According to the teleologist, there is no reason to deny that the system has successfully reidentified p.

As always, what is important to the teleologist is what explains the success of the system in helping the organism to find its way about. As we have seen, it will be a part of this explanation that the place that the system reidentifies on the basis of stored information should have been the source of that information. And this is indeed the case in the situation that we are considering. On the other hand, the fact that the information would not have been sufficient to allow the organism to distinguish that place from its counterpart is irrelevant: the fact that, had the organism encountered the counterpart of p, it would have misidentified it as p has nothing to do with the explanation for the system's success in reidentifying p when it has actually encountered p.

It is this informational link that ensures that the system's reidentification is correct. This is possible even when the information contained within the link is no longer sufficient to discriminate between p and its counterpart in the opposite area. Of course, if the organism continues to lose its way, and begins to misidentify the places that it encounters, the two sets of information relating to the two places will eventually become confused. Once this has happened, it will no longer be the case that the fact that the organism successfully reidentifies a place can be explained by the fact that the information that the organism used in making its identification was derived from that place. In that situation, the organism's capacity to mnemically identify that place will be lost, and we will no longer be able to assign determinate content to the representations that the system produces. But, until this happens, the system will continue to be able to mnemically identify places in its environment.

In order to mnemically identify a particular place, then, a topographic mapping system need not be in a position to discriminate that place from all other places in the environment. Nor is it necessary that the system should continue to be able to recognize that place as time passes. The system simply needs to represent that place as having features of some kind and as having some spatial position; and it must do so on the basis of an information link of the normal kind.

2.5. *Making Maps: Summary*

A topographic mapping system differs from a route mapper or a vector mapper in that it operates with a centreless frame of reference. It differs from a network mapper in that it represents space, not as an array of discrete locations, but as a continuous expanse. As a result, an organism that makes use of a topographic mapping system will be able to display a high degree of flexibility in navigating its environment.

In order to make use of a topographic map, a navigational system must be able to place the organism on the map. To do this, the system must be able to recognize particular places as places that the organism has encountered before, using information about their appearance and their location relative to other places. For this reason, we can characterize a topographic mapping system as representing places as particular items. Moreover, unlike the tracking systems considered in the previous chapter, a topographic mapping system is able to represent places in their absence. I have labelled this form of representation mnemic identification. The capacity to mnemically identify a particular place is grounded in the capacity to make use of information about the appearance of a place and about its location relative to the organism. But this leaves room for the possibility that the organism might misrecognize or mislocate a particular place, and for the possibility that it might not be able to discriminate a place from every other place in the environment. Finally, in order to count as representing particular places, rather than particular items of some other kind, the mapping system must normally operate in accordance with a set of rules that reflect the spatio-temporal properties of places.

3. Places and Objects

3.1. *Representing a Continuous Space*

In this section and the next, I would like to consider two issues that have to do with the relationship between the capacity to represent places and the capacity to represent objects. In this section, I will consider Campbell's suggestion that the capacity to represent space as a continuous expanse rests on the capacity to represent physical objects. In the next section, I will consider the claim that the capacity to mnemically identify particular objects rests on the capacity to identify particular places.

A topographic mapping system will have the capacity not only to represent a place in its absence, but also to represent a place that the organism has never encountered. It can do this because it is able to identify places by their spatial relations to other places that it has visited. The system may plan a route to a place that it has not previously visited; or it might make inferences about how things are at such a place on the basis of information that it has gathered about places nearby. It is in virtue of possessing abilities of these kinds that the system may be said to represent space as a continuous expanse, rather than as a set of discrete locations. In this section, I would like to say something about this capacity.

Campbell (1993) has suggested that our capacity to represent a space as continuous rests on a capacity to represent physical objects moving about in space. As we saw in the previous chapter, Campbell holds the view that physical objects are characterized, not only by their spatio-temporal continuity, but also by a kind of causal unity, which consists in the fact that the state of the object at one time causally depends on its states at earlier times. When we represent physical objects as moving about in a space, we conceive of that space as having a similar kind of causal unity: when an object moves from one place to another, how things are at its current location will causally depend on how things were at the locations through which it moved. According to Campbell, it is because we conceive of physical objects as characterized by this kind of causal connectedness that we are able to conceive of space as continuous.

I believe that Campbell is right to suggest that the capacity to represent space as continuous will often rest on the ability to make inferences that depend upon the continuing identity of particular objects (or spatio-temporal particulars of some other suitable kind). But I would like to argue that this need not be the case. Moreover, even when this is the case, the system need not have the capacity to represent particular objects, but only the capacity to operate in accordance with some assumption that concerns some particular object in the environment.

In order to represent a place that the organism has never visited, the system must exploit information it has gathered at other places, together with certain expectations about the ways in which places may be spatially related to each other. These expectations will be reflected by the rules in accordance with which the system normally creates and uses its map. In addition, the system will operate in accordance with certain assumptions about the way in which features or particulars are distributed in its environment. For example, it might operate with the following assumption: *if the organism has encountered a predator at a certain place, it is likely that there will be predators at other places nearby*. A system that operated with this assumption would be able to infer from the fact that a predator was seen at place p that there is likely to be a predator in the area just north of p. The system will be able to make this inference, even though the organism has never visited the area just north of p.

Let us assume that this inference is correct, and that there is likely to be a predator in the area just north of p. Unless the mapping system is a mere guessing system of the kind described in Chapter 4, there will normally be some causal connection between the fact that the predator was seen at p and the fact that there is likely to be a predator just north of p. This causal connection might involve a single predator that has its lair at p, or it might involve a family of predators living together. It is because this causal connection exists that the presence of a predator at p carries the information that there is likely to be a predator in the area just north of p.

In this case, then, the system is able to make inferences of this kind because it operates in accordance with an assumption that reflects a conception of space as occupied by spatio-temporal particulars of a certain kind— that is, items that are characterized by the kind of causal integrity that Campbell describes. But the system may operate in accordance with an assumption of this kind without representing any particular object or family. All that is required is that the system should make inferences whose success normally depends on facts about the properties of some particular item. These inferences need not themselves concern particular items of any kind; they may be concerned with the distribution of a certain feature in the organism's environment.

Moreover, it is not clear that the kind of causal connection on which these inferences depend will always involve some physical object, or group of objects. There may be causal processes that are distributed across locations but that do not involve any particular item. For example, the system might operate with the assumption that the presence of smoke and heat at a certain place is likely to indicate the presence of fire further on. In this case, the causal connection does not involve the states of a single object or family, but how things are at the places themselves: how things are at one place causally depends on how things are at another. Moreover, the causal connection between these two places depends in part on the spatial relation between them. It is because this is the case that the system is able to exploit information about conditions at one place in order to infer how things are at some other place, identified only by its relative location.

If this is right, then the capacity to make inferences about places that the organism has never visited need not depend upon the capacity to represent particulars of some other kind. It may often be the case that the success of such inferences will normally depend on the existence of some causal connection involving a single object or group of objects. But what is crucial is that the system should operate in a way that reflects a conception of *places* as causally connected; the mutual causal connectedness of places is no less basic than the internal causal connectedness of physical objects.

3.2. *Mapping Objects*

In this section I would like to consider the claim that the capacity to reidentify an object encountered on an earlier occasion requires the capacity to reidentify places. The idea will be that an organism can distinguish between similar objects only on the basis of their spatial position. When an object is beyond the range of the organism's sensory mechanisms, the organism cannot do this by tracking the object. The only recourse left is for the organism to locate the object on a topographic map of space: the object can be reidentified as the object that the organism encountered before, only if its current location on the map is compatible with its location when it was last encountered.

But there is another possibility. This is that a system might be able to form a map that records the spatial relations holding between objects that it has encountered. Of course, this could not be a topographic map, as I have defined it: for objects do not make up a continuous expanse in the way that places do. But a system might produce a network map on which it had recorded the relative positions of objects in its environment.

In most cases, a map of this kind would be of little use to the organism, since objects tend to change their position relative to each other. However, it is possible to imagine an environment in which important resources cluster around a few, relatively static objects. For example, a turtle might spend much of its life visiting large banks of seaweed where it finds food and shelter. If these banks of seaweed tended to stay in the same place, or drift without changing their relations to each other, the turtle might well benefit from the capacity to form a network map recording their relative locations.

How could we distinguish a network mapper that represents particular objects from a network mapper that represents particular places? One possibility is that an object map might be characterized by a certain degree of elasticity: in other words, the system might normally be prepared to reidentify a bank as one that the turtle had visited before, even though there has been some slight alteration in its location since the turtle's last visit. But this is not essential: the system might assume that the seaweed banks are static. If the system does make this assumption, then we need to consider what explains the system's success. What is important is that, in this environment, the presence of a seaweed bank at a particular location explains the presence of food and shelter there: the two conditions do not merely coincide. If so, the fact that the system guided the turtle to the bank will provide a more immediate explanation of its success than the fact that it guided the turtle to the place occupied by the bank.

Nevertheless, this is not to deny that an organism that possesses a topographic map of its environment will be able to use that map in order to re-identify particular objects. But there are circumstances under which an organism might possess the capacity to mnemically identify particular objects without having the capacity to represent particular places.

3.3. Places and Objects: Summary

In the previous chapter, I argued that the capacity to represent particular objects does not depend on the capacity to identify particular places, but only the capacity to determine the relative spatial position of objects. I also argued that the capacity to represent particular places by perceptually tracking them does not depend on the capacity to represent particular objects. In the same way, the account, given in this chapter, of the capacity to reidentify a place makes no appeal to the capacity to reidentify some object located at the place: the place can be distinguished on the basis of its spatial relations to other places. Moreover, I have argued that the capacity to represent space as continuous does not depend on a capacity to represent particular objects moving through space. Nor does the capacity to reidentify a particular object encountered on an earlier occasion require the capacity to identify the particular place that it occupies. It seems, then, that, in the case of special-purpose systems, at least, the capacity to represent places and the capacity to represent objects are independent of each other.[4]

4. Some Further Issues

I will end this chapter by considering three further issues relating to topographic mapping systems: the capacity to plan routes; the capacity for self-representation; and the capacity to represent space in an objective way. These are all issues that will receive further attention in the final part of the book, when I turn my attention to general-purpose systems. I will begin with the capacity to plan routes.

4.1. Forming Plans

The plans made by a topographic mapper will be complex, in that they will specify a sequence of behaviours, that, when put together in the right way,

---

[4] Contrast Strawson (1959: 62). See also Wiggins (1963), Woods (1963), and Campbell (1994: 33–4).

will help to satisfy some goal. Topographic mapping systems are not the only systems that will be capable of forming complex plans. Any system that functions to put together complex patterns of behaviour in a way that is sensitive to the organism's current surroundings will be a system that produces complex plans. For example, consider the case of an organism that builds nests out of twigs. The organism might build its nest by a process of trial and error; but it might approach the task more methodically, using longer, stiffer twigs to build a framework and then weaving in shorter or more flexible twigs to fill in the gaps. Since no two collections of twigs will be the same, the system will do better if it plans how to make the best use of the twigs in the organism's possession. Its plan will be subject to certain constraints—such as the constraint that no one twig can be used twice. Like the topographic mapping system, this system will exhibit a level of perspective-independence, in that it will be able to reach its destination—a finished nest—from many different starting points. We can extend the analogy even further if we suppose that the system can plan to produce nests of different shapes and sizes depending on the circumstances. In this case, we can say that the system will be able to aim at any (possible) destination from any (possible) starting point.

The plans produced by these systems may, like the executive devices considered in Chapter 6, possess imperative content: they will do so provided that they represent, not a certain sequence of bodily movements, but a sequence of goals that must be translated into bodily movements by some executive mechanism.

In translating goals into bodily movements, executive mechanisms of the kind considered in Chapter 6 need to rely on information about the environment, together with certain assumptions that govern the way in which the system would normally modify the organism's movements in the light of that information. These assumptions do not need to be represented by the system; it is enough that the system operates in accordance with them. There are two reasons for this. First, these assumptions are stable; hence the organism does not need to register whether they obtain at any one time. Secondly, they have a highly restricted and predictable effect on the workings of the system. As a result, they can simply be built into the architecture of the system, either innately or through a process of learning.

A topographic mapping system will also have to operate in accordance with a certain set of assumptions in planning its routes. These will include assumptions about the way in which the organism's environment fits together—these will include spatio-temporal assumptions similar to those that govern the way in which the system creates its map. But, because a route involves a sequence of behaviours, they will also include assumptions about the way in which the organism's behaviour at one stage of the route will alter its circumstances later on. For example, the workings of the system will normally respect the assumption that, if the organism has left a certain place, then it is no longer at that place.

These assumptions differ from the assumptions that govern the workings of other systems in that they appear to be hypothetical in form. Nevertheless, like the other assumptions that govern the operations of the executive systems considered earlier, they do not need to be represented by the system, for just the same reasons. In the next chapter, we will encounter systems that do need to represent background assumptions that are hypothetical in form; but there can be planning systems that do not have this capacity.

4.2. *Self-Representation*

Peacocke (1992: 90–1) suggests that an organism that is capable of forming and using a topographic map of its environment will be capable of representing itself. In this section, however, I will argue that this is not the case. Indeed, I will go on to suggest that a teleological theory of content might be thought to face a difficulty in accounting for the possibility of self-representation.

I take it that Peacocke's reason for supposing that topographic mapping involves self-representation has to do with the fact that, in order to be able to form and use a topographic map, the system must be able to locate the organism on the map. I take it that Peacocke's thought is that, in locating the organism, the system produces representations of the form 'I am now at p'. But it is not clear that this is the case: up until now, I have simply assumed that the system will operate by identifying places and by registering their spatial position relative to the organism. In order to represent the position of a place in a body-centred frame, the system does not need to represent the organism's body at the centre of the frame. The organism can represent a place as being over there to the right, without representing it as being over there to the right *of the organism*. Again, it might be thought that, in order to plan a route, the system must be able to represent the organism as following that route. But, again, there is no reason to suppose that this is so: the system might simply represent a certain set of goals, without representing those goals as goals to be achieved by the organism.

This might prompt us to ask what is required for an organism to be capable of representing itself. So far, I have accepted the Strawsonian claim that, in order to be able to represent particulars of some kind, a system must be able to identify particulars of that kind and to discriminate them from other particulars of the same kind. It seems natural to apply the same criterion to the capacity for self-representation: in order to be able to represent itself, an organism must be able to discriminate itself from other objects. For example, an organism might count as representing itself if it were able to discriminate a situation in which a tree, say, is to the left of a boulder, and a situation in which a tree is to the left of the organism; and if, in doing so, it treated *being to the left of* as a relation that could hold either between the tree and some other item in the environment or between the tree and the organism itself. But this is not a capacity that a topographic mapping system needs to have. It might treat the spatial relations that places in its environment bear to each other and the spatial relations that places in the environment bear to the organism as two quite different sets of relations.

Indeed, we might wonder how a teleological theory of content could ever allow for the possibility that an organism might represent itself. For an organism to be able to represent itself, it must be able to discriminate itself from other items—for example, from other members of its family group. But the teleologist will insist that the organism will have no need to make this discrimination unless the success of some pattern of behaviour depends on it. But this possibility will arise only if the organism is capable of producing some pattern of behaviour that may be directed either at the organism itself or towards some other family member. But, if a pattern of behaviour is identified by its function, then it is hard to see how there could be a single pattern of behaviour that could be directed either at the organism itself or towards some other item in the environment.

For example, suppose that an organism could decide whether to groom itself or whether to groom its neighbour, depending on whether it represents itself or its neighbour as needing to be groomed. We might conclude from this that there is a property that the organism is able to represent as belonging either to itself or to its neighbour. But, if patterns of behaviour are functionally identified, grooming oneself and grooming another organism will be two very different patterns of behaviour: self-grooming and other-grooming. Self-grooming has the function to promote hygiene; other-grooming has the function to maintain good social relations. These two patterns of behaviour will be controlled by different intentional systems. Hence, there is no intentional system that is able to represent both the fact that the organism needs to be groomed and the fact that a neighbour needs to be groomed. There will be one system that may be able to discriminate between neighbours and will produce representations of the form 'that neighbour needs to be other-groomed' and another, quite separate system that will produce devices of the form 'self-grooming needed now'. Moreover, it seems reasonable to expect that behaviour that is directed towards the organism itself will always have a different function to behaviour that is directed towards other organisms. If so, it seems that there will never be an organism that is able to discriminate between itself and other organisms, thereby succeeding in representing itself.

If this is right, then we can conclude that a capacity to use a topographic map does not confer the capacity to represent oneself. Indeed we seem to be faced with a reason to suppose that, given a teleological theory of content, self-representation is impossible. Fortunately, there is an answer to this objection. But it does not lie with the special-purpose systems that we have been considering in this part of the book. We will only be able to answer this objection once we have introduced systems that are capable of general-purpose representation.

4.3. *Topographic Maps and Objectivity*

The representations produced by the mapping systems considered in this chapter will possess a form of objectivity denied to the tracking systems considered in the previous chapter: they will be able to represent places that the organism is not currently perceiving. For these systems, the presence of a certain item in the environment does not depend on its being immediately accessible to the organism.

Nevertheless, there is no reason to suppose that any of these systems will be capable of representing items that could not be reached by the organism. This will include items that were once accessible to the organism but that have become inaccessible over time, perhaps because the organism has aged, or because some impassable obstacle has appeared. Once again, the reason will be that, although these systems may be competent to represent inaccessible items, the fact that they possess this competence will never benefit the organism. Hence, although we can characterize the system as operating with rules according to which an item may continue to be present even though the organism can no longer access it, these are not the rules with which the organism normally operates.

For example, we can characterize a topographic mapping system as operating with the following rule:

L If a place l_1 bears some spatial relation R to a place l_2 at some time t, and if the organism is currently at l_2, then l_1 bears R to the organism's current location.

There would be no guarantee that representations generated in accordance with L would correlate with places that were behaviourally accessible to the organism. It follows that a system that normally operated in accordance with L would be able to represent places outside the organism's behavioural reach. But, in fact, it will always be open to us to treat the system as normally operating with another, more modest rule. Suppose that, at each point in the organism's life, it is possible to define a distance that is the maximum distance that organism will be able to travel in what remains of its lifespan. If so, we can represent the system as normally operating in accordance with the following rule:

L* If a place l_1 bears some spatial relation R to a place l_2 at some time t, and if the organism is currently at l_2, then l_1 bears R to the organism's current location, provided that l_1 can normally be reached from l_2 within what remains of the organism's normal lifespan.

For a system that normally operates in accordance with L*, an object or a place that has become inaccessible to the organism has simply ceased to exist: there is no such (accessible) item.

The same point will apply to the inferences that the topographic mapper is able to make concerning places it has yet to visit. Once again, we can characterize the system as operating with a rule that makes no mention of the accessibility of places that the system represents. But we will always be able to characterize the system as normally operating with a more modest rule, one that restricts the places that the system is able to represent to include only places that can be reached from the organism's current location. This rule reflects a more precise account of how earlier organisms benefited from the capacity to identify places that they had not visited. They benefited because this enabled them to make inferences about locations that they would one day be able to visit.

If so, the capacity to map places and objects in the environment brings with it a very modest form of objectivity: the ability to represent items that the organism cannot currently perceive and that are not within the organism's immediate behavioural reach. Nevertheless, the representations produced by these systems cannot be credited with the kind of objectivity required for truth as the realist conceives it.

4.4. Further Issues: Summary

In this final part of the chapter, I have considered some further issues related to topographic mapping systems. I began with the capacity to form complex plans. I argued that a planning system will operate with certain assumptions that are conditional in form; but I denied that these assumptions need to be represented by the system. I argued against Peacocke's claim that the capacity to use a topographic map involves self-representation, and I suggested that the teleological theory faces a prima facie difficulty in explaining how an organism could ever be ascribed the capacity to represent itself. Finally, I suggested that the representations produced by mapping systems will be marked by a certain kind of objectivity, in that they are able to represent particular items in their absence; nevertheless, they do not possess the kind of objectivity required for truth as the realist conceives it.

PART III

General-Purpose Systems

9

General-Purpose Intentionality

1. Introduction

In the final part of this book, I would like to turn my attention to more sophisticated intentional systems, systems that bear a closer resemblance to the human mind than the systems examined in Part II. In particular, I would like to investigate a proposal made by Millikan, who suggests that one distinctive feature of the human mind is that it is a *general-purpose* intentional system.

In an early paper, Millikan (1986: 72–3) suggests that, while less sophisticated states belong to systems that are dedicated to the satisfaction of a particular need or set of needs, our own beliefs and desires may be used to help to satisfy almost any need. As Millikan (1986: 72) puts it, 'no strictures beyond relevance (some semblance of logic) determine which beliefs and desires may interact with which to form new beliefs and desires or help to produce actions; beliefs are not hooked to certain uses and unavailable for others. Contrast the toad's belief that these are bugs, which is fixatedly hooked to its desire to eat bugs.' Millikan's claim suggests a picture of the human mind as a general-purpose intentional system—a system that is capable of bringing information and patterns of inference to bear on a range of problems relating to a wide variety of biological needs; perhaps even problems that relate to no biological need, but that concern idiosyncratic interests of the individual organism.[1]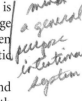

Millikan is not alone in distinguishing between special-purpose and general-purpose representation. Andy Clark and Annette Karmiloff-Smith (1993) offer an account of the process by which the information that guides a specific response is subsequently made available to serve a much wider variety of ends. Clark and Karmiloff-Smith differ from Millikan in that their aim is to offer an empirical account of how this transition takes place within a single organism, rather than to make a distinction between more and less

---

[1] In a later paper, Millikan (1989*b*) draws some further distinctions between primitive and sophisticated intentional devices.

sophisticated organisms. But it is the shared distinction between special- and general-purpose representation that is of interest here.[2]

I have two reasons for focusing on the distinction between special-purpose and general-purpose representation. First, I take it that the suggestion that human beliefs and desires are states of a general-purpose intentional system has some prima facie credibility. Nevertheless, a number of writers have suggested that a teleological theory of intentional content will not be able to allow for representational systems of this kind. If this objection were to succeed, it would be a serious blow to the teleological theory: it would suggest that the theory is unable to provide an account of precisely those intentional phenomena that are of greatest interest to us—namely, our own doxastic representations. I will attempt to rebut this objection in the next chapter.

Secondly, I would like to make a connection between this distinction and another, more familiar distinction—that is, the distinction between conceptual and non-conceptual content. A number of philosophers have argued that we need to make a distinction between conceptual representations—generally equated with our own doxastic representations—and non-conceptual representations—ascribed to more primitive intentional systems, such as the systems possessed by non-human animals or pre-verbal infants, or the perceptual and executive subsystems possessed by adult human beings. But there has been a great deal of disagreement about the nature and scope of the distinction.[3] A common suggestion, however, is that conceptual representations must meet a requirement, originally formulated by Evans and known as the Generality Constraint.

In this chapter, I will argue that there is an interesting connection between general-purpose representation and the Generality Constraint. This could be taken to suggest that the distinction between general-purpose and special-purpose representation has a role to play in helping us to understand the distinction between conceptual and non-conceptual representation.[4]

My purpose in this chapter is to investigate the distinction between special-purpose and general-purpose intentional systems. As usual, I will try to set out the minimal conditions a system must meet if it is to be classified as a system of this kind. Along the way, I will consider how the notion of general-purpose

[2] See also Stich (1978), Davies (1989), Sterelny (1990: 134), Bogdan (1994: 181), and Campbell (1994: 212–13).

[3] I cannot hope to do justice to the variety of positions to be found in the literature. For a range of suggestions, see Dennett (1978), Dretske (1981), Peacocke (1992), Cussins (1990, 1992), Martin (1992), and Bermudez (1995).

[4] Since the distinction between conceptual and non-conceptual representation is so controversial, I cannot say more than this. In particular, the suggestion that we should simply equate the two distinctions would not be acceptable to someone who held that there is a connection between conceptual representation and language.

intentionality relates to some familiar ideas in the literature, such as Fodor's distinction between modular and central systems.

I will begin by trying to make the distinction between special- and general-purpose systems a little more precise. This will turn out to be a rather more complicated task than one might expect. This is because there are at least two different features that an intentional system must exhibit if it is to count as a general-purpose system. I will label these two features *interest-independence* and *task-independence*, and I will dedicate a section to each.

2. In Search of General-Purpose Intentionality

2.1. *Interest-Independent Systems*

Millikan suggests that the frog's visual system may represent flies only as food; but a human being may represent flies as food, as frog bait, as nuisances, or just as objects of scientific curiosity. Indeed, there appear to be no limits to the way in which a human being may represent flies. This suggests that a general-purpose system is one that is capable of representing items or features in the environment in a way that is independent of some particular *context*. The first thing we need to do, then, is to investigate what the relevant type of context will be.

An obvious starting point is the idea that the frog's visual states are tied to a particular biological need—the need for food. In contrast, any belief that a human being might form about flies could, given sufficient ingenuity, be used to satisfy any basic biological need that the subject might possess. So one suggestion might be that we should think of contexts in terms of the organism's basic biological needs. But we have to be very careful here: although I have mentioned biological needs fairly frequently in this book, I have not yet said anything about how they are to be individuated. Until now, this question has not been important. But, if the suggestion is that general-purpose systems are systems that are capable of using representations in a way that cuts across the boundaries set by basic biological needs, then we need to give some indication of where those boundaries lie. Indeed, it might plausibly be argued that both frogs and humans have only one basic biological need—the need to produce fertile and healthy offspring. If so, the idea that humans are able to represent their environment in a way that is independent of a particular biological need will collapse.

For this reason, I would like to reject this initial suggestion. Instead, I will begin by focusing on the patterns of behaviour that the organism produces.

Any organism that is capable of representing its environment will be able to engage in certain activities: snapping at flies, threatening rivals, signing cheques, and so on. These behavioural patterns may be innate or they may be acquired during the organism's lifetime. Patterns of behaviour, so construed, are individuated by their functions, rather than by the bodily movements that realize them.

Behavioural patterns are sliced more thinly than needs: an organism may have a large number of different ways of satisfying a particular need. Nevertheless, patterns of behaviour cannot be cut infinitely finely: *moving halfway towards prey* may be something that an arrow worm does, but it will not count as a pattern of behaviour, because none of the bodily movements that the worm produces has the function to realize that behaviour. Conversely, there will be no danger that all behaviour will turn out to share the same function (helping the organism to reproduce, for example), because the ascription of a function to each pattern of behaviour will be governed by the independence condition.

The ability to engage in a certain pattern of behaviour could be said to generate certain sub-needs, which I shall refer to as *interests*. The frog needs food; but, given that it normally satisfies that need by catching flies, we can say that it has an interest in catching flies. Interests differ from basic biological needs in two important ways. First, they may be acquired during the organism's lifetime. Secondly, not all the interests that the organism develops will answer to its needs: when Freddie the rat learns to avoid dewberries because he mistakenly classifies them as poisonous, he acquires an interest—avoiding dewberries—that fails to protect him from ingesting poison.

My first suggestion is that a general-purpose intentional system must operate in a way that is independent of any particular interest or set of interests: there will be no particular set of interests that the system is supposed to serve. A number of the systems discussed in Part II could be characterized as operating in a way that is not tied to some particular interest. It is important to explain why these systems will not count as interest-independent in the required sense. By doing so, I hope to make the notion of interest-independence a little clearer.

To begin with, consider the example of a system that we might describe as a multi-purpose signalling system. This is a simple signalling system that functions to trigger a type of bodily movement that has a number of different functions. For example, suppose that, in eating a piece of fruit, the organism normally satisfies a number of different interests—its need for sugar, its need for water, its need for certain vitamins, and so on. The signalling system that controls this behaviour will also serve all these different interests. But the system will not count as operating in an interest-independent way: an interest-independent system is not simply a system that serves multiple interests. It is a system that is capable of serving any interest that the organism may acquire. In order to be sure that the range of interests served by an intentional system is a genuinely open-ended one, we need to be sure that it belongs to an organism that is capable of acquiring new interests through learning.

A more interesting comparison can be made with a system that is able to represent goals, for example, the bees' flight-planning mechanism, which was discussed in Chapter 6. We can describe this mechanism as controlling a single pattern of behaviour—*going to a nectar source*. But we could also describe it as controlling a range of different behaviours—*going to a nectar source at position p_1, going to a nectar source at position p_2,* and so on. Each flight will constitute a different pattern of behaviour, because each flight will have the function to take the bee to a different location. It might seem that the flight-planning mechanism exhibits at least a limited form of interest-independence, since it is able to control so many different patterns of behaviour.

Nevertheless, the flight-planning mechanism will not count as an interest-independent system in the intended sense. There are two reasons for this. The first is that, although the system is able to guide the bee to a very large number of different locations, the range of locations in the bees' repertoire is not an open-ended one. Secondly, although the system can be described as serving different interests on different occasions, it is possible to identify a single overarching interest—getting the bee to a nectar source—that the system as a whole functions to serve. When we are considering systems that are able to represent goals, we need to make a distinction between interests deriving from goals represented by the system on different occasions and the interests that are served by the system overall. The system will count as operating in an interest-independent way only if it cannot be described as serving a particular interest or set of interests overall.

This second point becomes particularly important when we consider the case of a topographic mapping system of the kind described in the last chapter. An organism might use a topographic mapping system to help it to locate a single type of resource—food, for example. Like the bees' flight-planning mechanism, this mapping system could be described as serving a single interest—the organism's need for food; or again, it could be described as serving many different interests—the need to get to place p_1 from place p_2, the need to get to place p_3 from place p_1, and so on. The mapping system differs from the bees' flight-planning mechanism in that it might control an open-ended range of behaviours. This is because a mapping system might be capable of learning about an indefinite number of places and of using that information to plan an indefinite number of routes. Nevertheless, so long as the system is used to locate a limited set of resources or hazards, it cannot be said to operate in an interest-independent way: so long as this is the case, it will be possible to describe the system as serving a specific set of interests overall.

A topographic mapping system, then, will not necessarily be a general-purpose intentional mechanism. Hence, the notion of interest-independence discussed here is not equivalent to Cussins's notion of perspective-independence introduced in the previous chapter. Perspective-independence concerns a system's flexibility in performing a particular task, whereas interest-independence concerns the system's flexibility in using information to help it to perform a range of tasks.

Finally, I would like to consider a perceptual system that belongs to an organism that is capable of developing new representational resources and new patterns of behaviour through learning. An example might be the olfactory system of the rat, which I discussed in Chapter 6. Once again, it might be tempting to describe this system as operating in an interest-independent way: the olfactory devices that it produces may come to serve many different interests over time, in a way that depends on the history of the individual organism. But, once again, we will come up against the fact that these devices are able to serve only a limited range of interests. This is because the learning mechanisms that make use of these devices are themselves special-purpose mechanisms. For example, the learning mechanism that ensures that the rat avoids eating food that in the past has made it sick has the function to prevent the rat from ingesting poisons. So long as the links between the organism's perceptual system and its executive mechanisms are controlled by a set of special-purpose learning mechanisms, the perceptual mechanism will continue to serve a restricted range of interests. And so it will not count as operating in an interest-independent way.

So far, I have characterized interest-independence in a negative way, by explaining why certain kinds of intentional system should not be regarded as operating in an interest-independent way. Later on, I will introduce some systems that can be regarded as interest-independent systems. We will find that the notion of interest-independence introduced in this section is in need of further clarification and refinement. In particular, I will argue that there are at least two grades of interest-independence, and that only systems that exhibit the higher grade will count as genuinely general-purpose intentional systems. But, first, I would like to introduce a second constraint that must be met by general-purpose intentional systems.

2.2. Task-Independent Systems

In the previous section, I argued that we should deny that the rat's olfactory system is a general-purpose intentional system on the grounds that it operates in conjunction with a special-purpose learning mechanism. But this leaves it open to us to classify our own perceptual subsystems as general-purpose intentional systems, on the grounds that our own perceptual states act as input to a general-purpose doxastic system. Yet philosophers commonly claim that there is a sharp distinction between perceptual and doxastic states. And many writers have found it natural to mark this distinction by stressing the commonalties between our own perceptual states and the perceptual states enjoyed by simpler organisms. If our own perceptual subsystems are classified as general-purpose intentional systems, we will be left wondering what this distinction is, and how it relates to the distinction between general- and special-purpose systems.

However, I would like to retain the idea that our perceptual systems are special-purpose systems, even though they operate in conjunction with a general-purpose doxastic system. They fail to be general-purpose systems, I would suggest, not because they operate in an interest-dependent way, but because they exhibit an analogous kind of context-dependence, which I will refer to as *task-dependence*.

A task-dependent system, like an interest-dependent system, will be a special-purpose system because the range of outcomes that it functions to produce is limited in a certain way. The difference between interest-dependent systems and task-dependent systems derives from the nature of the functions possessed by the two types of system. The functions performed by our perceptual subsystems are unlikely to bear much resemblance to the kinds of function performed by the sensorimotor systems possessed by simple organisms. This is because the former, unlike the latter, do not have direct control over the organism's behaviour. They control its behaviour only *via* the workings of the central, doxastic system. Hence, while the functions of the sensorimotor systems possessed by simple organisms will be tied directly to the creature's interests, this may not be true of the perceptual subsystems that operate in conjunction with a general-purpose doxastic system.

We classify the subsystems of the human visual system as line detectors, or edge detectors, or even human face recognizers, performing functions that might promote almost any interest. Nevertheless, these subsystems can be ascribed specific functions, individuated in terms of the informational tasks they normally perform. What I would like to suggest is that these systems will fail to count as general-purpose mechanisms because the representations that they produce will be used in a way that is tied exclusively to that informational task. The representations produced by my face recognition system, for example, will play a highly restricted, stereotypical role in my psychology—for example, to prompt beliefs about the identity of the person that I am looking at. In this respect, they contrast with the states of my doxastic system, which may enter into processes of reasoning in highly unpredictable ways.

In his much discussed book *The Modularity of Mind*, Jerry Fodor (1983) makes a rather different distinction between the workings of our central doxastic system and the workings of our perceptual and executive subsystems.[5] According to Fodor, these cognitive subsystems are characterized by a number of features: for example, they are dedicated to a particular task, their operation is mandatory and fast, and they exhibit characteristic and specific patterns of breakdown.[6] Most importantly, they are *informationally isolated modules*: in other words, although they may share computational resources, they have no access to a common pool of information. Conversely, other systems have no access to the information used by a particular module. The interface between these modular subsystems is provided by central doxastic systems. These central systems, Fodor argues, are non-modular: the mechanisms that govern belief fixation are able to draw on information in a way that cuts across cognitive domains.

Clearly there are some similarities between Fodor's distinction between cognitive modules and central systems and the distinction made here. Both distinctions trade on the idea that some systems, but not others, are restricted in the way in which they use the information available to the organism. But there is a crucial difference between the two distinctions. Fodor's distinction focuses primarily on the processes of belief *fixation*: the idea is that cognitive modules are unable to draw on certain kinds of information in representing the world. In contrast, the distinction made here focuses on the way in which the representations produced by different intentional systems are used in guiding the organism's behaviour.

Fodor argues that our perceptual subsystems are informationally isolated, in the sense that the representations produced by these subsystems are not inferred from our beliefs. The notion of task-independence is neutral on this matter. Whether a system counts as a general-purpose intentional system depends not on what sources of information it uses in producing its representations, but on what role those representations go on to play in producing new representations and in guiding behaviour. It might turn out that my beliefs about where I am have a strong effect on my ability to recognize a familiar face. But my face recognition system will continue to count as a task-dependent system, so long as the representations that it produces are excluded from playing the flexible role characteristic of beliefs. Of course, this is not to deny that Fodor might be right to claim that some or all of our perceptual and executive subsystems are informationally isolated modules. But whether these systems should be viewed as special-purpose or as general-purpose systems will not turn on the answer to this question.[7]

---

[5] For discussion of Fodor's view, see especially Shallice (1984), Marshall (1984), Cam (1988), Shannon (1988), and Bennett (1990).   [6] This is not an exhaustive list.
[7] Stich's earlier distinction between doxastic and subdoxastic states combines both ideas. According to Stich (1978: 507), subdoxastic states 'are inferentially impoverished, with a comparatively limited range of potential inferential patterns via which they can give

In the last two sections, I have argued that a general-purpose intentional system will be a system that is neither restricted to serving a limited range of interests nor confined to carrying out a specific informational task. Nevertheless, it is natural to view interest-independence as the crucial criterion: for, although interest-independence will not by itself distinguish between general- and special-purpose intentional systems, it will be both necessary and sufficient for an organism to be capable of general-purpose representation that it should possess at least one interest-independent intentional system. It is only when we have established that an organism meets this criterion that we need to apply the test of task-independence to determine which of its intentional systems are general-purpose systems. For this reason, I will continue to concentrate on the notion of interest-independence in what follows.

2.3. Integrated Systems: From Abel to Mabel

In this section, I will describe two systems that use interest-independent representations. I will argue that the first system exhibits only a limited form of interest-independence. For this reason, I will label this system a *first-order integrated system.* A first-order integrated system is a system that is normally able to use information about a certain category of items in order to help it to satisfy an indefinite range of interests relating to that category. A *higher-order integrated system,* on the other hand, is a system that is able to use information about a certain kind of item to help it to satisfy an open-ended range of interests relating to a range of different categories.

As an example of a first-order integrated system, I will use the imaginary case of Abel, an ape who lives in a forest, feeding on vegetation and insects. Like a chimpanzee, Abel uses twigs, which he gathers from trees and bushes, to make termite stickers. He is able to recognize suitable twigs by using visual information about their shape and colour, and tactile information that he gets by testing the twigs for strength and flexibility. As well as using twigs to make termite stickers, Abel also chooses strong and flexible twigs to make a nest each evening to keep him warm while he sleeps. In both cases, he strips the twigs of leaves before he uses them. Suppose, too, that Abel is capable of learning about twigs. Perhaps he is able to develop new ways of recognizing them or manipulating them. Again, he might be able to store general information

---

rise to beliefs and a comparatively limited range of potential inferential patterns via which beliefs can give rise to them'. Davies, on the other hand, treats these two forms of poverty as separate phenomena. See Davies (1989).

about twigs; for example, he might record the location of good sources of twigs on a topographic map of the area.

We might imagine that Abel operates with two quite separate representational systems—one relating to the twigs that he uses to make termite stickers (twigs$_1$) and one relating to the twigs that he uses to make nests (twigs$_2$). The two systems might use very different sensory and behavioural resources, or they might share the same resources on a kind of time-sharing basis: recognizing a twig as a twig$_1$ only when Abel is hungry; and recognizing a twig as a twig$_2$ only when he is ready to sleep. Whatever Abel learns about twigs$_1$ will be ignored when he is dealing with twigs$_2$; and he will operate with two separate maps, one for twigs$_1$ and one for twigs$_2$. If this is how Abel operates, we can conclude that he simply represents twigs$_1$ and twigs$_2$ as belonging to two quite separate categories.

But now suppose that this is not the case: in fact, Abel's twig-related behaviour is controlled by a single intentional system that treats information about twigs in a thoroughly integrated way. For example, suppose that one day when he is making a termite sticker, he discovers a quicker way to strip leaves from a twig. Next time he gathers twigs to make a nest, he uses the same method to get rid of the leaves. Again, suppose that one evening, when he is making a nest, Abel finds a good source of twigs at a certain location. The next time he needs a termite sticker, he looks for twigs at that location. Finally, suppose that Abel is capable of acquiring new twig-related interests over time: perhaps he is playing around with a twig one day and discovers that he can use it to dig up roots. Later, when he goes in search of a new digging tool (a twig$_3$), he begins his search in the location where he discovered twigs while looking for nesting material a few days earlier. If Abel can behave in this way, it must be because his 'twig' system is able to use any piece of information about twigs to guide any pattern of behaviour relating to twigs. Abel's 'twig' system is a first-order integrated system.

In operating in this way, Abel is conceiving of twigs, not as potential termite stickers or nest material or digging tools, but as *twigs*—brown, leafy objects that can be used to make termite stickers or nests or digging tools depending on the circumstances. In other words, Abel is representing twigs, and indeed, his own twig-related behaviour, in an interest-independent way. He is able to do so because his 'twig' system integrates information about twigs in a way that cuts across different twig-related interests.

Abel will use information about twigs with a degree of flexibility and coherence that we have not encountered before. One particularly interesting feature of an organism that produces interest-independent representations is that it will be able to display what we might think of as idle curiosity. Abel is in a position to engage in a special kind of interest-neutral exploratory behaviour—gathering information about twigs or trying out novel forms of twig-related behaviour, with no particular interest in view. The function of this exploratory behaviour will be to enable him to acquire information or skills that need be of no use to him at the time, but that might later turn out to be useful—depending in part on what interests he goes on to develop.

In order to engage in this kind of behaviour, Abel will need to be willing to persevere in a particular kind of behaviour—using a twig to prod around in the soil, for example—without any immediate reward. He will need to be encouraged by nothing more than his success in producing some novel or conspicuous effect. In this sense, Abel could be described as prodding the soil just for the sake of it. A tendency to engage in this kind of general curiosity might benefit Abel overall, but at the risk of developing habits that are irrelevant to, or even in conflict with, his basic needs.

Nevertheless, it is important to note just how primitive a first-order integrated system might be. Abel will be able to achieve first-order integration while being able to engage in only the simplest forms of inference: he might be able to do no more than infer from something's appearance that it is a twig and then respond appropriately, depending on his current goal or drive. The primary distinction between a first order integrated system and the special-purpose systems considered earlier is the ability to use information more efficiently.

Moreover, there is a strong sense in which the workings of a first-order integrated system are still tied to a particular context: they are tied to a particular subject matter—twigs. Abel's representational capacities remain fundamentally disunified: if he were to possess a second first-order integrated system, concerned with reeds, for example, his 'reed' system would be quite separate from his 'twig' system. Indeed, he might possess dozens of systems very similar to his twig system, all representing different kinds of object in an interest-independent way, but all quite separate from each other. These systems will remain separate because Abel can only use information about twigs to help him to satisfy interests to which twigs are directly related: he could not, for example, draw on experiences with twigs in order to develop a more efficient way of handling reeds. So, although Abel might be described as representing twigs in an integrated way, it would hardly be appropriate to describe him as representing his *environment* in an integrated way. His representations remain bound, not to a particular interest, but to a particular kind of interest—interests relating to a particular subject matter. We could describe him as operating in a category-dependent way.

Contrast this situation with what we might think of as the next model up. This is another ape, Mabel, who not only conceives of twigs$_1$ and twigs$_2$ as being the same kind of thing, but also thinks of twigs as being one kind of object among others. Mabel is capable not only of using information about twigs, but of using information about twigs in conjunction with information about other kinds of object: pebbles, reeds, fruit, and so on. I will refer to this kind of integration as *higher-order integration*.

It is important to note that higher-order integration cannot proceed on the same basis as first-order integration. Abel succeeded in representing twigs in an integrated way by recognizing that $twigs_1$, $twigs_2$, and $twigs_3$ are all the same kind of thing. Clearly this cannot be the strategy employed by Mabel if she is to be capable of thinking about twigs in conjunction with other kinds of object: an organism that conceived of eggs and reeds as the same kind of thing would simply be a less discriminating version of Abel. Rather, we need to suppose that Mabel distinguishes between twigs and reeds but assigns them to the same higher-order category. In other words, we must suppose that Mabel operates with a hierarchy of categories. At this stage, we have an organism that not only treats twigs as belonging to some more general category but also conceives of twigs as belonging to that category.

For this kind of integration to occur, Mabel must operate with at least a two-layered taxonomy. The fewer layers, the more likely she will be left with a fragmented view of the world resulting from the presence of discrete systems. For example, there might be an organism that treated twigs, reeds, and fruit as different kinds of small, passive object; and that treated beetles, lizards, and mice as different kinds of small active object; and yet did not treat passive objects and active objects as different kinds of object. Such an organism would possess two separate higher-order integrated systems.

I suggested earlier that a first-order integrated system will operate with a flexibility and coherence denied to simpler systems. Mabel will take this a stage further. She will be able to use information about twigs to satisfy interests that have nothing to do with twigs. For example, she might infer from the information that there are twigs at a certain location, together with the information that fruit is found in the same locations as twigs, that fruit might be found at that location too. Again, she might be able to use her past experience in snapping off twigs in attempting to snap off a reed for the first time.[8] Unlike Abel, Mabel will be in a position to make inductive leaps across categories, to see similarities between items that she classifies as items of different kinds. We might take this to amount to a very limited form of creativity.

Again, like Abel, Mabel will be able to engage in exploratory behaviour, gathering information about her environment or trying out a novel form of behaviour for the sake of it. However, Mabel will be able to exploit the results of her curiosity in a much more flexible way: learning to dig in the soil might help her to become better at finding roots—or it might suggest a way of enhancing a water source, or building a fortification, or hiding a precious

---

[8] Again, we need to suppose that Mabel not only conceives of twigs and reeds in an interest-independent way, but also makes use of an interest-independent conception of her own behaviour. In other words, she needs to think of snapping something off as a behaviour that could be applied to any small object with the appropriate properties, to satisfy any interest.

object. Moreover, as she explores her environment, Mabel will not only be able to acquire new information and new interests; she will be able to develop new categories. Just like the other products of her explorations, these new categories need be of no immediate use to her. Indeed it would be perfectly possible, though not very economical, for Mabel to develop a set of categories that did not reflect her current interests at all, but that were based purely on perceptually salient properties, such as shape or colour.

Nevertheless, as with Abel, it is important to bear in mind Mabel's limitations. In order to benefit from the workings of her representational system, Mabel must be able to learn new patterns of behaviour, to recognize similarities between items and behaviours of different kinds, and to perform simple inferences that exploit those similarities. One important ability that Mabel might lack is the capacity to engage in complex planning, of the kind discussed in the previous chapter. In a later section, I will investigate what we should say about a higher-order integrated system that does have the ability to plan its behaviour. For the present, we should note that the capacity to learn and to make connections of the kind I have described are all that is minimally required for the capacity to engage in higher-order integration.

Nevertheless, I would like to suggest that a higher-order integrated system possesses the degree of flexibility required to count as a general-purpose system of the kind characterized by Millikan. Mabel's representational system is able to use information to satisfy any interest that she may acquire, without any limitation.

2.4. In Search of General-Purpose Intentionality: Summary

A general-purpose intentional system must meet a number of distinct criteria. First, it must operate in an interest-independent way. In other words, the representations that it produces must be capable of being used to serve an open-ended range of interests. For this to be the case, it must be possible for the organism to acquire new interests through learning. Secondly, the system must operate in a task-independent way. That is, the representations that it produces must be involved in a variety of cognitive tasks. This requirement is needed to distinguish general-purpose systems from the task-dependent subsystems that serve them. Finally, a general-purpose system will be a higher-order integrated system. That is, it will be able to use information about items that it encounters in dealing with items of other kinds. It will be able to do this only if it operates with a conception of those items as belonging to certain ontological category—for example, it might conceive of twigs and reeds as two different kinds of *object*. A higher-order integrated system, then, will operate with a hierarchy of categories.

3. The Capacities of General-Purpose Systems

3.1. *General-Purpose Representation and the Generality Constraint*

In the remaining part of the chapter I would like to investigate some unique features of general-purpose representational systems. I will begin by attempting to make explicit the connection between general-purpose representation and Evans's Generality Constraint. I will argue that it is a distinctive feature of a general-purpose system that it will *normally* satisfy the constraint.

Evans (1982: 104) phrases the constraint as follows: 'if a subject can be credited with the thought that *a* is *F*, then he must have the conceptual resources for entertaining the thought that *a* is *G*, for every property of being *G* of which he has a conception.' As Evans introduces it, the constraint is a constraint on the attribution of singular thoughts to a subject. But it could be treated as a constraint on the capacity for conceptual thought in general. Read in this way, the constraint requires that there should be no restrictions on the ways in which concepts may be combined in representations produced by a conceptual system, except, of course, restrictions arising from logical or metaphysical considerations.[9]

The constraint captures two central features of human thought: its systematicity and its productivity. In doing so, it reflects one sense in which human thought may be regarded as objective: a system that fails to satisfy the Generality Constraint will represent the world in a subjective way, in the sense that its operations will reflect a conception of the world that is determined in part by arbitrary features of the system's own psychology. A system that meets the constraint will operate in a way that reflects the objective structure of the world, and not contingent features of the representational system itself.

It is clear, however, that, as characterized here, the Generality Constraint could be seen only as a necessary, not as a sufficient condition on conceptual thought. This is because, as Martin Davies (1989) points out, the constraint can be satisfied by a very simple intentional system simply in virtue of the poverty of its representational resources.[10] For example, consider a simple sensorimotor system, such as the frog's fly-detecting system. We might say of

---

[9] Not everyone agrees that our thoughts are subject to the Generality Constraint. Travis (1994) argues that we often think and form categories in a context-dependent way. I agree that we should allow for a degree of context-dependence in accounting for actual human capacities, but I would prefer to do so by suggesting that the human doxastic system does not always operate as a general-purpose system. This need not be taken to imply that context-dependent thought is abnormal: the human doxastic system will count as a general-purpose system in so far as it is normal for the system to operate in a general-purpose way under certain circumstances.

[10] Davies is talking about our own subdoxastic states.

this system that, if it is capable of representing something as being to the left of the frog, then it is capable of representing a fly as being to the left of the frog. But this is only because flies are the only thing that the system is capable of representing.

Davies (1989) suggests that what distinguishes doxastic from subdoxastic systems is that it is an essential, not an accidental feature of a doxastic system that it should meet the Generality Constraint. In a similar way, I would like to suggest that what distinguishes the higher-order integrated system from less sophisticated systems is not that it *actually* satisfies the Generality Constraint—the simplest system could do that—but that it is *supposed* to satisfy the constraint: failure to do so would be abnormal for the system.

It is clear that there is nothing to preclude the possibility that a higher-order integrated system will sometimes fail the Generality Constraint. Consider the piece of inference described earlier, when Mabel reasoned from the presence of twigs at a certain location to the presence of fruit at that location. There is no guarantee that a higher-order integrated system will be able to produce the conclusion that fruit will be found at a particular location. The system may happen to suffer from some arbitrary limitation, preventing it from representing fruit at a position where it had not discovered them before. This would be an arbitrary limitation because, given that the system generally represents fruit as spatio-temporal objects, there is no reason for it to ignore the possibility that fruit might be found at a particular place. Such a limitation would suggest that the system did not conceive of fruit in a completely context-free way—in a way that is independent of its current recognitional and behavioural schemes.

Nevertheless, there is an essential connection between the capacity to represent the world in an integrated way and the capacity to represent the world in a coherent way. We can assume that the system's capacity to engage in these kinds of inference is present partly because the organism's ancestors benefited from the capacity to perform inferences of this kind. In other words, this is a normal feature of the system. The system could have benefited from this capacity only in so far as it was able to produce novel representations as a result. The system is able to produce novel representations precisely because it is able to apply information about one kind of thing in helping it to deal with another. And it is able to do this only because it is able to represent two different kinds of thing as having the same property. In other words, satisfying the Generality Constraint will be a *normal* feature of the system.[11]

Contrast this situation with one involving a less sophisticated system—for example, the first-order integrated system described earlier. It is perfectly possible for a system of this kind to fail the constraint: suppose that the system

---

[11] My position differs from Davies's only in that I am proposing a teleological view of what it means to say that a system is answerable to the Generality Constraint.

uses a spatial map, and that it normally relies on olfactory cues to recognize twigs, but not to recognize places: the system will be able to recognize twigs as musty smelling but it might not be able to represent places as musty smelling. There will be nothing abnormal about this situation: there is nothing in the way the system normally operates that requires it to conceive of twigs and places as having properties in common.[12]

Of course, this leaves the possibility of a higher-order integrated system that does frequently fail the constraint: a system for which successful inference is rather a hit and miss affair. Such a system might possess a notably incoherent and subjective view of its environment. Nevertheless, satisfaction of the Generality Constraint will still be a normal constraint on the system. Indeed it is important to emphasize this point. A system that is capable of interest-independent representation may continue to operate in an interest-dependent way for much of the time. For example, it might organize its memory or apply patterns of inference in a highly context-bound way. All that is important is that the system should sometimes be able to use information across contexts, and that this ability should play a sufficiently significant part in explaining the system's survival.

In this sense, then, the workings of a general-purpose intentional system will be characterized by the coherence and objectivity captured by the Generality Constraint. If so, it seems to me to be reasonable to conclude that such systems meet at least one significant constraint on the possession of conceptual content. If meeting the Generality Constraint is the only require-ment that a conceptual system must meet, then it will be reasonable to infer that general-purpose systems are conceptual systems.[13]

In what remains of this chapter, I would like to draw attention to two capa-cities that might be exhibited by organisms that possess general-purpose intentional systems. I will argue that it will be open to organisms of this kind to form simple causal theories about items in the environment and to represent themselves.

These two claims are interesting in themselves. But they also have a role to play in my defence of the teleological theory for two reasons. First, as we saw in the previous chapter, it is possible to make a prima facie case for the claim that the teleological theory will not be able to account for self-representation. If I can show that an organism that possesses a general-purpose representational system will be able to represent itself, I will have rebutted this objection. Secondly, as we will see in the final chapter, the capacity to engage in

---

[12] There is evidence that rats ignore colours, textures, and smells in reidentifying places, relying only on information about the overall shape of the environment. If so, a rat may represent a piece of cheese as smelling a certain way, but it will not normally represent a place as smelling that way. See Gallistel (1990: 189).

[13] The issue will hang on what kind of objectivity is taken to be constitutive of concep-tual content. I will not attempt to adjudicate this issue here.

theory-building will be of vital importance when we turn our attention to Peacocke's claim that the teleological theory is incompatible with realism.

3.2. Making Plans and Forming Theories

In the previous chapter, we encountered systems that are able to form behavioural plans. The prime example of such a system was the topographic mapping system, which is able to plan routes from place to place. As we have seen in this chapter, there is no reason to suppose that systems of this kind will need to operate in an interest-independent way. In this section, however, I would like to consider what would happen if we were to give a higher-order integrated system a capacity for complex planning. I will argue that a general-purpose system that is capable of forming complex plans will need to form simple theories about its environment.

At this point, I will introduce a third primate whom I will call Pablo. Pablo differs from Mabel in the following way: he is able to represent to himself the consequences of his behaviour. Because he is able to do this, he can form complex plans, at each stage taking account of how actions at earlier stages of the plan will have affected the situation. For example, suppose that Pablo is planning how to eat some fruit. He knows that, if he breaks the stem that attaches the fruit to the branch, the fruit will drop. He also knows that, if the fruit lands on the hard ground below, it will smash, and the pulp inside will get dirty. He might think of putting leaves on the ground so that the fruit will not smash, or of washing the pulp in a nearby stream; and so on.

Pablo will differ from an organism that possesses an interest-dependent planning mechanism in that he will be able to use a particular piece of information to help him to plan an open-ended range of activities. For example, suppose that he has learnt that leaves are soft to land on: he can use this information to help him to solve the problem of the fruit; but he could also put it to use in working out how to build a more comfortable nest. An interest-dependent planning mechanism cannot, by definition, use information in this way.

What I would like to argue, however, is that there is another way in which Pablo will differ both from Mabel and from an organism that possesses an interest-dependent planning system. Pablo will be able to form simple theories about his environment. My argument rests on three propositions.

(1) Pablo needs to make assumptions about the explanatory relations that hold between properties in his environment.

(2) Pablo will *represent* these explanatory principles.

(3) Pablo will need to represent the *precise nature* of these explanatory relations.

I will argue for these propositions in turn. I will begin by contrasting Pablo with Mabel.

As we have seen, in order to transfer information from one context to another, Mabel needs to make inductive inferences of an appropriate kind. For example, suppose that she realizes that, if she can use a reed to fish a dead frog out of a pool, she might be able to use a twig to knock some berries down from a branch. This inference will normally succeed only if it reflects a correct understanding of what makes the reed good for reaching—that is, its length and rigidity, and not its being hollow or wet. Mabel, it seems, needs to be able to recognize which kinds of property go with which. But there is no need to suppose that she will conceive of these relations between properties as *explanatory* relations: she does not need to realize that it is *because* the reed is long and rigid that it is a good for reaching with. She can simply rely on a set of rules linking properties together. Mabel's world could be a Humean world, in which certain properties are constantly conjoined.

But this is not true of Pablo. This is because he needs to know about the likely consequences of actions that he has not actually carried out. To know this, it is not enough to know which properties actually go with which. He also needs to know which properties would go with which in certain merely possible circumstances. And to know this, it seems, he needs to conceive of the relations between properties not merely as constant conjunctions that hold as things actually are, but as explanatory relations that link properties both actually and counterfactually. Pablo's plans need to be governed by simple explanatory principles.

I will now argue for the second proposition—the claim that Pablo will represent these explanatory principles. Again, my argument will exploit a contrast, this time a contrast with an interest-dependent planning system of the kind considered in the previous chapter. In the previous chapter, I suggested that the workings of any planning system will presuppose the existence of a certain set of causal or other regularities that govern events in the environment. The workings of a topographic mapping system, for example, will reflect a set of assumptions about the way in which places in the environment fit together. But, as we saw in the previous chapter, we do not need to describe the topographic mapper as representing these spatial principles. This was not only because these assumptions concern stable states of affairs in the environment, but also because they influence the workings of the system in highly restricted and predictable ways. For this reason, these principles, whether learnt or innate, do not need to be represented. They can be built into the normal workings of the system. In Pablo's case, on the other hand, there is no telling in advance how the explanatory principles on which he relies will influence the plans that he makes. And so these principles cannot be built in; they must be represented.

But I have not yet done enough to show that Pablo will form *theories* about his environment. To take this last step, I need to establish my third proposition—the claim that Pablo will represent the nature of these explanatory relations. To do this, I need to contrast Pablo with a first-order integrated system that is capable of making plans. Suppose that Abel is capable of planning a range of different twig-related behaviours. Some of his plans might make use of a learnt assumption that twigs make good reaching tools. Like Pablo, Abel will need to represent this information explicitly if he is to use it to plan a variety of behaviours. In other words, Abel might be capable of representing a causal regularity. For example, he might record the information that there is a connection between being a twig and being good for reaching with.

Nevertheless, it does not seem appropriate to describe Abel as having a *theory* about twigs. The problem is that he does not need to isolate the features that explain the fact that twigs have this property. Theorizing seems to involve a little more than identifying that a causal connection holds: it requires the capacity to specify the nature of the connection. Pablo, on the other hand, does have this capacity: as we have already seen, he shares with Mabel the ability to apply information in a way that cuts across categories. And this requires him to know not only *that* twigs are good for reaching with, but *why*. In learning about these explanatory relations, Pablo can be described as forming simple causal theories. And, of course, the more integrated his representational system is, the more comprehensive and coherent the theories he will be able to form.

If this is right, then we can describe Pablo as forming simple causal theories about items in his environment. This possibility arises because of the intersection of three different features of Pablo's representational system. First, he shares with any organism capable of forming plans the need to speculate about outcomes of merely possible actions. Secondly, he shares with Abel the need to represent explicitly the principles that guide these speculations. And, finally, he shares with Mabel the need to represent principles that identify very precisely the connections between properties in the environment. Only a general-purpose system that has the capacity to plan a range of different behaviours will be characterized by all three of these features.

3.3. Self-Representation

In the previous chapter, I suggested that a teleologist theory of intentional content might have difficulty in accounting for the possibility that an organism might represent itself. The problem was that an organism will be able to represent itself only if it needs to distinguish itself from other organisms. To do this, however, it needed to think of certain behaviours as behaviours that could be directed either towards another organism or towards itself. But it seemed impossible to find a pattern of behaviour that could be applied both to other organisms and to the organism itself: grooming oneself and grooming a conspecific, for example, will count as different patterns of behaviour because they have quite different functions. So it seems that, although an organism might need to identify other individuals, it will never need to identify itself.

I would like to suggest that we are now in a position to solve this problem. Organisms such as Mabel and Pablo that are capable of general-purpose representation might be able to represent themselves. For example, suppose that Mabel is normally able to detect and respond to situations involving social threats. She distinguishes between situations in which another member of the group is being threatened (threats$_1$) and situations in which she is being threatened (threats$_2$). But she treats both these situations as belonging to the same higher-order category.[14] As a result, she will be able to apply what she learns in situations involving threats$_1$ to a situation involving a threat$_2$. For example, suppose that she sees Abel pacifying an angry Pablo by going over to groom one of Pablo's allies. The next time she is threatened by Pablo, she tries a similar strategy.

Mabel does not conceive of these two situations as belonging to two quite unrelated categories: she must think of *being threatened* as a property that could be shared by Abel and herself. Similarly, she must think of grooming Pablo's ally as a piece of behaviour that could be performed by Abel or by herself. Nevertheless, she does not respond to both situations in the same way. So, she must be able to distinguish situations in which Abel is being threatened from situations in which the threat is directed at her; and she must be able to distinguish Abel's behaviour from her own. To do this, she needs to be able to produce representations whose content concerns herself and her own behaviour. She must be able to represent herself. She is able to do this because she conceives of the property *being threatened* in an interest-independent way.

There is another connection between general-purpose representation and selfhood. Throughout this chapter, I have found it increasingly natural to ascribe representations and processes such as learning and making inferences to organisms rather than to their intentional systems. The more integrated we suppose an organism's intentional capacities to be, the more appropriate it becomes to regard the organism as itself a possessor and user of representations, as the proud owner of a mind.

---

[14] The ability to treat all threats as belonging to a single category and yet to distinguish between different kinds of threat would not be open to a first-order integrated system.

3.4. The Capacities of General-Purpose Systems: Summary

I have argued that general-purpose intentional systems will normally satisfy the Generality Constraint. Thus, they meet at least one condition on the capacity for conceptual representation. I have also identified two other significant features of these systems: they are capable of self-representation; and they are capable of building theories about their environment. The first of these claims enables us to answer an objection raised in the previous chapter. As we will see in the final chapter, both the capacity for self-representation and the capacity to form theories will have a crucial role to play in solving the objectivity objection raised by Peacocke.

10

General-Purpose Content

1. Introduction

In this chapter, I would like to investigate how a teleologist might go about assigning content to the representations produced by a general-purpose system. This is a particularly pressing question for the teleologist, because it has been suggested, with some plausibility, that a teleological theory cannot be applied to systems of this kind.[1]

It is not difficult to see the nature of the problem. The teleological theory tells us that the content of the frog's visual devices relates to flies (in part) because it is the function of those devices to guide the frog's snapping responses, and the function of the frog's snapping responses relates to flies. This ascription of content depends on the claim that the frog's visual system functions to serve an identifiable interest. The content of the devices produced by a general-purpose, doxastic system cannot be determined by considering the interests that they are supposed to serve because there is no such set of interests. This might be taken to cast considerable doubt on the claim that a teleological theory will be able to account for the content of these devices.

There are a number of different ways in which it would be possible to develop this kind of objection. In the next section, I will outline four preliminary versions of the objection, and I will suggest an initial response to each one. In the end, though, the only satisfactory way for a teleologist to answer these objections is to develop an acceptable account of doxastic content. In this chapter and the next, I will provide an outline of such an account.

---

[1] See especially Sterelny (1990: 123-4), Bogdan (1994: 181), and Campbell (1994: 212–13).

2. Four Problems about General-Purpose Content

I will consider four versions of the objection raised in the previous section. As we shall see, some of these difficulties are more cogent than others. Still, it is important to stress that my responses here are preliminary responses. More work needs to be done, in this and the next chapter, to make these responses stick.

We could summarize the objections as follows:

(1) It is impossible to give a teleological account of doxastic content, because general-purpose intentional systems do not have a function.

(2) It is impossible to give a teleological account of doxastic content, because, although general-purpose intentional systems do have a function, that function is too broad to support specific ascriptions of content to particular thoughts.

(3) It is impossible to give a teleological account of doxastic content, because we are able to assign content to thoughts that have no biological utility.

(4) It is impossible to give a teleological account of doxastic content, because we are able to assign content to thoughts that involve the exercise of concepts that have no biological utility.[2]

Why might someone suppose that a general-purpose intentional system lacks a function? The thought might be that there is no unified explanation for how a general-purpose system helps to ensure the survival of the organism. And so its operation cannot be characterized in functional terms. But there is no need to accept that a general-purpose intentional system has no function: its function will be to ensure that the behaviour under its control helps to satisfy the interests of the organism. It will perform this function by ensuring that the organism's behaviour bears an appropriate informational relation to the environment. And it will do this by producing representations in a way that is sensitive to information picked up by the organism's perceptual mechanisms. Moreover, the way in which it produces these devices and uses them in processes of inference will normally be governed by an identifiable set of principles and assumptions. There is no reason to deny that a general-purpose intentional system has a function or that it works in accordance with a normal explanation.

---

[2] When I use the term 'concept' in this chapter, I am talking about a capacity—that is, the capacity to produce doxastic representations whose content concerns some property or item in the environment.

Nevertheless, it is certainly true, as the second version of the objection states, that any function that it would be reasonable to ascribe to a general-purpose intentional system will be far too broad to assist us in assigning content to specific representations produced by the system. The system's function is to ensure that the organism's behaviour is appropriate to its environment. But we would not wish to say that our thoughts are about nothing more specific than our environment.

But this is not enough to show that we should abandon the project of developing a teleological account of doxastic content. When I considered how to assign content to the special-purpose devices in Part II, I did not suggest that we could rely solely on the function of the system that produced them. Rather, I accepted Millikan's suggestion that we should appeal to the function of the system, together with the rules that normally govern its workings. The teleologist can make the same move in the case of a doxastic system: the content of doxastic devices will be determined by the procedures and assumptions that govern the way in which they are produced or used by the system. What is important for the teleologist is to spell out what those normal procedures and assumptions are, and what kind of content they produce.

It is at this point that someone might raise the third version of the objection. The worry will be that we cannot appeal to the normal workings of a doxastic system in giving an account of doxastic content because it is perfectly possible for a human being to make judgements and to form desires about matters that are quite irrelevant to our biological needs. A love of medieval church music or a desire to know the origins of the universe might, arguably, be interests of this kind. Moreover, it is possible for humans to produce representations that are quite inimical to their biological needs, such as the desire to commit suicide or the belief that lifelong celibacy is the only path to paradise. The worry will be that, in producing devices of this kind, the system is not working normally. And so the teleologist will not be able to assign content to these devices. Indeed, she will not be able to treat them as representations at all.

Similarly, the fourth version of the objection questions whether the teleologist will be able to allow for the possibility that a human being might be able to form *concepts* that are biologically useless. As we saw in the previous chapter, the capacity to engage in idle curiosity carries with it the risk of forming new representational capacities of this kind. For example, curiosity may lead me to speculate about the properties of distant galaxies, without any biological reward. The worry will be that a doxastic system will not be operating normally when it forms concepts of this kind.

In order to resolve these difficulties, we need to distinguish between two different ways in which a relational device, such as an intentional device, may be defective: a relational device may be defective because it has been produced in an abnormal way—by a mechanism that is malfunctioning. Or it may be defective because it has been produced under abnormal circumstances. For example, a bee dance might indicate the presence of a nectar source at a certain location, even though the source was destroyed during the bee's flight back to the hive. The production of the dance under these circumstances will not normally benefit the bees. Nevertheless the dance is produced in a perfectly normal way; so there is no difficulty in assigning content to it.

We could treat the desire to commit suicide in a similar way. In producing a desire to commit suicide, my doxastic system will be behaving inappropriately, given my biological needs. Nevertheless, the system can produce this desire without malfunctioning. The capacity to produce judgements or wishes about suicides other then one's own might well have biological utility; moreover, a doxastic system will normally satisfy the Generality Constraint. It follows that, if I am normally able to wish that someone else would kill herself, I will normally be able to desire my own suicide.[3] Such a desire would have an abnormal outcome, and, in producing it, the system would not be performing its function. But it might still be operating in its normal way. So there need be no problem in assigning content to it.[4]

We can respond to the fourth problem in a similar way. My learning mechanisms normally operate by ensuring that my beliefs and desires are (informationally) related to the environment in the appropriate way. So long as my astronomical beliefs bear the appropriate informational relation to distant galaxies, my learning mechanisms will have operated normally in enabling me to produce beliefs of this kind, even though beliefs about distant galaxies will never help me to satisfy any biologically useful interest.

Both these responses depend on the assumption that we can treat the capacities for reasoning and curiosity exhibited by doxastic systems, not as a set of discrete capacities, exercised in different contexts, but as unified *strategies* exercised by the system; although particular applications of these strategies fail to benefit, and may even harm, the organism, this is quite compatible with the claim that they are beneficial overall. In this respect, the behaviour of a doxastic system might be compared with the behaviour of a tree that each year entrusts its seeds to the wind: many, perhaps most, of the seeds may fall

---

[3] Papineau (1996) appeals to compositionality to answer Peacocke's objectivity objection. At this point in my argument, however, the appeal to compositionality is simply a preliminary response to a preliminary objection. As I will make clear in the next chapter, I do not believe that a straightforward appeal to compositionality will answer Peacocke's development of this type of objection.

[4] It would be an objection to the teleological theory if we could credit people with desires or beliefs that could be reached only in an abnormal manner. But it will not matter to the teleologist if there are beliefs or desires that are generally reached in an abnormal way, provided that they *can* be produced in a way that approximates a normal manner. The content of an intentional device is determined by the rules that normally govern its production, not the rules that generally do so.

on infertile ground, but the release of these seeds will count as normal, because it is an instance of a strategy that, in general, benefits the plant. In both cases, the wastefulness of the strategy is balanced by its effectiveness in dealing with a demanding environment (some of the tree's seeds may reach very fertile ground) and by its flexibility in dealing with an unpredictable environment (the tree could not have known where the fertile ground was likely to be).

Still, it is important once again to stress the preliminary nature of this response. It leaves important questions about how strategies are to be individuated and what justifies the ascription of a certain strategy to an intentional system. There is a close connection between questions of these kinds and Peacocke's objectivity objection. For this reason, I will return to these issues in the next chapter, where I will discuss Peacocke's objection for the last time. For the time being, I will operate on the assumption that these questions can be answered.

The account of special-purpose content that I developed in Part II depended on the idea that an intentional mechanism serves a specific need or interest. This raises the question whether the teleologist will be in a position to account for the content of devices produced by general-purpose intentional mechanisms. I have argued that the teleologist need not concede this point in advance: for the teleological account developed earlier rested on an appeal, not only to the function of the intentional mechanism, but also to the way in which it normally operates. Nevertheless, we have yet to see how such an account would work in detail. A fully developed account will have to show how to get from the idea that a doxastic system will normally operate in accordance with certain rules and assumptions to specific claims about the content of doxastic devices. And it will have to leave room for the possibility that a doxastic system might produce judgements, wishes, and concepts that have no biological utility.

3. Some Preliminaries

3.1. *Doxastic Representations*

Before we can begin the task of assigning content to doxastic devices, we need to get a little clearer about what kinds of doxastic representations there might be. It is important to emphasize that my project in this section is not to attempt a little armchair psychology: I am not trying to identify a set of doxastic states that human beings actually possess. Nor am I trying to offer an account of the psychological concepts with which we operate in everyday life.

My purpose in this chapter is not to give an account of the content of doxastic devices that we actually have or that we regard ourselves as having; but rather to establish the general possibility of ascribing content to the devices produced by *some* doxastic system, given a teleological theory of content. To do this, I need to identify a set of devices that we might plausibly ascribe to *some doxastic system or other*.

In order to keep things as simple and as uncontroversial as possible, I will pick on an imaginary and relatively unsophisticated system, such as that possessed by Pablo. In the previous chapter I characterized Pablo as capable of producing general-purpose representations about items in his environment and of forming plans based on simple theories about the environment. I have not suggested that Pablo is capable of thinking about non-empirical matters, such as mathematics or ethics; or that he is able to develop more than the very simplest explanatory hypotheses about the workings of his environment; or that he enjoys a particularly subtle emotional life. The problem set by Pablo is to assign content to a set of doxastic devices that concern the organism's immediate environment and a set of interests that are closely connected to the organism's needs in that environment.

Imagine that Pablo is exploring a new area when he starts feeling thirsty. He wishes he had some water, but remembers that there was no water in any of the places he has been exploring. So he plans to look for some. But he is in a dense patch of forest that makes searching difficult. He remembers an earlier occasion, when he saw Mabel climb a boulder to get a better view of an intruder. He realizes that climbing the boulder allowed Mabel to see further just because the boulder was tall. He concludes that, if he were to climb a tall object, he would be able to look for water. There are no boulders nearby, but he can see a tall tree. He decides to climb the tree.

Many different kinds of intentional device are involved in this sequence of thought. I would like to divide them into three groups: judgements, conjectures, and aims. Judgements include non-inferential judgements that are formed on the basis of perception, memory, or testimony, and judgements that have been arrived at by inference, including induction. Conjectures include explanatory insights ('Mabel could see further when she had climbed the boulder *because* the boulder was tall') and conditional expectations ('If I were to climb something tall, I would see further'). Aims include wishes, plans, and decisions to act.[5]

These different kinds of representation will be differentiated by their functions. Since Pablo's doxastic system normally operates by engaging in processes of inference, we can identify the functions of these devices with the

---

[5] Note that all these representations are intended to be understood as occurrent, rather than dispositional, representations. I will not offer an account of beliefs and desires in this book.

inferential role that they normally play. And, since processes of inference may normally draw on representations of any of these kinds, we will identify the inferential role normally played by each kind of representation only by considering what it contributes to such processes, given the contributions made by the others.[6] As a result, the functions of these kinds of representation can be identified only in relation to each other.[7]

Earlier, I suggested that we could characterize the function of a doxastic system as follows: the function of such a system will be to ensure that the organism's behaviour is appropriate, given its interests and the way in which things are in its environment. And I suggested that doxastic systems, like other intentional systems, will perform this function by exploiting informational relations between events in the environment. This suggests that some doxastic devices, at least, will carry information about the organism's surroundings.

It is natural to suppose that judgements will be devices of this kind. Moreover, I take it that judgements will, like the indicative devices produced by special-purpose systems, represent the information that they normally carry. The different kinds of judgements that I identified earlier will differ from each other in their origin and in the kind of information they carry: some judgements will carry information about particular items or events; others will carry information about general states of affairs. But all judgements will function to enter into processes of inference in such a way as to ensure that the organism's behaviour is appropriate, given the aims directing that process, and the truth of the conjectures involved, to the features actually possessed by particular items in the environment. In the case of an organism that is capable of planning, judgements will also have the additional function of ensuring that the explanatory insights that the system produces are likely to be true.

Aims, like the imperative devices considered in Chapter 6, represent states of affairs or patterns of behaviour that they are supposed to produce. Aims will include decisions to act—that is, the executive devices that are the output of processes of practical inference and represent pieces of behaviour. Their function is to prompt executive subsystems to select bodily movements that, in the circumstances, will realize behaviour of that kind. Other types of aim become involved in practical reasoning at an earlier stage: these include wishes and plans to do such-and-such. The function of wishes and plans is to enter into processes of inference in such a way as to ensure that the organism

---

[6] The abstractness condition and the independence condition will be important here, of course: the former to prevent us from slicing the function of each type of device too thinly, the latter to ensure that we slice it thinly enough.

[7] This will be true to some degree of the components of any system: we cannot specify the function of the sinoatrial node without mentioning the heart; and we cannot specify the function of the heart without mentioning the blood.

produces behaviour that is likely, given the truth of the judgements and conjectures involved, to satisfy one or more of the organism's interests.

Conjectures include explanatory insights and conditional expectations. Insights are produced in response to judgements about how things are in the environment and give rise to the conditional expectations that the organism needs in order to make plans and decisions in particular circumstances. The function of conjectures is to enter into processes of inference in such a way as to ensure that the organism's behaviour is appropriate, given the aims directing that process, and the truth of the judgements involved, to the existence of certain explanatory connections in the environment.

Conjectures differ from judgements in that they cannot be said to represent the information that they carry. This is because informational relations hold between events; but the assumptions that are represented by conjectures do not concern particular items or events in the environment, but the explanatory connections between those items or events. The most we can say is that the events about which these devices normally carry information will count as *evidence* for the explanatory connections that they represent.

My next task is to explain how we should go about assigning content to some of these different kinds of doxastic representation. This is a task that will occupy me for the rest of the chapter.

3.2. *Two Disputes about Content*

There are many different kinds of theories of content on the market. It is certainly not part of my project to set out a comprehensive taxonomy of existing theories. Nevertheless, in developing an account of content, it is important to make it clear how the suggested account stands with respect to the most important controversies in the area. In particular, I would like to locate the account with respect to two familiar disputes: the dispute between externalists and internalists; and the dispute between atomists and holists. Before outlining my account, then, I would like to make it clear what I take these positions to be.

The dispute between externalists and internalists could be characterized in the following way. An internalist holds that the content of a representation is fully determined either by its intrinsic properties or by the relations (causal, rational, or other) that it bears to other representations produced by the same system. On the strongest possible view, we will be able to ascribe content to a set of representations without taking any account of the actual environment, or even assuming that there is a world external to the mind at all. An externalist, on the other hand, holds that the ascription of content to a representation depends on some relation (causal or other) that it bears to items or features in the environment. On the strongest possible view, the content of a representation will be determined entirely by some relation that it bears to some item or feature in the environment.

There is, of course, room for intermediate positions. Someone might hold, for example, that representations have content because the internal relations between them somehow *model* the relations between items and features in the environment. On this view there are two different sets of relations: the causal (say) relations that representations bear to each other and the modelling relation that the whole system of representations bears to the environment. Again, someone might hold that the content of representations is determined by the causal relations that they bear to each other *and* to items in the environment: on this view, only one type of relation is involved, but it can hold both between representations and between representations and external items. We might characterize these intermediate positions as *weakly externalist* positions.

The account of simple content that I suggested in the central part of the book could be characterized as a weakly externalist account. The account that I developed was an externalist one, in that I took the content of these devices to be determined, first and foremost, by the informational relations that they normally bear to items in the environment. Nevertheless, the internal workings of these simple systems were given some role to play in determining the ontological category of the items that they represent. The account, I take it, is externalist in spirit, in that it is driven by a conception of intentionality as grounded in information. But it does not present these devices as simply mirroring the environment. As we shall see, the account of doxastic content that I shall outline may also be characterized as a weakly externalist account.

A related dispute is the dispute between content holism and content atomism.[8] An atomistic account of content takes it that, in ascribing content to a representation, we are not committed to any claim regarding the content of other representations produced by the system. This is not to say that the atomist is committed to the claim that there could be a doxastic system that possessed a single belief. If it were constitutive of a doxastic system that it is capable of engaging in complex forms of inference of the kind I have described here, for example, then such a system must possess a wide range of beliefs. But it would be possible to accept this without accepting that the content of one belief in any way depends on the content of another.

Holism, on the other hand, is the view that the content of any representation ascribable to a system is answerable to the content of any other representation that it produces. Again, this view must be distinguished from the view

---

[8] There are a number of different disputes in the philosophy of mind that could be characterized as disputes between holists and atomists; I am interested in just one kind of dispute here. For a survey of the territory, see Fodor and Lepore (1992).

that it is impossible for a doxastic system to have just one belief, since it implies nothing about how many beliefs the system must have.

The idea that a doxastic system is a general-purpose system might seem to indicate that we should be committed to a holistic approach to content. As we saw in the previous section, we can understand the different functions of judgements, aims, and conjectures only by seeing how they work together to ensure that the organism's behaviour is appropriate to its environment. In this sense, our account of what it is for a doxastic device to count as a judgement, say, is a holistic account. But it need not follow from this that when we come to ascribe *content* to the devices of a doxastic system we will have to proceed in a holistic way. As Fodor (1987: 69–71; 1990: 10) points out, it may be that what makes a judgement a *judgement* has to do with the way in which it is supposed to interact with other devices of the system; but that what determines its *content* is something quite independent of the content of other devices of the system. Indeed, as we shall see, the account of doxastic content that I will develop is an atomistic account.

3.3. The Shape of the Account

Earlier, I suggested that we can divide Pablo's doxastic representations into three categories: judgements, conjectures, and aims. I would now like to introduce another distinction, between peripheral and inferred devices. Peripheral devices are the devices with which processes of practical inference begin and end. I take it that these should be identified with perceptual judgements, episodic memory judgements, decisions to act, and a subclass of wishes and plans. This subclass will consist of wishes and plans from which processes of inference start, rather than those that are produced in the course of such processes. Other kinds of judgements and aims and all conjectures will be produced as a result of some process of inference, and so will count as inferred representations.

My strategy is to begin by explaining how we can ascribe content to peripheral devices. I will focus on perceptual judgements, though I will explain very briefly how to apply the same strategy to peripheral wishes and decisions to act. I will then attempt to account for the content of inferred devices by appealing to the relations that they normally bear to these peripheral representations. The content possessed by inferred devices will be *parasitic* on the content possessed by peripheral devices.

Underlying my account is the thought that it is possible to characterize doxastic systems and general-purpose learning mechanisms as normally operating in accordance with certain very abstract rules. These rules will be abstract in the sense that they will not classify devices in terms of some interest that they are supposed to serve or the kind of item they are concerned with: they will not specify how judgements *about trees* will interact with wishes *about trees*, for example. They will classify doxastic devices only in terms of their general type (as perceptual judgements, wishes, and so on) and in terms of the ontological category of the items that they represent.[9]

As we saw earlier, in giving an account of content, we need to take seriously the idea that doxastic devices have a structure that relates them to other devices produced by the system. For example, the production of the perceptual judgement 'That tree is tall' will involve the exercise of three distinct capacities: the capacity to identify a particular object in the environment; the capacity to recognize an object as a tree, and the capacity to recognize an object as tall. Any of these capacities might be exercised on other occasions to produce judgements of a different kind, such as 'That rock is heavy' or 'Mabel is tall'.

It follows that, if we take the content of a judgement of the form 'That a is F' to concern a tree, then we had better take the content of other judgements of the form 'That a . . .' to concern trees as well. This is an important point, if only because it explains how a doxastic device can be ascribed a determinate content on the first occasion on which it is produced. This will be possible, provided that the production of a device of that kind involves the exercise of capacities that the system possesses innately or has already developed through learning.[10]

4· An Account of General-Purpose Content

4.1. Perceptual Judgements

I will begin by considering how we are to go about ascribing content to a perceptual judgement, such as 'That tree is tall'. I will refer to this judgement as J_p. We can characterize J_p as having the form 'That a is F'.

The account of simple content developed in Part II exploited three separate factors: the information carried by simple intentional devices; the behaviour that they prompt, and the normal workings of the intentional system itself. My account of doxastic content will have just the same structure: we will need to consider the information that J_p or related judgements carry; the inferen-

---

[9] Once again, this is not to deny that some of the rules with which a doxastic system operates may once have been selected to do a very specific job. But where it is a normal feature of this system that its procedures may be commandeered for other tasks, these rules will no longer normally concern a particular subject matter or interest.

[10] The point here is no different from the point made about bee dances in Chapter 4.

tial role they play; and the normal workings of the mechanisms that produced them. I will discuss these three factors in turn.

I will begin with J_p's informational origins. When all is going normally, instances of J_p will carry the information that a particular tree is tall. There may be a number of different ways in which instances of J_p may normally be informationally related to a tall tree. This is because J_p will be produced in response to output from some perceptual subsystems, and the organism may possess a number of subsystems that are capable of registering information of this kind. Each of these subsystems will exploit a different kind of information channel: visual, auditory, tactile, and so on. Nevertheless, there will be a determinate range of ways in which J_p may normally be informationally linked to tall trees. I will refer to this range of information links as R.

It is important to point out that we could not account for the content of J_p simply by appealing to the information that J_p or related judgements *normally* carry. It may be perfectly true that the content of J_p is equivalent to the content it normally carries, but to point this out will bring us no nearer to having an account of the content of J_p. This is because we have no independent account of what makes it that case that instances of J_p and its related judgements normally carry information of this kind.

Someone might suggest that we could appeal to the occasions on which J_p or related judgements have prompted successful behaviour in the past. It is not unreasonable to suppose, for example, that, whenever judgements of the form 'That a . . .' have given rise to successful behaviour in the past, this was partly because those judgements carried information about trees. But, if we were to attempt to account for the content of J_p in this way, we would be open to the fourth version of the objection that I outlined at the beginning of the chapter. It is perfectly possible for a doxastic system to develop concepts that never benefit the organism in any way. Hence, we cannot determine the normal informational content of these judgements by setting out how such judgements have helped to prompt successful behaviour in the past.[11]

It follows from this that we cannot account for the content of a perceptual judgement by focusing purely on its normal informational origins. It may be

[11] A more promising move might be to consider the rules that normally govern the production of judgements of that kind. For example, we might consider the rules that govern the way in which judgements are produced in response to output from the perceptual subsystems that serve the doxastic system. The idea might be that an instance of J_p will normally carry information about some condition in the environment if it is normally produced in response to some perceptual device that itself normally carries information about that condition. But this proposed solution will not work. This is because the function of the perceptual subsystems that serve a doxastic system is to provide information *for the doxastic system*. There is no way of specifying what kind of information these subsystems are supposed to provide until we know what kind of information the doxastic system normally uses.

perfectly true that the content of a perceptual judgement is equivalent to the information that it normally carries, but this alone will not help us to determine what its content actually is. We need to look elsewhere.

The second factor that we need to consider is the inferential role that J_p and its related judgements normally play. We can expect that, when all is going normally, J_p will feature in processes of inference that eventuate in behaviour that is appropriate, given the aims driving that process of inference, to the presence of a tall tree. More generally, we can say that judgements of the form 'That a . . .' will normally feature in processes of inference appropriate to the presence of a tree; and that judgements of the form '. . . is F' will normally feature in processes of inference appropriate to the presence of some tall item.

It might be suggested that we could give an account of the content of J_p that worked by equating the content of a perceptual judgement with its normal inferential role. One way to do this would be to specify all the ways in which J_p or related judgements will normally interact with other representations produced by the system. If we were to accept an account along these lines, we would be committed to a holistic approach to content, since the content of J_p would depend in part on the content of other doxastic devices possessed by the system. But we might question whether it would be possible, even in principle, to produce an account of this kind. The problem arises from the fact that doxastic systems are general-purpose systems. It follows from this that it would be extraordinarily difficult to specify the inferential role that would normally be played by any particular doxastic device.[12] It could be argued that this worry relates only to our practical ability to specify J_p's normal inferential role, not to the claim that there is some specific inferential role that J_p does actually play.[13] But at the very least, this constitutes a significant prima facie difficulty for this kind of account.

But there is an alternative. This is to suggest that J_p can be characterized as the judgement that 'That tree is tall' because J_p normally features in processes of inference that are such as to ensure that the organism's behaviour is appropriate to the presence of a tall tree in the vicinity. This account would not be a holistic one, because it does not require us to specify how J_p or related judgements interact with other doxastic devices, but only to say how these interactions, whatever they may be, normally help to ensure the success of the organism's behaviour.

Unfortunately, however, there is a more general problem that confronts any attempt to account for the content of J_p by appealing to its normal inferential

---

[12] Millikan (1986) emphasizes this point.

[13] This is not a very promising response: after all, we are able to ascribe content to doxastic devices in practice, and not just in principle. It is hard to see how we could do this if the considerations and assumptions governing our ascriptions were not specifiable in practice.

role—just the same problem, in fact, that we encountered when we tried to equate the content of J_p with the information that it normally carries. The claim that we can equate the content of J_p with its normal inferential role will be no help to us, unless we have some independent way of identifying the inferential role that it normally plays. We cannot appeal to the past history of J_p or its related devices: if we were to do this, we would again be open to the objection that a doxastic system may issue judgements that have never assisted the organism to satisfy its biological needs, and never will.[14]

If we are to give an informative account of the content of J_p, we need to explain how we are to *identify* the information that it is supposed to carry and the inferential role that it is supposed to play. To do this, we need to investigate how the doxastic system came to have the capacity to produce devices of this kind. There are two possibilities: the first is that the capacities that the system exercises when it produces an instance of J_p are innate; the second is that they are the result of a process of learning governed by some general-purpose learning mechanism ancillary to the doxastic system. I will begin with the possibility that these capacities are learned.

If the organism does possess some general-purpose learning mechanism, what will the function of this mechanism be? I take it that one function of this mechanism is to ensure that, when judgements produced by the system become involved in processes of inference, they will do so in a way that is appropriate, given the information that they carry. In other words, this mechanism will function to produce a kind of *harmony* between the rules in accordance with which the doxastic system produces judgements and the rules in accordance with which it employs those judgements in reasoning about the environment.

I will label this kind of harmony *J-harmony*. The two sets of rules will J-harmonize with each other if the doxastic system is operating in a way that accords with the following principle: where J is a type of judgement produced by the system; L_1 is the set of rules governing the way in which judgements are used in inference, L_2 is the set of rules governing the way in which judgements are produced by the system, and C is some condition in the environment; then, if J, when used in accordance with L_1, tends to give rise to behaviour that would be appropriate if C obtained, then it will also be true

---

[14] Earlier on in this chapter, I did make an appeal to the normal inferential role played by various doxastic devices. I did so when I explained how we are to differentiate between different kinds of doxastic device—judgements, aims, and so on. Hence I am indeed committed to the claim that J_p would not count *as a judgement* unless earlier judgements featured in successful processes of inference in the way that judgements do. The claim we are considering here, however, is a much stronger claim: it is the claim that J_p would not count as the judgement *about a tree* unless earlier judgements featured in successful processes of inference in the way that judgements about trees normally do. This claim is far too strong to be tenable.

that J, if produced in accordance with L_2, will carry the information that C obtains.

We can bring all these considerations together as follows. First, the doxastic system that produced J_p will normally assign to J_p a certain role in inference. Secondly, J_p or related judgements are produced in accordance with a set of rules that has ensured that judgements of this kind sometimes bear R to trees or to tall things. Finally, the fact that J_p has been assigned this inferential role is explained by the fact that J_p or related judgements sometimes bear R to trees or tall things; and this explanation goes via the normal workings of a learning mechanism that has the function to ensure that the doxastic system operates in a J-harmonious way. It is in virtue of these facts that J_p normally carries the information that some tree is tall; and it is in virtue of this that J_p can be said to represent this information.

It could be objected that this account runs into the first objection I raised against the attempt to equate the content of J_p with its normal inferential role: that is, that the inferential role assigned to J_p and related judgements by the learning mechanism will not be specifiable in practice. But, in fact, this is not a difficulty for this more complex account. This is because there is no need for us to specify the role that J_p actually plays: the important point is that the learning system assigns a certain inferential role to J_p, *whatever that may be*, just because J_p or related judgements sometimes carry a certain kind of information.[15]

Another possibility is that the capacity to produce judgements such as J_p is innate for this system. If so, we cannot appeal to the operation of some learning mechanism to determine the content of J_p. Instead we will have to appeal to the way in which J_p or related judgements were used by earlier systems in the past. The idea will be that the system has the capacity to produce these judgements because the exercise of this capacity by earlier systems enabled them to produce behaviour that satisfied the organism's interests; and this is because the system assigned a certain inferential role to judgements that sometimes bore R to items of those kinds.

There is one final piece of the jigsaw. None of the constraints that I have put on the content of J_p so far will determine whether the content of J_p concerns trees, places occupied by trees, tree lineages or items belonging to some other ontological category. When we were ascribing content to the devices of special-purpose intentional systems considered in Part II, we resolved this problem by appealing to the rules that normally governed the way in which the system identifies items of that kind. The cheetah's tracking system can be said to represent antelopes as particular objects if it normally operates in

---

[15] Although, as we shall see in a moment, we do have to say something about the *kind* of role that J_p normally plays.

accordance with a set of rules Ω that reflects the status of antelopes as particular objects.

We can make the same move here: the role that J_p normally plays in inference will normally reflect some set of assumptions appropriate to the ontological status of the items represented by these judgements. If the system conceives of trees as particular objects, for example, then these processes of inference will reflect certain assumptions about the spatio-temporal properties of objects. If it conceives of them as living things, then it will normally operate in accordance with certain assumptions about the ways in which trees, as living things, can grow and change. These assumptions will also determine the ways in which the system produces judgements and other kinds of devices: a system that conceives of trees as particular objects, for example, might normally judge that 'That tree is tall' or 'That tree is to the left of Mabel'. But it will not normally produce judgements such as 'That tree occurred at the same time as that flash of light' or 'That tree is blocked by rubble'.[16]

This gives us the following analysis (where the content of J_p is the result of learning): where S is a doxastic system; J_p is a perceptual judgement issued by S that has the form 'That a is F'; $IR(J_p)$ is a role that might normally be played by some judgement produced by S; R is some set of informational relations that may hold between devices of S and states of affairs involving particular objects in the environment; J_p will be the judgement that 'That tree is tall' if only if:

(J.1) J_p bears (a member of) R to some item in the environment.

(J.2) Perceptual judgements produced by S that have the form 'That a ... ' sometimes bear (a member of) R to trees.

(J.3) Perceptual judgements produced by S that have the form ' ... F' sometimes bear (a member of) R to tall things.

(J.4) It is a normal feature of the operation of S that J_p would normally play $IR(J_p)$.

(J.5) It is a normal feature of the operation of S that $IR(J_p)$ reflects the ontological status of trees as particular objects and living things; and that it reflects the ontological status of *being tall* as a property that may be possessed by particular objects and living things.

(J.6) (J.4) and (J.5) are true because (J.2) and (J.3) are true; and these explanations go via the normal operation of a learning mechanism

---

[16] This requirement in turn puts a constraint on the perceptual subsystem that give rise to judgements of these kinds: these subsystems will need to provide information of the kind the doxastic system needs to operate in this way. For example, these perceptual subsystems must provide the spatio-temporal information needed to discriminate between and to reidentify particular objects.

that has the function to ensure that the way in which S employs judgements in processes of inference J-harmonizes with the way in which those judgements are produced.

If we were to assume that the content of J_p is determined innately, we would need to adapt this analysis accordingly. We could do so by referring to ancestors of S rather than S in clauses (J.2) and (J.3) and by rewriting (J.6) to:

(J.6*) (J.4) and (J.5) are true because (J.2) and (J.3) are true; and these explanations go via the fact that, in the past, ancestors of S produced judgements of the form 'a ...' and '... is F' and used them in processes of inference of the kind described in (J.4) and (J.5).

It is not difficult to see how this account aims to avoid the objections that I considered at the beginning of this chapter. One objection was that the teleological account will be able to ascribe content only to intentional devices that serve a specifiable need. The account that I have presented here sidesteps this difficulty. The fact that a perceptual judgement may be ascribed a certain content is dependent on the fact that it is (normally) assigned a certain role just because it carries a certain kind of information. But we do not have to specify exactly what that role is. In particular, we do not need to specify what kinds of interest the judgement is supposed to serve. The content of the judgement depends on the information that it, or related judgements, carry and on the rules that normally govern the operation of the doxastic system and the learning mechanisms that serve it.

Another objection was that a doxastic system may produce a representation of a certain kind, even though the production of a representation of that kind never benefits the organism. This objection is answered by the fact that, on this account, the content of a perceptual judgement does not depend on the fact that the production of a judgement of that kind has ever helped to satisfy a biological need. All that is required is that earlier systems sometimes prompted successful behaviour by producing perceptual judgements of some kind or other.

Earlier, I said that the account of doxastic content that I was about to give would be a weakly externalist and atomistic account. I would like to end this section by explaining why the account of perceptual judgements satisfies both these descriptions. The view is an externalist one in that the content of perceptual judgements is determined by the causal relations that they normally bear to items in the environment—that is, by the information that they normally carry. Nevertheless, it is a weakly externalist account, because it will also be true that the content of perceptual judgements will be determined in part by the nature of the inferential role they normally play, which will determine the ontological category of the item or feature that they represent. The account, I take it, is externalist in spirit, in that it is driven by a conception of intentionality as grounded in information. But it does not present the mind as simply reflecting the environment.

I take it that the account I have sketched here should be regarded as an atomistic account. This is because the content of a perceptual judgement will be determined, not by the inferential role that it normally plays, but by some feature (that is, its sometimes carrying a certain kind of information) that explains why it comes to play the inferential role that it does. None of this puts any constraints on the content of other devices produced by the system.

One question that might be raised is whether the constraints I have introduced in order to deal with ontological categories introduce a form of holism. The thought might be that it will follow from my account that, in order to make judgements about trees, I must be able to have thoughts about living things; and in order to make judgements about living things I must at least be able to make judgements about living things of various kinds. But this would be a misunderstanding of the account. For it to be the case that a process of inference reflects the status of trees as living things, it does not need to be the case that the organism judges that trees are living things. It is enough that the process normally reflects certain assumptions that need not be represented by the organism. It is, therefore, quite possible for the organism to make judgements about trees without making judgements about living things.

Nevertheless, it is possible that there are certain categories with which an organism might operate that do require the organism to possess more than one concept falling under that category: perhaps the organism could not be said to conceive of *being the mother of* as a kinship relation unless it regarded this relation as belonging to a complex network of relations having a certain structure.[17] If so, we might come across what Peacocke (1992: 10) terms *local holisms*. There is room for local holisms within an otherwise atomistic theory.

4.2. Decisions to Act and Peripheral Wishes

This account of the content of perceptual judgements may be extended to cover other peripheral doxastic devices. We can generalize the account in the following way: the content of a peripheral doxastic device will depend upon the existence of an explanatory connection between the fact that devices of that kind, or related devices, are sometimes causally related to the environment in a certain way and the fact that devices of that kind are normally assigned a certain role in inference.

In this section, I would like to explain how this principle may be applied to peripheral wishes and decisions to act. I will use the example of a decision, D_p,

---

[17] See Atran (1987).

which I will take to be the decision 'To climb that tree' and a wish, W_p, which I will take to be the wish that 'Some tree is tall'. For brevity's sake, I will ignore the possibility that the capacity to produce these devices might be innate. Instead, I will concentrate on the possibility that these capacities were acquired through learning. I will begin with D_p. As we will see, a decision to act may be treated as more or less the converse of a perceptual judgement.

The function of a decision to act is to give rise to a certain pattern of behaviour. Its function is analogous to that of the imperative devices produced by special-purpose systems, which I discussed in Chapter 6. A decision functions to ensure that the executive subsystems that control the organism's movements select movements of the right kind to realize a certain pattern of behaviour, taking into account how the organism judges the environment to be. It is via this connection with the organism's behaviour that decisions are causally connected to the environment.

As we saw earlier, decisions to act are always the output, and never the input, of processes of practical inference. A decision to act will normally be produced in response to judgements and conjectures that, if true, would suggest that the production of a certain kind of behaviour by the organism would conduce to the satisfaction of some wish or plan directing that process of inference. Being produced in this way constitutes D_p's normal inferential role.

I am assuming that the system acquired the capacity to produce D_p through learning. This process of learning will have been controlled by a learning mechanism that functions to maintain a certain kind of harmony between the way in which decisions are produced and the way in which they are used. The learning mechanism will function to ensure that, when decisions are produced as a result of some process of inference, they are produced in a way that is appropriate, given the behaviour to which they give rise. They will be produced in an appropriate way, if the judgements and conjectures that feature in that process of inference together imply that behaviour of that kind could help to satisfy the wish or plan with which that process is concerned. I will label this kind of harmony D-harmony.

We can now say that D_p may be characterized as the decision 'To climb that tree' because the fact that D_p and related decisions sometimes give rise to behaviour that is directed towards trees, or that involves climbing, explains the fact that D_p would normally be produced by a certain kind of inference; and this explanation goes through the normal workings of a mechanism that has the function to ensure that the doxastic system operates in a D-harmonious way.[18] It is because this is the case that we can say that this is the kind of behaviour that D_p normally produces. And so this is the behaviour that D_p represents.

---

[18] Again, we will have to insist that the inferential role normally played by D_p (or related decisions) is one that reflects the ontological status of trees as living things, and of *climbing* as a behaviour that may be directed towards physical objects.

I will now turn my attention to the wish that I labelled W_p: that is, the wish that 'Some tree is tall'. As we saw earlier, the function of a wish is to feature in processes of inference in such a way as to ensure that the organism produces behaviour that is likely to satisfy its interests. It is tempting to suppose that we should treat wishes in the same way as decisions to act: that is, that we should claim that wishes are causally linked to the environment via the behaviour to which they give rise. But I think that this would be an error. There need be no particular kind of behaviour that a desire normally prompts: for example, a desire to impress people might manifest itself in all sorts of ways. I think that the same point will apply to wishes, as I am characterizing them here. For this reason, I will take it that the inferential role normally assigned to W_p will depend on the way in which W_p, or related judgements, are sometimes produced.

Not all the wishes and plans issued by a doxastic system can be the result of a process of practical inference carried out by the system: the system must sometimes issue such devices at the start of such a process. This will be possible if the system operates in accordance with a set of motivational subsystems that function to ensure that the processes of inference in which the system engages are directed by aims that are appropriate to the organism's interests.

The interests of the organism might make themselves felt through sensations, such as hunger or disgust, or through emotional states, such as fear. Subdoxastic motivational devices of this kind might interact with perceptual and mnemic devices in complex ways. For present purposes, I will say only that devices of these kinds will interact *in some way or other* with perceptual and mnemic devices to prompt the formation of wishes and plans. These wishes and plans will normally be appropriate to the organism's interests, given how the organism represents the environment and the organism's own body to be.

I am assuming that the system acquired the capacity to produce W_p through a process of learning. As before, we must assume that this process has been controlled by a learning mechanism whose function is to maintain a certain kind of harmony between the way in which wishes are produced and the way in which they are used in inference. To be more precise, the learning mechanism will function to ensure that, when the wishes produced by the system become involved in processes of inference, they do so in a way that tends to give rise to behaviour that would be appropriate to the content of the perceptual or mnemic devices that prompted them. We could call this kind of harmony W-harmony.

We can now explain why it is that W_p can be characterized as the wish that 'Some tree is tall'. This is because the fact that W_p normally plays a certain inferential role is explained by the fact that W_p (or related wishes) are sometimes produced in response to subdoxastic devices of a certain kind—that is, representations whose content implies that the occurrence of some state of affairs involving a tree or a tall item would conduce to the satisfaction of one of the organism's interests. Moreover, this explanation goes through the operation of a learning mechanism that has the function to ensure that the doxastic system works in a W-harmonious way.[19] It is because this is the case that we can say that W_p is supposed to bring it about that there is a tall tree. And so this is the state of affairs that it represents.

4.3. Inferred Representations

At the beginning of the previous section, I formulated a principle that, I suggested, could be taken to govern the ascription of content to all peripheral doxastic devices. The principle turned on the existence of an explanatory connection between the fact that a given device is sometimes causally related to the environment in a certain way and the fact that devices of that kind normally play a certain role in inference. Unfortunately, this principle will not help us to ascribe content to inferred doxastic representations. This is because inferred representations need never be causally related to the environment in the appropriate way.

In ascribing content to a perceptual judgement we needed to suppose that judgements of that kind, or related judgements, do sometimes carry the information that they are supposed to carry. Again, in ascribing content to a decision, we needed to suppose that decisions of that kind, or related decisions, do sometimes give rise to the behaviour to which they are supposed to give rise. But it would be possible for a system to produce an inferred judgement of a certain kind, without ever producing a judgement of the same kind, or a related judgement, that carries the information that it is supposed to carry. For example, suppose that an organism judges that lichen is likely to be found on trees. It produces this judgement because it has seen a number of telegraph poles splashed with yellow paint, and has mistaken them for lichen-covered trees. It never produces any other inferred judgement about trees or about lichen. In this case, neither this inferred judgement nor any related inferred judgement will carry information about trees or about lichen.

Moreover, it will also be possible for a system to produce an inferred judgement in response to judgements that are true, but do not support the inference made by the system. For example, the system might infer from the presence of a number of lichen-coloured boulders in its environment that lichen is to be found on all boulders. Again, it seems that it is possible for a

---

[19] We will, of course, also have to insist that the inferential role normally played by W_p (or related wishes) is one that reflects the ontological status of trees as living things, and of *being tall* as a property of physical objects.

system to produce a judgement of this kind even though it never produces any other inferred judgements about lichen or about boulders.

We can make just the same points about inferred plans or wishes and about conjectures. This suggests that, in giving an account of the content of inferred representations, we will need to make room for the possibility that the inferential processes that generate these representations may be faulty, or founded on misinformation.

The obvious way to deal with this problem is to treat these devices as having what we might term *parasitic content.* In other words, the content of these devices will be determined in part by the relations that such devices would normally have to the wishes and perceptual judgements that help to prompt them, and the decisions to act to which they normally give rise. Of course, it is important to bear in mind that the relation between an inferred device and these peripheral devices may be more or less direct: for example, inferred judgements may be produced in response, not only to perceptual judgements but also in response to other inferred judgements. But, of course, once we have an account that sets out how we can ascribe content to inferred representations that are produced directly by peripheral devices, we will be able to apply the account recursively to other inferred representations.

As before there will be two sets of rules that govern the behaviour of inferred representations. The first set of rules will govern the procedures by which the system produces inferred devices of various kinds in response to information about the environment. And the second set of rules will govern the way in which inferred devices are themselves used in inference. Once again, the system will be working normally only when there is harmony between these two sets of rules. In the case of a judgement of any kind, it will be important that, where a judgement normally carries the information that a condition of some kind occurs, that judgement is used to ensure that the organism's behaviour is appropriate given that the condition occurs. In the case of an aim, it will be important that the behaviour or state of affairs that the aim would normally produce is one that conduces to the satisfaction of some interest or goal. In the case of a conjecture, it will be important that the conjecture normally modifies the organism's behaviour in a way that would be appropriate if the environment worked in a way that is likely to be true, given the content of the judgements on which a conjecture of that kind would normally be based. I will call this kind of harmony I-harmony.

Once we have these ideas in play, we can proceed much as before. The content of an inferred representation will depend on the fact that there is an explanatory connection between the fact that a representation of that kind would normally be produced by peripheral devices having a certain content, and the fact that it would normally be assigned a certain inferential role by the system. To give an example, consider the inferred judgement that 'That tree is very old'. The inferential role normally played by this judgement will be explained by the fact that it would normally be prompted by judgements that imply that a particular tree is very old. In addition, this explanation must go through the workings of a system—in this case, the doxastic system itself—that normally operates in an I-harmonious way. Finally, we will need to mention that the inferential role normally assigned to the inferred device is appropriate both to the type of device that it is and to the ontological status of the items or properties that it represents.

The crucial difference between this account and the account of the content of peripheral devices offered earlier is that the inferential role that would normally be assigned to the device is determined by the way in which it would *normally* be produced, and not by the information that it *actually* carries. In this way we can leave room for representations produced by faulty reasoning or by misinformation.

Clearly, the need to treat the content of inferred devices as parasitic on the content of peripheral devices further weakens the externalist credentials of this account. The account will have a further seasoning of internalism in that the content of inferred devices will be determined by the relations they normally bear to other intentional devices. Nonetheless the point remains that the content of these peripheral devices will be determined, to some extent, by the causal relations they bear to items in the environment.

It might be thought that this account of the content of inferred devices introduces an element of holism into the account. But I think that this would be incorrect. It is true, of course, that the content of inferred devices does depend on their sometimes being prompted by other devices that have a certain content. But the relations involved are importantly asymmetrical: the content of an insight depends on the content of the judgements that prompt it; but the content of those judgements does not depend on the insights that they prompt. There is a dependency here, but not a holism.

4.4. *An Account of General-Purpose Content: Summary*

My purpose in this chapter has been to answer this objection that a teleological theory will be unable to provide an account of general-purpose content. The objection turned on the fact that there is no specific role that general-purpose representations function to play. My response has centred on the following idea: that the content of such a device might depend on the fact that the way in which it is normally used in inference, whatever that may be, is explained by some feature that it possesses. We can appeal to this fact without assuming that there is some specifiable role that the device would normally play. In the case of peripheral devices, the relevant feature will have to do with the causal relations they bear to the environment. In the case of inferred devices, it will have to do with the content of the representations that would normally trigger their production.

Although the account does not require us to specify a precise inferential role for each general-purpose device, I have suggested that we should put some constraints on the way that such devices are used in inference. The inferential role normally played by each device will be appropriate to the type of device it is (perceptual judgement, plan, insight, and so on) and to the ontological status of the properties and items represented by the device.

None of this amounts to a fully developed theory of doxastic representation. To provide such an account, I would have to consider a much wider range of issues: issues about the relation between thought and language, about the epistemology of content, and about consciousness, for example. And I would have had to consider a much wider range of representations. My purpose here has been to try to answer the objection that teleology has no role to play in such an account, and to lay the foundations for a fully developed teleological theory of doxastic content.

Nevertheless, my project is not yet complete. In the last chapter of this book, I will return to the issues about truth that I first raised in Chapter 5. Once again we will have to consider whether a teleological account has the resources to ground content that is both determinate and objective.

11

Utility and Truth

1. Introduction

In the Introduction to this book, I listed three objections to the teleological theory that I regard as especially acute: (1) the objection that the teleologist is unable to ascribe determinate content to intentional devices; (2) the objection that the teleological theory is incompatible with a thoroughgoing metaphysical realism; and (3) the objection that the teleological theory is unable to account for the content of general-purpose intentional mechanisms. Over the last two chapters, I have outlined a response to the third of these objections. In this final chapter, I would like to return to the first and the second.

In Chapters 5 and 6, I argued that the teleologist is able to answer the determinacy objection, at least as it applies to special-purpose intentional devices. My response depended on the claim, defended in Chapter 3, that it is possible to ascribe determinate functions to biological devices. Nevertheless, I would like to raise the issue of determinacy once again. This is because we need to examine the possibility that the account developed in Part II will not apply to the representations produced by general-purpose, doxastic systems. In particular, the worry will be that the function of the doxastic system plays a less direct role in determining the content of the devices that it produces. For this reason, it might be questioned whether determinacy of function will be sufficient to secure determinacy of doxastic content.

The second objection was also raised in Chapter 5. I concluded that the teleologist has no reason to insist that the intentional devices produced by special-purpose systems have utility-transcendent truth conditions: these systems are able to register only states of affairs that are normally accessible to the organism. In Chapters 7 and 8, I have argued that this will be true, not only of minimally intentional signalling systems, but also of systems that are able to represent particular items in the environment. In this chapter, I will examine the possibility that doxastic systems, unlike special-purpose systems, are capable of representing an environment that extends beyond the subject's practical reach.

2. Determinate Doxastic Content

2.1. The Determinacy Objection Revisited

I will illustrate the determinacy objection using the example of Pablo's perceptual judgement J_p: J_p is the judgement 'That tree is tall'. Once again we can identify four versions of the objection:

(1) *The distality problem (close-up version)*: the teleologist cannot decide between the claim that the content of J_p concerns the presence of a tall tree and the claim that it concerns the nature of the proximal stimuli reaching the organism.

(2) *The distality problem (far-out version)*: the teleologist cannot decide between the claim that the content of J_p concerns the presence of a tall tree and the claim that it concerns some state of affairs that occurred in the past, such as the germination of a seed that was genetically disposed to produce a tall tree.

(3) *The description problem (input version)*: the teleologist cannot decide between the claim that J_p is the judgement 'That tree is tall' and the claim that J_p is the judgement that 'That brown, tree-shaped object is tall'.

(4) *The description problem (output version)*: the teleologist cannot decide between the claim that J_p is the judgement 'That tree is tall' and the claim that J_p is the judgement that 'That object that is strong and stable and has branches low enough for me to reach is tall'.

The Distality Problem arises because J_p will normally carry information, not only about trees, but also about the proximal stimuli reaching the organism and the past history of the trees that the organism encounters. The source of the description problem, again, is the fact that J_p will normally carry information, not only about trees, but also about items that look like trees and about items that have the features that make trees useful to Pablo. In order to answer these objections, we need to show that it was because J_p carried information about trees, and not about any of these other items, that it normally enters into processes of inference in the way that it does.

2.2. The distality problem

The distality problem will be relatively easy to resolve. In fact, we can answer it by using exactly the same principles as those we used in Chapter 5. The only difference will be that we will need to apply these principles to the workings of the system as a whole, rather than examining the way in which it helps to satisfy specific interests.

To resolve the distality problem, then, we need to appeal to the normal workings of the doxastic system, or of the learning mechanisms that control how judgements are used in processes of inference. As we saw in the previous chapter, the doxastic system will be working normally only when judgements are used in inference in a way that is appropriate to the information that they carry. The processes of inference in which Pablo engages will help to satisfy his interests by ensuring that his behaviour is appropriate to states of affairs in the environment that favour its success. This will normally be the case only if Pablo's behaviour is hooked up in the right way to perceptual judgements that carry information about states of affairs of just that kind. So, if we want to know what kinds of states of affairs Pablo's perceptual judgements represent, we need to find out what kinds of state of affairs generally help to ensure the success of his behaviour.

I take it that, in Pablo's case at least, the success of the behaviour controlled by his perceptual judgements will depend on states of affairs that involve middle–sized objects and that occur at the time that the judgement was produced. I will label states of affairs of this kind *M-conditions*. If so, we can conclude that the content of Pablo's perceptual judgements will concern the occurrence of some M-condition.[1] The presence of a tall tree is an M-condition; the occurrence of some set of proximal stimuli and the occurrence of some event in the distant past are not.

A proponent of the far-out version of the distality problem might attempt to argue that, if the organism's behaviour is generally appropriate to M-conditions in the environment, then it will also be appropriate to earlier events that explain why those M-conditions obtain. But, just as in Chapter 5, we can appeal to the fact that the most immediate explanation for the success of the organism's behaviour will be that it is appropriate to some M-condition. The extended immediacy condition will answer this version of the distality problem for doxastic content just as it did for special-purpose content.

Again, a proponent of the close-up version of the distality problem might claim that the success of Pablo's behaviour can be explained by the fact that it is generally appropriate to the proximal stimuli reaching the organism at each moment. Again, we can reply to this in just the same way as before. Although the occurrence of proximal stimuli of these kinds will often coincide with the production of some piece of behaviour, this coincidence does not explain why the behaviour succeeds. This version of the objection involves a violation of the first clause of the abstractness condition: it confuses the way in which the doxastic system normally operates with what it functions to bring about.

Of course, this is not to deny that a sophisticated thinker might produce judgements about conditions other than M-conditions. Pablo will be able to make inferences about the proximal stimuli reaching his sense organs and

---

[1] Compare Davies (1983: 420–1).

about events in the past. But this is irrelevant to the content of the perceptual judgements that he produces. More interestingly, Pablo might be able to learn to make non-inferential judgements about conditions other than M-conditions. For example, he might learn to shift his attention away from the tree in front of him and towards the quality of the light reaching his eyes. But this will involve a process of self-education that will have the effect of modifying the content of the perceptual judgements involved. In the absence of such a process, the content of perceptual judgements will concern only M-conditions.[2]

2.3. The Description Problem

The description problem will not be so easy to solve. This is because this version of the problem concerns the categories that Pablo employs in representing his environment. In the case of special-purpose systems, the organism's categories are determined by its interests.[3] The frog's fly-detecting system serves the organism's need for food. Hence, the frog represents flies as packages of biochemical properties—just those properties that make flies nutritious to frogs. But a doxastic system, by definition, is not dedicated to the service of a specifiable interest or set of interests. Hence, we cannot solve this problem for doxastic systems by appealing to the function of the system.

How, then, are we to determine how Pablo divides up the world? How can we determine whether Pablo's concept 'tree' picks out members of a certain biological kind; or whether it picks out items that have a certain appearance; or whether it classes together items that have certain useful features? Our answer to this question ought not to exclude the possibility that Pablo's repertoire of concepts will include concepts that fit any of these patterns. Our own concepts, after all, include a mix of biological, phenomenal, and practical concepts, and many others besides.

Once again, we will need to appeal to the normal workings of the doxastic system. In the previous chapter, I suggested that the processes of inference carried out by a doxastic system will normally be governed by rules that reflect the ontological category of the items and properties concerned. The distinction between a biological concept and an observational concept has to do with the ontological category of the items represented. Which type of concept Pablo is using will depend on the rules that normally govern the way in which

---

[2] This has some interesting implication about what we should say about the perceptual judgements made by human beings about items that are very distant from them, such as stars. It implies that the content of an uneducated perceptual judgement about a star will concern what the star is like *now*. Consequently, many of these judgements will be false.

[3] Or, in the case of auxiliary properties, by the normal workings of the organism's perceptual systems.

the devices concerned are used by the system. And this will be determined by the history of those devices or by the operation of the learning mechanisms that control the way in which Pablo's perceptual judgements become involved in inference. The ontological categories that Pablo uses may be innate, or they may themselves be learned, as Pablo discovers which are the most productive and convenient types of category to use.

The idea that the way we think is governed by the ontological categories that we use has been explored by Susan Gelman, Frank Keil, and others.[4] Gelman (1988) argues that the nature of the inductive inferences made by children is sensitive to the nature of the concepts involved. Her subjects expected members of a biological kind to be similar to each other in a wide variety of ways: in behaviour, internal structure, and life history. Membership of an artificial kind did not give rise to the same expectations, suggesting that ontological category constrains the kinds of inductive inference that her subjects were prepared to make. Keil (1989) identifies differences in the kinds of evidence that subjects take to indicate membership of a kind, depending on the type of concept involved. In the case of artificial kinds, use counts for more than appearance. In the case of natural kinds, internal structure and origin are the key factors.[5]

These are all empirical claims about how the doxastic systems possessed by human beings actually operate. Nevertheless, they are suggestive of the kinds of consideration to which we could appeal to distinguish between different categories of concept. For example, if Pablo's concept 'tree' is a biological concept, then we would expect that his identification of some item as a tree will not normally turn on its appearance alone. Again, we would expect that he might normally judge of a tree that it is tall, or healthy, or even threatening, but not that it is a trick of the light. And, again, we would expect that he might normally be prepared to infer that all trees grow from seed, but not that all trees are precisely 22 feet tall.

Clearly, there is a great deal more to be said here. A complete account of doxastic content would have to include a detailed analysis of what is involved in operating with concepts belonging to a wide range of categories. That would be a book in itself. My aim here has simply been to indicate how a teleological account of doxastic content might appeal to the notion of an ontological category in order to resolve the description problem for doxastic content.

---

[4] The notion of a biological kind term employed by Gelman and Keil can be traced back to the philosophical account proposed by Kripke (1972) and Putnam (1975). See also Atran (1987, 1989).

[5] Gelman and Keil are primarily interested in investigating the way in which concepts alter as a child learns more about its environment.

2.4. Determinate Doxastic Content: Summary

A teleological theory of doxastic content will be able to answer the problem of determinacy raised in Chapter 5. The solution to the distality problem will turn on the claim that the behaviour of doxastic subjects will generally be directed towards middle-sized objects currently found in the subject's environment; and it rests on the same appeal to the extended immediacy condition and the abstractness condition on which I relied in Chapter 5. The description problem, on the other hand, requires a new solution—one that appeals to the role of ontological categories in structuring the subject's thought. Here, I have invoked ideas presented by Gelman and Keil to support the ascription of determinate content to doxastic systems.

3. Objective Doxastic Content

3.1. The Objectivity Problem Revisited

In Part II, I argued that the content of the devices produced by special-purpose intentional systems will concern some state of affairs that is normally accessible to the organism. This is because the explanation of how these devices helped to ensure the success of the organism's behaviour will need to mention the fact that the features or items about which those devices carried information were within the organism's behavioural reach. In arguing this, I endorsed Peacocke's claim that the teleological theory faces a prima facie difficulty in accounting for the possibility that some intentional devices may be ascribed truth conditions that transcend their normal biological utility.

I suggested there that we should not be too concerned to discover that special-purpose intentional systems suffer from this limitation. Nevertheless, I took the view that it would be fatal for the teleological theory if the same restriction were found to apply to all intentional systems. Although I believe that it might be possible for a teleological theorist to reduce truth to normal utility, this is not a version of the teleological theory that I would find acceptable.

I will begin by formulating what I take to be the most plausible version of the objection. Once again, I will concentrate on the question whether the system—in this case a doxastic system—will be able to represent a place that is inaccessible to the organism. A teleological account of doxastic content will start from the claim that a doxastic system normally operates by producing states that correlate, in some specifiable way, with items in the subject's environment. Peacocke's point will be that the success of earlier systems will be explained, in part, by the fact that the states that they produced correlated with items that were normally within the subject's behavioural reach.

For example, suppose that a teleologist identifies some relation R, which, she claims, any judgement that represents a particular place will normally bear to that place. She might attempt to characterize the system as normally operating in accordance with the following rule:

> E A judgement j will represent a place p only if j bears R to p.

But now suppose that, for some reason, the subject normally has access only to places that lie within a certain distance of the subject. We might begin by supposing that this is the furthest distance that the subject would normally be able to travel in what remains of her lifetime. If Peacocke is right, it looks as if we should treat the system as operating in accordance with the following rule:

> E* A judgement j will represent a place p only if j bears R to p and p is normally reachable by the subject in what remains of her lifetime.

Once again, the idea will be that we should treat the system as operating in accordance with E*, rather than E, because the subject could never benefit from representing places that are inaccessible to her. If this is right, it will follow that a doxastic system cannot represent inaccessible places: the capacity to produce states that correlate with such places is not normally of use to the subject. Such a capacity, if it were to arise, would have to be classified as abnormal, and the states that resulted could not be classed as genuine representations.

As we saw in Chapter 5, in formulating Peacocke's challenge we need to be clear about what is meant by the term 'inaccessibility'. I have already introduced a distinction between fortuitous and normal inaccessibility. Once we are dealing with a general-purpose system, we will need to introduce two further refinements. This is because subjects who are capable of general-purpose representation have some additional capabilities that we need to take into account.

First of all, a subject who possesses a general-purpose intentional system will be capable of a high degree of behavioural flexibility. There is no telling in advance what new interests or patterns of behaviour she will develop during her life. As these new interests and abilities develop, places that were previously of no interest to her may gain new significance; or she may discover how to gain access to places that were previously outside her reach. Such a subject will be able to benefit from the capacity to gather information about places that are *currently* inaccessible to her, since this information may become useful later on. For this reason, the teleologist can allow that such a subject will be able to represent places that are *currently* outside her behavioural reach.

Nevertheless, there remains the possibility that there are places that are *in principle* inaccessible to the subject, perhaps because of their very great distance or because they are shielded from her by a physical barrier of some kind. The objector will insist that the subject can benefit only from the capacity to think about places that are at least in principle accessible to her. The challenge will now be to show that doxastic systems can represent places that are normally and in principle inaccessible to the subject.

There is a second distinctive feature possessed by at least some doxastic systems that we need to consider: human beings have the capacity to form theories about their environment. A consequence of this is that a human being may be able to receive information about a place that she cannot in principle visit or act upon, information that, nonetheless, helps her to make useful inferences about her environment. For example, it may help to confirm or disconfirm some more general theory—a theory that has practical implications with respect to locations that she *can* in principle visit.

Once again, this will force us to refine what we mean by 'inaccessibility'. In the case of the special-purpose systems discussed in Part II, a place will count as accessible to the organism only if it is able to use some item located there. In the case of a human being, on the other hand, a place will count as accessible if the subject is able to act on it *or* if she is able to gather information about how things are at that location.[6] I will label this very weak form of accessibility *practical accessibility*.

In what follows, I will refer to places that are, normally and in principle, practically inaccessible to a subject as places that are *closed* to that subject; and I will refer to places that are, normally and in principle, practically accessible to a subject as places that are *open* to her. The objection may now be phrased as follows: it is possible that there are places that are closed to us. And, since we could never benefit by speculating about closed places, the teleologist cannot allow that we could represent them. It is easy to see how this objection could be generalized to apply to all aspects of the workings of a doxastic system.

David Papineau (1996: 429) has attempted to answer Peacocke's objection as it applies to doxastic systems by appealing to the fact that doxastic systems obey the Generality Constraint. The idea will be that a subject who is able to exercise the concepts *place* and *closed to someone* in forming biologically useful

---

[6] This is in need of further clarification. There may be some things that a subject is able to know about any place, no matter how inaccessible. As we saw in Chapter 8, space is a causal unity: hence causal laws that hold in one region of space will hold in all. A subject who knows, say, that $E=MC^2$ will know that $E=MC^2$ even in regions that are inaccessible to her. All places, then, are epistemically accessible to us, at least in this minimal sense. Moreover, it may be possible to know quite specific facts about a place that is informationally inaccessible to us by making inferences based on information about neighbouring places. A place will be informationally inaccessible to us if we cannot know anything about it except by inference; informational inaccessibility makes for practical inaccessibility because nothing we could know about such a place will help us to find out anything *new*.

beliefs or desires will be able to put those concepts together to form beliefs and desires that represent places as closed to her. This response takes the same form as my reply, in the previous chapter, to the objection that the teleologist will not be able to allow for the possibility that I might form biologically harmful doxastic states.

However, I do not think that, in the end, this appeal to the Generality Constraint will provide us with an answer to Peacocke's objection. This is because we cannot assume that, in forming biologically useful beliefs and desires, the subject is exercising the concept *place* at all. She may be operating with a narrower ontological category, one that includes only places that are open to her. We might refer to such entities as 'open-places', or 'o-places' for short. If the subject's concept is the concept of an o-place, her belief that such a place is closed to her will be incoherent.

Papineau (1996: 430) attempts to block this riposte. He accepts that Peacocke's objection turns on the claim that the success of the subject's behaviour will be explained by her capacity to represent only items that are accessible to her. But, he suggests, the properties to which this explanation appeals are 'gruelike' or gerrymandered properties.[7] This suggests that Papineau would claim that the ontological category *o-place* is a gerrymandered category.

This response is not compelling: there is nothing odd or contrived about the claim that a subject who has the capacity to represent space will benefit from that capacity only because she is able to represent places that are open to her.[8] Of course, the category *o-place* will seem contrived to us: that is because it is not a category with which we normally operate. But there seems to be no good reason to rule out in advance the possibility that there might be subjects that operate with a category of this kind; and, if so, we need to explain how we differ from subjects of that kind.

The failure of Papineau's response raises some difficult questions about my response to some of the worries with which I began the previous chapter. In particular, it threatens to undermine the claim that the teleologist can treat biologically useless beliefs and concepts as the outcome of strategies that benefit the subject overall. Peacocke's objection prompts us to ask *which* strategy the subject is employing. Is it a strategy that allows the generation of beliefs or

---

[7] See Goodman (1955).

[8] Explanations that appeal to 'gruelike' properties generally appear contrived because they introduce a redundancy into the explanation. For example, if I were to attempt to explain why it is hard to find an emerald that has been dropped on a lawn by saying that emeralds are green-and-expensive, this explanation would appear contrived because the reference to monetary value is surplus to requirements. The explanation that Papineau has in mind does not seem to involve the same kind of redundancy. The fact that the place represented by the subject's beliefs is a place that is open to her is not redundant in an explanation of the success of her behaviour.

concepts even in circumstances under which they will prove useless or harmful? Or is it one that will allow the subject to generate only beliefs or concepts that are at least normally and in principle of practical benefit to the subject? Until we have resolved this worry, we cannot assume that, when a subject forms a biologically useless belief, she is exercising the same strategy as when she forms a belief that might in principle help her to satisfy some biological need.

In this section, I have attempted to present a prima facie case for the claim that Peacocke's objection will apply to a teleological theory of doxastic content. However, this is not enough to show that the case cannot be answered. In order to answer it, we need to give some plausible account of what it is for a subject to represent space in an objective way. And we will need to be confident that this account can be accommodated inside the teleological theory.

3.2. Verity and Prudence

I will centre my response on the example of two cousins, whom I shall name Verity and Prudence. The cousins are both capable of doxastic representation, and both use a topographical map to help them to navigate around their environment. Prudence, I will stipulate, is capable of representing only places that are open to her. She would regard the idea that a place might be closed to her as incoherent. Indeed, she could not come to conceive of openness as a property of places. Hence, it does not seem appropriate to regard Prudence as representing *places* at all. Rather, we should characterize her as representing o-places. Verity, on the other hand, is capable of representing places, rather than o-places. She is in a position to develop a concept of openness and to discriminate between places that are open to her and those that are not.

In order to answer Peacocke's objection, we need to find a way to defend the idea that Verity is a coherent possibility. To do this we need to show two things. First, we need to show that Verity is minimally competent to represent places that are closed to her.[9] And, secondly, we need to show that she is capable of benefiting in some distinctive way from this competence.[10]

What does it mean to say that Verity benefits in some distinctive way from her competence? One thing that is certainly not required is that she is more successful in negotiating her environment than Prudence. It may be that Verity and Prudence are equally successful at finding their way about, but that they do so in different ways. What is important is that Verity *as it turns out*

---

[9] Note that we do not need to show that Prudence is not minimally competent to represent places—it may be that she is competent to do so, but that she does not benefit from that competence. [10] Or, to be more precise, her ancestors.

benefits from her competence, not that she would not have fared so well if she had not had that competence.[11] Nevertheless, we must be certain that the competence that she is exercising on these occasions is genuinely distinct from any competence from which Prudence is able to benefit.

Our first task, then, is to consider what conditions Verity must meet for it to be true that she is minimally competent to represent places. A complete answer to this question would be very long, and would involve developing a detailed account of doxastic content. Fortunately, it is not essential to do this in order to answer Peacocke's question. What is important here is simply that Verity is capable of producing states that correlate with there being some place that is closed to her. If Verity can produce states of this kind, she is minimally competent to represent a place as being closed to her. Hence, she will be minimally competent to represent places, as opposed to o-places.

What we now need to consider is how Verity might be thought to benefit by exercising this competence. I will start by considering a capacity that Verity and Prudence share. Prudence, like Verity, can distinguish between places that are actually accessible to her and places that are only potentially accessible to her. Hence, she can represent how things are at a place that she cannot immediately reach. She will be able to use this information in deciding whether it is worth expending the effort required to make that place accessible to her. Moreover, she might use information about a place that is currently out of reach in order to plan how to get there. For example, she might realize that she cannot currently reach a certain place because it has been flooded. Knowing this, she might wait until the waters have receded, or she might build a boat.

Clearly, much of this will be irrelevant when we consider how Verity benefits from the capacity to discriminate between open and closed places. Given that she can never visit a closed place, she cannot have information that would help her to do so; nor does she need to know whether there is anything useful awaiting her there. Nevertheless, she may benefit from knowing that a place is closed to her: knowing this might prevent her from wasting time trying to get there. Moreover, it is possible for a place to become closed to her over time; or even for her to make a place closed to her by acting or failing to act in a certain way. We might suggest, then, that Verity may benefit from the capacity to discriminate between places that are open to her and places that are not, because the capacity to represent a place *as* closed might save her from wasted effort, or help her to prevent a place from becoming closed to her, and so on.

But at this point a problem arises. We have shown that it is possible for Verity to benefit from the capacity to discriminate places that are closed to her from places that are open to her. But the worry will be that we have not yet established that it is this capacity that she is exercising on these occasions. For,

---

[11] The heart has the function to move the blood around the body, regardless of whether we would have done better if our blood corpuscles had been able to move themselves.

after all, Prudence also has a way of saving herself from wasted effort—that is, by recognizing that there is no o-place that she could try to reach. Moreover, Prudence might think of o-places as sometimes ceasing to exist; and she might sometimes take steps to ensure that this does not happen. Of course, it may simply be that Verity and Prudence are solving the same problem in different ways. But we need to establish that this is the case.

Unfortunately, there is an obstacle in our way: the problem is that there is nothing to prevent us from *reinterpreting* Verity's representation as having the same content as the one produced by Prudence.[12] Suppose that Verity produces a representation of the form 'p is-N'. We could treat 'is-N' as a predicate that assigns a property—being closed—to the place denoted by 'p'. But we could also treat 'is-N' as a negated existential quantifier, and to take Verity to be judging, like Prudence, that there is no such o-place.

The problem arises because we have not established that Verity produces any other type of judgement of the form ' . . . is-N' to which we could appeal to resolve the ambiguity. If we are to insist on interpreting 'is-N' to mean 'is closed', we need to find a range of judgements in which it appears that cannot be reinterpreted in this way. But what other kinds of judgements might Verity produce that would require her to represent a place as being closed to her?

At this point I would like to refer to a recent discussion by John Campbell (1994: 201–22). Campbell's target is the form of anti-realism characterized by Michael Dummett (1969, 1991), which centres on the claim that truth may be equated with warranted assertability. Campbell argues that the anti-realist fails to take account of the way we think about our capacity to perceive and to act upon our environment. He suggests that we operate with a simple theory of perception and agency that captures the causal constraints that govern our interactions with our environment. This theory, he argues, embodies a realist conception of the relationship that holds between the subject and her surroundings.[13] As Campbell (1994: 217) puts it:

We need the idea that the reason that we did not find out about something, or that we could not affect an appropriate outcome, was some limitation on our own powers. . . . This kind of point appeals to our reflective understanding of our own place in the world. It exploits our grasp of a simple theory of perception and action. This theory explains our perceptions as the joint upshot of the way things are in the world and the way things are with us, and it explains the effects of our actions as the joint consequences of our bodily movements and the way things were around us to begin with.

Campbell (1994: 218) goes on to suggest that this theory carries with it a distinction between truth and assertability. This is because it implies that assertability and truth may come apart: truth requires that things should be as

---

[12] I owe this point to Rowland Stout.
[13] This is a line of thought that can be traced back to Peter Strawson. See especially Strawson (1966: 104–5). See also Evans (1980).

they are asserted to be, whereas assertability requires that the subject should be in a position to discover that this is the case. Moreover, assertability does not entail truth—the evidence available to the subject may be misleading. This gap between assertability and truth is intelligible in the light of our reflective understanding of the causal constraints that govern our capacities to perceive and to act upon the world.

What I would like to extract from Campbell's discussion is the idea that we think of our perceptual and practical capacities as explained not only by facts about ourselves but also by facts about our surroundings. If we regard these abilities as partly dependent on how things are in the environment, we cannot at the same time suppose that how things are in the environment depends in part on what we are able to perceive and to do.

I suggested earlier that Prudence might sometimes be inclined to explain the fact that she is currently unable to obtain access to a place by appealing to how things are at that place. Moreover, Prudence may operate with a theory of perception and agency—a theory that enables her to make inferences and predictions about the extent of open space. She may realize, for example, that open space is shrinking as she becomes older. But Prudence can explain such changes only by appealing to changes in her own perceptual and practical capacities. What she cannot do is explain the fact that a place is closed to her by appealing to how things are *at that place.* She is not able to do this because she is not able to represent places as being closed to her.

Verity, on the other hand, will be able to formulate explanations of this kind. Suppose that Verity believes that, given the technology available to her, any place that is more than 100 feet underwater is closed to her. And suppose that Verity has dropped her favourite rock into a pool that is known to be more than 100 feet deep. It is possible for Verity to infer that, *because* the current location of the rock is more than 100 feet underwater, it is closed to her.

Nevertheless, it might now be suggested that we have simply pushed the problem one stage back, for, once again, it could be objected that we do not *have* to understand Verity's explanation in this way. We can represent Verity's explanation as having the following form: 'p is-N because p S o'. And it has been suggested that we should identify it with the insight:

> (I) The rock's current location is closed to me because it is more than 100 feet from the surface of the water.

But the objector will suggest that we could equally well identify it with the insight:

> I* There is no such o-place as 'the rock's current location' because there is no such o-place within 100 feet of the surface of the water.

In this case, however, the objection is less pressing. This is because we can reasonably refuse to interpret the judgement 'p S o' as meaning that there is no such o-place within 100 feet of the surface of the water. This is because Verity may produce other judgements of the form ' . . . S . . . .' that can be identified only as judgements that some item is more than 100 feet from some other item. In other words, Verity's insight that that place is closed to her need not stand alone. It may be a part of a network of judgements about the spatial relations that items in her environment bear to each other. These judgements may have all sorts of different uses for her. For example, they may have a role in formulating a wider physical theory, of which her theories of perception and agency form a part. But the important point is that these judgements and insights will belong to a unified reasoning system—one that obeys the Generality Constraint—so that our ascription of content to one judgement must answer to our ascription of content to other judgements with which it shares constituents.

Note that my argument here is not equivalent to Papineau's appeal to compositionality that I mentioned earlier on. The idea is not that Verity's capacity to represent places that are closed to her rides piggyback on the fact that she is able to benefit from her capacity to represent places that are open to her. Rather, I have claimed that Verity may benefit in a distinctive way from her capacity to represent places that are closed to her. I have appealed to compositionality only to undermine the attempt to reinterpret what Verity is doing when she benefits in this way.

To block this appeal to compositionality, an objector would have to insist that ' . . . S . . . ' has different meanings in different contexts. But it would be reasonable, I think, to view this suggestion as violating Millikan's generality requirement. This is because there *is* available a single, unified explanation of how Verity benefits from the capacity to produce judgements of the form ' . . . S . . . ' that presents Verity as exercising exactly the same capacity each time: that is, the capacity to produce judgements that correlate with states of affairs that consist in one item being more than 100 feet from another. Moreover, there is no redundancy in this explanation, and so no pressure to seek another, more precise, way of characterizing what she is doing on these occasions.

The solution that I have suggested may be summarized as follows. Verity is competent to represent places, as opposed to o-places, because she is able to discriminate between places that are open to her and places that are not. She is able to benefit from this competence because it enables her to explain the fact that a certain place is closed to her by appealing to properties of that place. In formulating an explanation of this kind, Verity is operating with a conception of her own capabilities as dependent, to some extent, on facts about her environment and her position in it. These explanations cannot be interpreted away, because they form an integrated part of a wider network of judgements and insights that Verity can produce. Moreover, the capacity to produce judgements that correlate with closed places is a normal feature of her representational system, because it enables her to modify her behaviour in a way that is appropriate, given her interests, to the fact that a certain place is (or may become) closed to her.

I have suggested that the capacity to represent space in an objective way depends on the capacity to develop theories of perception and of agency, which purport to explain our perceptual and practical capacities partly in terms of the intrinsic or relational properties of items in the environment. If this is right, then it follows that the capacity to represent places, as opposed to o-places, is a fairly sophisticated capacity—one that is restricted to subjects capable, not only of doxastic thought and of theory-building, but of building theories about their own capacities as knowers and as agents. If so, we will have to concede that Peacocke is right to claim that the teleologist is unable to ascribe this kind of capacity to a wide range of intentional systems. But he is wrong to claim that the teleologist will be unable to ascribe this kind of content to any kind of intentional system whatsoever.

When I first introduced Peacocke's objection in Chapter 5, I characterized it as an objection raised by a realist against other realists. I left it open that a teleologist might wish to respond to Peacocke's objection by embracing some form of anti-realism. While I am strongly sympathetic to Campbell's defence of realism, nothing I have said here demonstrates that a teleological theory of content is incompatible with anti-realism. In order to resolve the issue between realism and anti-realism it would be necessary to investigate the truth of Campbell's claims about human thought.

3.3. *Objective Doxastic Content: Summary*

My second task in this chapter has been to find a solution to the objectivity problem. I have argued that neither the capacity to engage in general-purpose representation nor the capacity to form theories is sufficient to secure the kind of objectivity required for utility-transcendent truth. Instead, I have argued that it is the capacity to form simple theories of perception and agency that underlies the capacity for objective representation.

CONCLUSION

Constructing Content

I began this book with a problem: how to develop a naturalistic theory of content that leaves room for the fact that intentional explanations have a normative ring. This problem is important, I suggested, because failure to answer it would leave a naturalist open to the objection that the notion of intentionality as an explanatory concept is intrinsically incoherent, and so ripe for elimination in favour of a more scientifically respectable notion. My purpose in this book has been to lay the foundations for a teleological theory of content—a theory that might be thought to have the resources to resolve this difficulty.

On the account that I have developed, the point of an intentional explanation is to make sense of the agent's behaviour as normal or appropriate response, in the light of the content of the intentional states that prompted it. For example, when we explain a piece of behaviour by appealing to some belief of the agent, we make sense of that behaviour as appropriate to the content of that belief, given the function or purpose of the behaviour. When we explain a piece of behaviour by appealing to the agent's wish or purpose in acting, we make sense of it as an appropriate response to the content of that wish or purpose, given how the agent believes the world to be. Explanations of this kind are causal explanations: they present the agent's behaviour as the product of a causal history that has a certain kind of structure. But they have a normative ring, because they rest on a teleological notion of normality of which we conceive via a metaphor of social obligation. On this view, there are no intentional norms in nature, because there are no biological norms in nature. Claims about function and content are claims about objective causal relations between natural items; normativity is a feature of the language that we use to describe those relational states of affairs.

In the course of this book, I have proposed a teleological approach to content that will underpin this view of intentional explanations. In developing this approach, I have set out three major objections, the determinacy objection, the objectivity objection and the objection from general-purpose content. My responses to these objections are woven through the chapters of this book. I have argued that the determinacy objection can be answered provided

that we begin from a well-developed theory of functions, and I have
attempted to show how the theory that I have proposed will help us to answer
this objection. I have contrasted my response with the response proposed by
Karen Neander, who begins from a theory of functions that differs from the
theory proposed here. In the third part of the book I have attempted to defuse
the objection from general-purpose content by illustrating how a teleologist
might go about ascribing content to the devices produced by a general-purpose intentional mechanism. My solution is designed to show how we might
go about determining the content of such devices without specifying the
inferential role that they are supposed to play. Finally, I have suggested that the
objectivity objection can be answered only for devices that are produced by
intentional systems of a highly sophisticated kind: systems that are capable of
formulating theories about the organism's perceptual and behavioural relations to the environment. It is only for systems of this kind that we can find
room for a gap between utility and truth.

The story of this book has been a story of intentional systems of increasing complexity producing devices of increasingly sophisticated kinds. In
Chapter 4, I began with signalling systems, including systems that function
simply to signal the occurrence of a certain feature nearby. I have attempted
to elucidate the distinctions between primitive mechanisms of this kind and
a range of increasingly sophisticated systems: systems that are able to signal
a range of different states of affairs; systems that are able to learn; systems
that are able to represent goals; systems that are capable of representing particular items, including tracking and mapping systems; and, finally, general-
purpose, doxastic systems.

At no point, however, have I claimed to have given an account of the doxastic states produced by human beings. This is because I am acutely aware of
the limitations of the account I have offered. Part II offers a reasonably
detailed account of special-purpose systems; Part III a rather sketchier
account of general-purpose systems. In order to turn this into a fully-fledged
account of our own intentional capacities, a number of further tasks would
have to be completed. First, such an account would have to say a great deal
more about the nature of the ontological categories that human beings use
when we think about the world. There is room to develop a detailed account
of our conceptions of basic categories, such as *object, place, time,* as well as our
capacity to represent ourselves. Secondly, there is much more to be said about
the role of language and culture in the development of our intentional capacities. The account of general-purpose content that I proposed in Chapter 10
invokes only the most basic perceptual and behavioural relations to the world.
Yet many of the concepts that we develop are shaped by our linguistic interactions with each other; and much of our behaviour can be understood only
in a cultural context. Much more needs to be said about how the linguistic and
cultural aspects of human thought may be integrated into the picture that I

have sketched here. Finally, a fully developed theory of content would have something to say about the relationship between mental representation and consciousness, and about the epistemology of content. These are issues that I have skirted here.

Nevertheless, my intention is that the account that I have developed here will act as a springboard for further investigation, and will provide the resources to underwrite a fully developed theory of content. This can be taken as an admission of how much further there is to go, but also as a claim about what I hope to have achieved.

APPENDIX

In Chapters 4 and 5, I argued in support of the claim that the content of the frog's visual signal is (something like) 'Catchable fly within range now!' (The term 'fly' here is being understood as shorthand for a catchable item having just those biochemical properties that make flies nutritious to frogs.) In order to make this claim I have had to rule out an array of rival content ascriptions. In this appendix, I would like to summarize the different elements of the account in order to provide a consolidated statement of my view. I will focus on the example of the frog's visual system rather than the slightly more complex case of the bee dance mechanism, where we have to appeal not only to the function of the system but to the rules by which the system normally works.

The account that I offered in Chapters 4 and 5 can be summarized as follows: the content of the frog's visual signal concerns the presence of a fly nearby because (i) signals of that kind normally carry the information that there is a fly within range, (ii) the fact that in the past signals produced by the system carried that information helps to provide a suitable abstract and immediate explanation of the fact that snaps prompted by those signals coincided with the presence of a fly within range, and (iii) the fact that those snaps coincided with the presence of a fly within range helped to explain their success.

In the course of Chapters 4 and 5, we encountered a number of rival content ascriptions. I will list them and explain briefly how each one is excluded by the account.

(1) 'The content of the visual signal concerns the absence of a predator close to the frog.' This ascription violates (i)—the signal does not normally carry this information.

(2) 'The content of the visual signal concerns the fact that the sun is shining.' This ascription violates (iii)—the fact that the sun is shining is irrelevant to the success of the frog's snaps.

(3) 'The content of the visual signal concerns the fact that acceleration due to gravity at the earth's surface approximates 9.81 metres per second.' This proposal violates (iii)—the fact that the signal carries information about the condition does not help to *explain* the fact that the frog's snaps coincide with it.

(4) 'The content of the visual signal concerns the presence of something small and dark within range.' This ascription violates (iii)—the fact that the signal carries information about this condition does not provide a suitably abstract explanation of the success of the frog's snaps. It is equivalent to the claim that the function of the heart is to make squeezing motions.

(5) 'The content of the visual signal concerns the arrival of a certain pattern of light at the frog's retinae.' This ascription can be excluded for exactly the same reason as (4).

(6) 'The content of the visual signal concerns the presence of something less than 1 centimetre across and moving at less than 50 kilometres per hour.' Again, this violates (iii)—the fact that the signal carries information about this condition does not

provide a suitably abstract explanation of the success of the frog's snaps. It is equivalent to the claim that the function of the heart is to move blood that is free from clots. Note the distinction between this rival ascription and the one that I have proposed, on which the content of the signal concerns the presence of a *catchable* fly. My proposed ascription contains no allusion to *specific* features of the frog's fly-catching equipment.

———(7) 'The content of the visual signal concerns the presence of a fly in the area a few seconds ago.' This proposal violates (iii)—the fact that the signal carries this information fails to provide a suitably immediate explanation of the success of the frog's snaps. It is equivalent to the claim that the function of the chameleon's pigment-arranging mechanism is to ensure that the colour of the chameleon's skin matches the chemical composition of the surface on which it is standing.

REFERENCES

Achinstein, P. (1977). 'Function Statements'. *Philosophy of Science*, 44: 341–62.

Agar, N. (1993). 'What Do Frogs Really Believe?' *Australasian Journal of Philosophy*, 71: 1–12.

Amundson, R., and Lauder, G. (1993). 'Function without Purpose: The Uses of Causal Role Function in Evolutionary Biology'. *Biology and Philosophy*, 9: 443–69.

Armstrong, D. (1973). *Belief, Truth and Knowledge*. London: Cambridge University Press.

Atran, S. (1987) 'Ordinary Constraints on the Semantics of Living Kinds: A Common-Sense Alternative to Recent Treatments of Natural-Object Terms'. *Mind and Language*, 2: 25–63.

—— (1989). 'Basic Conceptual Domains'. *Mind and Language*, 4: 7–16.

Ayers, M. (1974). 'Individuals without Sortals'. *Canadian Journal of Philosophy*, 4: 113–48.

Beckermann, A. (1988). 'Why Tropistic Systems are not Genuine Intentional Systems'. *Erkenntnis*, 29: 125–42.

Bedau, M. (1991). 'Can Biological Teleology be Naturalized?' *Journal of Philosophy*, 88: 647–55.

—— (1992a). 'Where's the Good in Teleology?' *Philosophy and Phenomenological Research*, 52: 781–806.

—— (1992b): 'Goal-Directed Systems and the Good'. *Monist*, 75: 43–51.

Bennett, L. (1990). 'Modularity of Mind Revisited'. *British Journal for the Philosophy of Science*, 41: 428–36.

Bermudez, J. L. (1995). 'Nonconceptual Content: From Perceptual Experience to Sub-personal Computational States'. *Mind and Language*, 10: 333–69.

Bigelow, J., and Pargetter, R. (1987). 'Functions'. *Journal of Philosophy*, 84: 181–96.

Black, M. (1954). 'Metaphor'. *Proceedings of the Aristotelian Society*, 55: 273–94.

Bogdan, R. (1994). *Grounds for Cognition: How Goal-Guided Behaviour Shapes the Mind*. Hillsdale, NJ: Lawrence Erlbaum Associates.

Boorse, C. (1976). 'Wright on Functions'. *Journal of Philosophy*, 85: 70–86.

Bredin, H. (1992). 'The Literal and the Figurative'. *Philosophy*, 67: 69–80.

Buller, D. (1998). 'Etiological Theories of Function: A Geographical Survey'. *Biology and Philosophy*, 13: 505–27.

Cam, P. (1988). 'Modularity, Rationality and Higher Cognition'. *Philosophical Studies*, 53: 279–94.

Campbell, J. (1993). 'The Role of Physical Objects in Spatial Thinking', in N. Eilan, R. McCarthy, and B. Brewer (eds.), *Spatial Representation*. Oxford: Blackwell, 65–95.

—— (1994). *Past, Space and Self*. Cambridge, MA: MIT Press.

Churchland, P. (1984). *Matter and Consciousness*. Cambridge, MA: MIT Press.

—— (1992). *A Neurocomputational Perspective*. Cambridge, MA: MIT Press.

Clark, A., and Karmiloff-Smith, A. (1993). 'The Cognizer's Innards: A Psychological and Philosophical Perspective on the Development of Thought'. *Mind and Language*, 8: 487–519.

Cummins, R. (1983). *The Nature of Psychological Explanation*. Cambridge, MA: MIT Press.

Cussins, A. (1990). 'The Connectionist Construction of Concepts', in M. Boden (ed.), *The Philosophy of Artificial Intelligence*. Oxford: Oxford University Press, 368–440.

—— (1992). 'Content, Embodiment and Objectivity: The Theory of Cognitive Trails'. *Mind*, 101: 651–88.

Davidson, D. (1963). 'Actions, Reason and Causes', reprinted in Davidson (1980), 3–19.

—— (1969). 'The Individuation of Events', reprinted in Davidson (1980), 163–80.

—— (1978). 'What Metaphors Mean'. *Critical Inquiry*, 5: 31–47.

—— (1980). *Essays on Actions and Events*. Oxford: Oxford University Press.

—— (1982). 'Rational Animals'. *Dialectica*, 36: 318–32.

Davies, M. (1983). 'Function in Perception'. *Australasian Journal of Philosophy*, 61: 409–26.

—— (1989). 'Tacit Knowledge and Subdoxastic States', in A. George (ed.), *Reflections on Chomsky*. Oxford: Blackwell: 131–52.

Dawkins, R. (1986). *The Blind Watchmaker*. London: Penguin.

Dennett, D. (1978). 'Why You can't Make a Computer that Feels Pain'. *Synthese*, 38: 415–49.

—— (1987). *The Intentional Stance*. Cambridge, MA: MIT Press.

Dretske, F. (1981). *Knowledge and the Flow of Information*. Oxford: Blackwell.

—— (1986). 'Misrepresentation', in R. Bogdan (ed.), *Belief: Form Content and Function*. Oxford: Oxford University Press, 17–36.

—— (1988). *Explaining Behavior: Reasons in a World of Causes*. Cambridge, MA: MIT Press.

—— (1994). 'Reply to Slater and Garcia-Carpintero'. *Mind and Language*, 9: 203–8.

—— (1995). *Naturalizing the Mind*. Cambridge, MA: MIT Press.

Dummett, M. (1969). 'The Reality of the Past'. *Proceedings of the Aristotelian Society*, 69: 239–58.

—— (1991). *The Logical Basis of Metaphysics*. London: Duckworth.

Evans, G. (1980). 'Things Without the Mind', in Z. van Straaten (ed.), *Philosophical Subjects: Essays Presented to P. F. Strawson*. Oxford: Clarendon Press, 76–116.

—— (1982). *The Varieties of Reference*. Oxford: Oxford University Press.

Fodor, J. (1983). *The Modularity of Mind*. Cambridge, MA: MIT Press.

—— (1986). 'Why Paramecia Don't Have Representations', in P. French, T. Uehling, and H. Wettstein (eds.), *Midwest Studies in Philosophy*, vol. 10. Minneapolis: University of Minnesota Press, 3–23.

—— (1987). *Psychosemantics*, Cambridge, MA: MIT Press.

—— (1990). *A Theory of Content and Other Essays*. Cambridge MA: MIT Press.

—— (1991). 'Reply to Anthony and Levine', in B. Loewer and G. Rey (eds.), *Meaning and Mind*. Oxford: Blackwell, 255–7.

—— and Lepore, E. (1992). *Holism: A Shopper's Guide*. Oxford: Blackwell.

Gallistel, C. (1990). *The Organization of Learning*. Cambridge, MA: MIT Press.

258   *References*

Gelman, S. (1988). 'The Development of Induction with Natural Kind and Artifact Categories'. *Cognitive Psychology*, 20: 65–95.

Godfrey-Smith, P. (1991). 'Signal, Decision, Action'. *Journal of Philosophy*, 88: 709–22.

—— (1992). 'Indication and Adaptation'. *Synthese*, 92: 283–312.

—— (1994). 'A Modern History Theory of Functions'. *Noûs*, 28: 344–62.

Goldman, A. (1967). 'A Causal Theory of Knowing'. *Journal of Philosophy*, 64: 355–72.

—— (1977). 'Perceptual Objects'. *Synthese*, 35: 257–84.

Goodman, N. (1955). *Fact Forecast and Fiction*. London: University of London Press.

—— (1968). *Languages of Art*. Oxford: Oxford University Press.

Grice, H. P. (1961). 'The Causal Theory of Perception'. *Proceedings of the Aristotelian Society*, supp. vol. 35: 121–52.

Griffiths, P. (1993). 'Functional Analysis and Proper Functions'. *British Journal for the Philosophy of Science*, 44: 409–22.

—— (1996). 'Darwinism, Process Structuralism, and Natural Kinds'. *Proceedings of the Biennial Meeting of the Philosophy of Science Association, Philosophy of Science*, 63, supp. vol. : 1–9.

—— and Goode, R. (1995). 'The Misuse of Sober's Selection for/Selection of Distinction'. *Biology and Philosophy*, 10: 99–107.

Hall, (1990). 'Does Representational Content Arise from Biological Function?' *Proceedings of the Biennial Meetings of the Philosophy of Science Association*, i: 193–9.

Jacob, P. (1997). *What Minds Can Do*. Cambridge: Cambridge University Press.

Keil, F. (1989). *Concepts, Kinds and Cognitive Development*. Cambridge, MA: MIT Press

Kripke, S. (1972). *Naming and Necessity*. Oxford: Blackwell.

Kukla, R. (1992). 'Cognitive Models and Representation'. *British Journal for the Philosophy of Science*, 43: 219–32.

Lewis, D. (1980). 'Veridical Hallucination and Prosthetic Vision'. *Australasian Journal of Philosophy*, 58: 239–49.

—— (1986) 'Causal Explanation', in *Philosophical Papers*, vol. ii, Oxford: Oxford University Press, 214–40.

Lloyd, D. (1989). *Simple Minds*. Cambridge, MA: MIT Press.

MacDonald, G. (1992). 'Reduction and Evolutionary Biology', in D. Charles and K. Lennon (eds.), *Reduction, Explanation and Realism*. Oxford: Oxford University Press, 67–96.

McGinn, C. (1989). *Mental Content*. Oxford: Blackwell.

Mackie, J. (1974). *The Cement of the Universe*. Oxford: Oxford University Press.

Marshall, J. (1984). 'Multiple Perspectives on Modularity'. *Cognition*, 17: 209–42.

Martin, M. (1992). 'Perception, Concepts and Memory'. *Philosophical Review*, 101: 745–63.

Millikan, R. (1984). *Language, Thought and Other Biological Categories*. Cambridge, MA: MIT Press.

—— (1986). 'Thoughts without Laws; Cognitive Science with Content'. *Philosophical Review*, 95: 47–80.

—— (1989a). 'In Defence of Proper Functions'. *Philosophy of Science*, 56: 288–302.

—— (1989b). 'Biosemantics'. *Journal of Philosophy*, 86: 281–97.

—— (1990a). 'Compare and Contrast Dretske, Fodor and Millikan on Teleosemantics'. *Philosophical Topics*, 18: 151–61.

—— (1990*b*). 'Truth, Rules, Hoverflies and the Kripke–Wittgenstein Paradox'. *Philosophical Review*, 99: 323–53.

—— (1990*c*). 'Seismographical Readings for *Explaining Behavior*'. *Philosophy and Phenomenological Research*, 50: 807–12.

—— (1991). 'Speaking up for Darwin', in B. Loewer and G. Rey (eds.), *Meaning in Mind*. Oxford: Blackwell, 151–64.

—— (1993*a*). 'On Mentalese Orthography', in B. Dahlbom (ed.), *Dennett and his Critics*. Oxford: Blackwell, 95–123.

—— (1993*b*). *White Queen Psychology and Other Essays for Alice*. Cambridge, MA: MIT Press.

—— (1995). 'A Bet with Peacocke', in C. MacDonald and G. MacDonald (eds.), *Philosophy of Psychology*. Oxford: Blackwell, 285–92.

—— (2000), *On Clear and Confused Ideas*, Cambridge: Cambridge University Press.

Nagel, E. (1977). 'Function Explanations in Biology'. *Journal of Philosophy*, 74: 280–301.

Neander, K. (1991*a*). 'The Teleological Notion of a Function'. *Australasian Journal of Philosophy*, 69: 454–68.

—— (1991*b*). 'Functions as Selected Effects: The Conceptual Analyst's Defence'. *Philosophy of Science*, 58: 168–84.

—— (1995). 'Misrepresenting and Malfunctioning'. *Philosophical Studies*, 79: 109–41.

O'Keefe, J. (1993). 'Kant and the Sea Horse: An Essay in the Neurophilosophy of Space', in N. Eilan, R. McCarthy, and B. Brewer (eds.), *Spatial Representation*. Oxford: Blackwell, 43–64.

Papineau, D. (1987). *Reality and Representation*. Oxford: Blackwell.

—— (1993). *Philosophical Naturalism*. Oxford: Blackwell.

—— (1996). 'Discussion of Christopher Peacocke's *A Study of Concepts*', *Philosophy and Phenomenological Research*, 56: 425–32.

Peacocke, C. (1983). *Sense and Content*. Oxford: Oxford University Press.

—— (1992). *A Study of Concepts*. Cambridge, MA: MIT Press.

—— (1993). 'Intuitive Mechanics, Psychological Reality, and the Idea of a Material Object', in N. Eilan, R. McCarthy, and B. Brewer (eds.) *Spatial Representation*. Oxford: Blackwell, 162–76.

Pettit, P. (1986). 'Broad-Minded Explanation and Psychology', in J. McDowell and P. Pettit (eds.), *Subject, Thought and Context*. Oxford: Oxford University Press, 17–58.

Pietroski, P. (1992). 'Intentionality and Teleological Error'. *Pacific Philosophical Quarterly*, 73: 267–81.

Price, C. (1998). 'Function, Perception and Deviant Causal Chains'. *Philosophical Studies*, 89: 31–51.

Prior, E. (1985). 'What is Wrong With Etiological Accounts of Function?' *Pacific Philosophical Quarterly*, 66: 310–28.

Putnam, H. (1975). 'The Meaning of "Meaning" ', in K. Gunderson (ed.), *Language Mind and Knowledge*. Minnesota Studies in the Philosophy of Science, 7. Minneapolis: University of Michigan Press, 215–71.

Reimer, M. (1986). 'The Problem of Dead Metaphors'. *Philosophical Studies*, 82: 13–25.

Ross, D., and Zawidzki, T. (1994). 'Information and Teleosemantics'. *Southern Journal of Philosophy*, 32: 393–419.

Scholz, O. (1993). ' "What Metaphors Mean" and How Metaphors Refer', in R. Stoecker (ed.), *Reflecting Davidson*. Berlin: De Gruyter, 161–71.

Sehon, S. (1994). 'Teleology and the Nature of Mental States'. *American Philosophical Quarterly*, 31: 63–72.

Sellars, W. (1962). 'Truth and "Correspondence" ' *Journal of Philosophy*, 59: 29–56.

Shallice, T. (1984). 'More Functionally Isolable Subsystems But Fewer "Modules"?' *Cognition*, 17: 243–52.

Shannon, B. (1988). 'Remarks on the Modularity of Mind'. *British Journal for the Philosophy of Science*, 39: 331–52.

Shapiro, L. (1992). 'Darwin and Disjunction: Optimal Foraging Theory and Univocal Assignments of Content'. *Proceedings of the Biennial Meetings of the Philosophy of Science Association*, ii. 469–480.

Shoemaker, S. (1984). 'Identity, Properties and Causality', in S. Shoemaker, *Identity, Cause and Mind*. Cambridge: Cambridge University Press, 234–60.

Slote, M. (1979). 'Causality and the Concept of a "Thing" ', in P. French, T. Uehling, and H. Wettstein (eds.), *Midwest Studies in Philosophy*, vol. 4. Minneapolis: University of Minnesota Press, 387–400.

Spelke, E., and Van de Valle, G. (1993). 'Perceiving and Reasoning about Objects: Insights from Infants', in N. Eilan, R. McCarthy, and B. Brewer (eds.), *Spatial Representation*. Oxford: Blackwell: 132–61.

Sterelny, K. (1990). *The Representational Theory of Mind*. Oxford: Blackwell.

Stich, S. (1978). 'Beliefs and Subdoxastic States'. *Philosophy of Science*, 45: 499–578.

—— (1983). *From Folk Psychology to Cognitive Science*. Cambridge, MA: MIT Press.

Strawson, P. (1959). *Individuals*. London: Methuen.

—— (1961). 'Perception and Identification'. *Proceedings of the Aristotelian Society*, supp. vol. 35: 97–120.

—— (1966). *The Bounds of Sense*. London: Routledge.

Sullivan, S. (1993). 'From Natural Function to Indeterminate Content'. *Philosophical Studies*, 69: 129–37.

Tirell, L. (1991). 'Seeing Metaphor as Seeing-As'. *Philosophical Investigations*, 14: 143–54.

Travis, C. (1994). 'On Constraints of Generality'. *Proceedings of the Aristotelian Society*, 94: 165–88.

Walton, K. (1970). 'Categories of Art'. *Philosophical Review*, 79: 334–67.

Wiggins, D. (1963). 'The Individuation of Things and Places (I)'. *Proceedings of the Aristotelian Society*, supp. vol. 37: 177–216.

—— (1980). *Sameness and Substance*. Oxford: Blackwell.

Wittgenstein, L. (1961). *Tractatus Logico—Philosophicus*, trans. D. Pears and B. McGuiness. London: Routledge & Kegan Paul.

Woodfield, A. (1976). *Teleology*. Cambridge: Cambridge University Press.

—— (1990). 'The Emergence of Natural Representations'. *Philosophical Topics*, 18: 187–213.

Woods, M. (1963). 'The Individuation of Things and Places (II)'. *Proceedings of the Aristotelian Society*, supp. vol. 37: 203–16.

Wright, L. (1976). *Teleological Explanations*. Berkeley and Los Angeles: University of California Press.

INDEX